English words
from
Latin and Greek
elements

English words

from Latin and Greek elements

DONALD M. AYERS

SECOND EDITION

Revised and Expanded
by
THOMAS D. WORTHEN

with the assistance of
R. L. CHERRY

The University of Arizona Press
TUCSON

About the Authors

Donald M. Ayers received both his B.A. and M.A. in classics from Stanford University and his doctorate in classics from Princeton. One of his special concerns was the classical background of the English vocabulary and the value of a knowledge of this in vocabulary building for both technical and general studies. He taught classics at Vanderbilt University before joining the Classics Department at the University of Arizona in 1951. He was also a graduate of Navy Japanese Language School (Boulder, Colorado) and was on active duty with the U.S. Naval Reserve for three years. He published several articles on technical terminology in addition to his book *Bioscientific Terminology,* published by the University of Arizona Press in 1972.

Owing to Dr. Ayers's untimely death in 1969, the revision of this book became incumbent upon **Thomas D. Worthen**, who received his M.A. and Ph.D. in classics from the University of Washington and has been teaching classics at the University of Arizona since 1965. **R.L. Cherry** is the author of the *Instructor's Manual* that accompanies this textbook.

NOTE

Words used in this text that the authors have reason to believe constitute trade names have been designated as such. However, neither the presence nor absence of such designation should be regarded as affecting the legal status of any trademark.

THE UNIVERSITY OF ARIZONA PRESS

Copyright ©1986
The Arizona Board of Regents
All rights reserved

This book was set in 10/12 Compugraphic Times Roman.
Manufactured in the U.S.A.

Library of Congress Cataloging in Publication Data

Ayers, Donald M.
  English words from Latin and Greek elements.

  Includes index.
  Summary: Presents an overview of the development of the English language and examines the formation of words expecially from Greek and Latin roots. Also discusses definitions and usage.
  1. English language--Foreign elements--Latin. 2. English language--Foreign elements--Greek. 3. English language--Roots. 4. English language--Word formation. 5. Vocabulary. [1. English language--Foreign elements--Latin. 2. English language--Foreign elements--Greek. 3. English language--Roots. 4.Vocabulary.] I. Worthen, Thomas D. II. Cherry, R.L. III. Title.
  PE1582.L3A9 1986   422'.48   85-28919

ISBN 0-8165-0978-6
ISBN 0-8165-0899-2 (pbk.)

This revised edition
is dedicated to
Esther Ayers
and Mary Worthen

CONTENTS

PART TWO: WORD ELEMENTS FROM GREEK

PREFACE TO THE SECOND EDITION

Dear Reader:

Congratulations! You hold in your hands the best available key for cracking the code behind the English vocabulary. I can claim this without boasting, for the same could have been said of Donald Ayers's *English Words from Latin and Greek Elements* before the current revision was undertaken. I do not wish to pursue with you my reasons for thinking this to be the case; my concern through fifteen years of teaching the course developed by Professor Ayers and through the revision of his textbook has been my ever-growing awareness of the necessity for introducing the materials presented in this book into our school curriculums, universally and early.

I was once asked to help in the grading of writing-proficiency examinations given to university juniors and seniors. The experience was eye-opening for me. We are failing to teach our students enough about their own language to enable them to construct an essay of minimum competency. I am sure—at least, I hope—that high-school seniors in France, Russia, China, or Denmark could do better.

I am not going to level the finger of blame at television, the system of compulsory education found in the United States, or any other cultural fact unique to our way of life. Television, in fact, can be of great assistance to public education, and I am sure that the essays that all instructors will be reading in about 1987 will be better as the students who were the first to be reared on *Sesame Street* and *Electric Company* pass into the college domain. No, I will put most of the responsibility for our educational quandries upon a fact of life which we cannot alter for ourselves—the English language itself.

Linguists may tell us that all languages are created equal, that language acquisition is no more difficult for the native speakers of one language than it is for those of another. I will not contest the point; I am sure that English *was* created equal. But after its nativity, it lacked the benefit of being reared by dutiful parents during its formative years, and, rather like Topsy in the novel *Uncle Tom's Cabin*, it "just growed."

In rather sharp distinction to other languages, English grew by the gradual addition of extraneous elements (discussed in detail in the Introduction), and this fact has created peculiar difficulties for those who would wish to learn English, which is truly a linguistic melting pot.

The particular difficulties I have in mind, although there are others of the same origin, are the problems one encounters when trying to acquire a vocabulary. In any language, words are built up according to formal rules. As an infant passes into fully articulate adulthood, the basics of these rules are acquired, very simply, by rote. Only minimal instruction need be given in school in order that these rules of word formation be thoroughly mastered.

In English instruction, however, the need is a great deal more than minimal, and this fact goes largely not only unnoticed but unattended, or worse, in that the student is often given over-simplified rules of thumb which are downright wrong—such as the insistence on the part of some grammar-school and high-school teachers that the highway sign *Drive Slow* is bad grammar and should read *Drive Slowly*; and I myself was taught that *-tion,* rather than the correct *-ion,* is a noun suffix which we ought to recognize. The need is not minimal because instead of the *one* set of rules for word formation adequate for learning most languages, in English there are at least *four* to master: those of Latin, Greek, French, and our native English.

If we could learn our language in strictly stratified layers so that only English words were first encountered, then French, then Latin, and so on (take any order you wish), the problem would not be so unwieldy to deal with. But there is, in fact, such an oversupply of foreign vocabulary in English that outlandish words are often learned before their native English synonyms; indeed, some native words are dropping from our vocabularies, ousted by polysyllabic intruders for which there is no native sensitivity or understanding. A linguistic student down from Mars would think that the English-speaking nations had been under continuous invasion from the outside for the last thousand years, when in fact thousands of imports have been dragged in by the English-speaking peoples themselves. The result is a nightmare of inappropriate diction, even in colloquial speech. One stutters before the range of possible choices of words while the opportunity to speak flies by!

Only the brightest and best-educated can learn to crack this code by rote. Yet there is no longer room in the curriculum for French, Latin, and Greek per se. But we can overcome the deficit by teaching the significant elements of these languages in our grammar and secondary schools. In Philadelphia and Los Angeles in 1985, great progress in teaching two of the three Rs had been seen, owing to the introduction of Latin-based materials into the curriculums of these school systems. The remainder of the nation needs to fall in step with what has been successful, and while I applaud the foresight of the directors of high-school instruction in English for introducing this subject matter through the adoption of this book for their students, superintendents need to be aware that already by the senior year of high school such instruction is remedial. Nothing would please me more than to receive a telegram at least by the year 2005 (after my retirement) stating that my "words course" is no longer necessary because the freshman students have been well instructed in cracking the English code.

The changes undertaken in this revised edition are too numerous to set forth in detail. A few bases have been added or deleted. Indexes have been compiled for the words used in the context sentences, some of which have been exchanged for new ones, especially those which dealt with subjects or people that are no longer topical. A list of prefixes has been added at the end of each section. The list of bases at the end of each section has been reformatted for quick reference and often does not (since it does not have to) follow the format of the presentation of the bases in the text. I have expanded the Introduction to Part I, which now offers a more detailed overview of the development of the English language in the context of its Indo-European heritage. I have rewritten the introduction to semantic change at Lesson XI, providing, I hope, a more clear analysis of the mechanisms by which words undergo changes in meaning. The discussion of the process of retrogressive assimilation in Lesson III has been elaborated upon. Treatment of the Latin verbal suffix in -at(e)/-it(e) has been considerably expanded and moved to Lesson II from Lesson XX so as to allow students to begin generating words with this suffix earlier in the course.

Mr. Cherry generously agreed to transfer certain materials—on back formations, reduplication and ricochet expressions, circumlocution, onomatopoeia, and acronyms—from his 1983 *Instructor's Manual* (to the first edition) into this revised edition, in addition to fleshing out and/or updating material on the discussion of blends, homonyms, clips, doublets, and words from religion, much of this also from the *Manual.* He has also composed new opening material for the chapters so that most chapters are now so prefaced. These include sections on abbreviations, dissimilation, phonetic changes that are concerned with differing forms of the same Latin verb (as VERT-, VERS- "to turn"), apheresis and aphesis, metathesis, loan words, and combining forms (Part II, Lesson XII). These alterations and expansions perpetuate Professor Ayers's unswerving intention to produce a book which was not a mere "vocabulary builder," but one which would stimulate the student to become interested in his own language—the greatest incentive of all for improving skills.

1986   T.D.W.

FROM THE PREFACE TO
THE FIRST EDITION

It has been stated on the basis of a study of student academic mortality at one large university that the lack of an adequate vocabulary is the most important single factor contributing to failure in college.* There has consequently been a general recognition of the need for word study even at the university level. The present book, which is the result of several years' experience in teaching a vocabulary course at the University of Arizona, is devoted primarily to the study of Greek and Latin stems (or bases) and affixes. This approach to vocabulary building, since it can be largely systemized, lends itself especially to classroom procedure. Also, since this method of word study is general in its application, it is better suited to the needs of students with varied backgrounds and interests.

It seems likely, however, that a combination of methods will yield the best results in vocabulary building. I have therefore tried to incorporate insofar as possible the benefits derived from other approaches. The learning of specially prepared word lists is valuable because the student concentrates on words which occur rarely enough to be unfamiliar but are found sufficiently often in college reading to cause difficulty. If the words to be studied are carefully chosen, the immediate gains from this procedure are quite large, though there is of course little transfer in the case of words not specifically considered. In order to include the advantages derived from this type of training I have chosen for the main exercises, wherever feasible, words with which the majority of students are likely to be unfamiliar but which it would be desirable for them to know.

The recognition of meaning from context clues has the merit of concentrating the student's attention on the use of a word in a sentence, for the precise meaning of a term can only be understood from its context. I have tried to introduce into the main exercises some of the advantages from this type of approach by generally including the words to be studied there in a sentence or phrase. Such words, however, are always to be defined with the aid of a dictionary.

The basic emphasis of this book nevertheless remains on Greek and Latin prefixes, stems or bases, and suffixes. The difficulty which is most frequently encountered in this approach to word study arises from the fact that often there is a considerable difference between the

---

*G. Rexford Davis, *Vocabulary Building,* New York, 1951, p.1.

etymological or root meaning of a word and its current meaning. Thus, in determining the meaning of *urbane,* it is not of much help to know that the Latin word *urbs* means "city." Some vocabulary-building textbooks have attempted to avoid this problem by omitting from consideration those words in which such a wide variation between root meaning and current meaning occurs. The present book, however, does not make an attempt to do so. There are several reasons for this. First, the problem can be overcome to some extent by instruction in the general patterns of semantic change, which are discussed in several of the lessons in this book. Second, examples of change in meaning furnish one of the most interesting and instructive aspects of word study. Not only does the student gain some insight into the patterns of human thought by studying words which have changed their meaning, but often such words reflect something of the history of ideas. After all, one of the best ways for a book such as this to achieve its goal is to make the student interested in words themselves and not merely to hold out to him as an incentive the practical rewards to be gained from having a large vocabulary. Not the least of the reasons for learning Greek and Latin elements is their mnemonic value; a knowledge of these will serve as an excellent device for fixing words in the memory once their meaning has been determined, and this should be true even when semantic change has taken place.

Although most textbooks devoted to vocabulary building give some attention to Greek and Latin word elements, I have felt that there is need for such a book as this. Many texts, while they list all of the important prefixes and suffixes and a great many stems or bases, confine consideration of these to only a few lessons, and they do not give sufficient practice in recognizing these elements ever to make the knowledge of them an effective tool for increasing vocabulary. The exercises in this book are therefore designed to give systematic drill in these elements as well as to acquaint the students with words which it will be useful for them to know. In each lesson the basic exercise consists of words which contain the roots and affixes studied in that lesson and in previous ones. The student is expected to be able to analyze these words fully and to define them. In addition, one or two other exercises of varying nature are usually included, which the instructor may assign at will. A number of these are suitable to be done in class.

Several excellent textbooks (which are among the books listed farther on) do treat very adequately the classical element in English and give thorough practice in applying this knowledge. Their aim, however, is somewhat different from that of the present work; they attempt to impart some knowledge of the Latin and Greek languages. They consequently tend to be written more from the standpoint of Latin and Greek than of English and give considerable attention to Latin and Greek grammar, a matter which, I have found, the student who is primarily trying to improve his vocabulary regards as extraneous.

The material in this book has therefore been presented insofar as possible from the point of view of English. Stems or bases (e.g., DUC-, NOMIN-) have been given rather than actual Latin and Greek words (e.g., *ducere, nomen, nominis*), and the meanings attached to them are not necessarily those of the Latin but rather those which they have when used in English derivatives. Suffixes are treated not so much with regard to their origin as to their present form and meaning. Thus, for example, no distinction has been made between the English adjectival suffixes -*ary*, derived from Latin -*aris* (as in *military*), and -*ary,* derived from -*arius* (as in *arbitrary*). For the same reason the discussion of grammatical points has been kept to a minimum.

1965   D.M.A.

ACKNOWLEDGMENTS

I would like to express my appreciation to my colleagues at the University of Arizona who were kind enough to read sections of the manuscript of this book and who offered many valuable suggestions. My especial thanks are due Professor G.D. Percy of the Department of Classics; Professors Robert H. Hurlbutt (now of the University of Nebraska) and Charles F. Wallraff of the Department of Philosophy; Professors Marie P. Hamilton, William F. Irmscher (now of the University of Washington), and Jack W. Huggins of the Department of English; and Professor Loyal A.T. Gryting of the Department of Romance Languages.

I would also like to express my gratitude to the University of Arizona for most generously granting me a sabbatical leave in order to complete this work.

I likewise take this opportunity to thank the editors of *The Atlantic Monthly, Harper's Magazine,* and *Time* for their kind permission to quote sentences from these magazines to illustrate the use of the words studied in the exercises.

1965   D.M.A.

The reviser, too, owes a debt of gratitude to many individuals for their help and support in preparing this second edition, especially to Professors Helena Dettmer and Marcia Lindgren of the Department of Classics at the University of Iowa for their many useful suggestions and for their close scrutiny of the manuscript, and to Professor Sigmund Eisner of the English Department of the University of Arizona. To my students in the course Classics 115, many thanks for your wholehearted participation.

My last words of praise are devoted to R.L. Cherry, who has assisted me in the latter stages of this revision. Mr. Cherry brought to the task skills and judgments developed in his various careers as a teacher in the United States and abroad, a lexicographer who over a period of twenty years contributed to the New Supplement to the *Oxford English Dictionary* and to Houghton Mifflin's and Funk & Wagnalls' dictionaries, as dictionary maker in his work for the University of Arizona Press, and as author of the *Instructor's Manual* for both the original and revised editions of this text.

1986   T.D.W.

BOOKS ON THE STUDY OF WORDS

The following list is by no means exhaustive but contains a number of useful books dealing with various aspects of the material covered in the revised edition of this volume. It includes popular works as well as those which are technical and scholarly.

Ayers, Donald M.
   1972 *Bioscientific Terminology.* Tucson: University of Arizona Press.
Bambas, Rudolph
   1980 *The English Language.* Norman: University of Oklahoma Press.
Barfield, Owen
   1954 *History in English Words.* New ed. London: Faber and Faber.
Baugh, Albert C., and Thomas Cable
   1978 *The History of the English Language.* 3rd ed. New York: Prentice Hall.
Blackie, C.B.
   1968 *A Dictionary of Place Names (Giving Their Derivations).* Detriot: Gale Research (reprint).
Boulton, W.F.
   1972 *A Short History of Literary English.* London: Butler and Tanner.
Brown, Roland W.
   1956 *The Composition of Scientific Words.* Rev. ed. Washington D.C.: The Smithsonian.
Burriss, Eli E., and Lionel Casson
   1949 *Latin and Greek in Current Use.* 2nd ed. New York: Prentice Hall.
Farb, Peter
   1983 *Word Play—What Happens When People Talk.* New York: Alfred A. Knopf.
Funk, Charles E.
   1948 *A Hog on Ice (and Other Curious Expressions).* New York: Harper and Brothers.
   1950 *Thereby Hangs a Tale.* New York: Harper and Brothers.
Funk, Wilfred
   1950 *Word Origins and Their Romantic Stories.* New York: Bell Publishing Co.

Groom, Bernard
1949 *A Short History of English Words*. London: Macmillan.

Hudson, Kenneth
1977 *The Dictionary of Diseased English*. Southampton, England: Camelot Press, Ltd.

Jennings, Charles, Nancy King, and Marjorie Stevenson
1957 *Weigh the Word*. New York: Harper and Brothers.

Jespersen, Otto
1956 *Growth and Structure of the English Language*. New York: Doubleday and Co.

Johnson, Edwin L.
1931 *Latin Words of Common English*. Boston: D.C. Heath.

Lewis, C.S.
1960 *Studies in Words*. Cambridge: Cambridge University Press.

McKnight, George H.
1923 *English Words and Their Background*. New York: Appleton.

Marckwardt, Albert
1980 *American English*. Rev. by J.L. Dillard. Oxford: Oxford University Press.

Nist, John
1968 *A Structural History of English*. New York: St. Martin's Press.

Nurnberg, Maxwell
1981 *I Always Look Up the Word 'Egregious.'* Englewood Cliffs, N.J.: Prentice-Hall.

Nybakken, Oscar E.
1959 *Greek and Latin in Scientific Terminology*. Ames: Iowa State College Press.

Partridge, Eric
1948 *The World of Words*. 3rd ed. London: Hamish Hamilton.

1950 *Name into Word*. New York: Macmillan.

1958 *Origins: A Short Etymological Dictionary of Modern English*. London: Routledge and Paul.

Pyles, Thomas, and John Algeo
1982 *The Origins and Development of the English Language*. 3rd ed. New York: Harcourt Brace Jovanovich.

Saffire, William
1980 *On Language*. New York: Quadrangle/The New York Times Book Co.

Savory, T.H.
1953 *The Language of Science*. London: Andre Deutsch.

Serjeantson, Mary S.
   1936 *A History of Foreign Words in English*. New York: Dutton; and New York: 1961, Barnes and Noble.
Sheard, J.A.
   1954 *The Words We Use*. London: Andre Deutsch.
Shipley, Joseph
   1984 *Origins of English Words: A Discursive Dictionary of Indo-European Roots*. Baltimore: Johns Hopkins.
Simon, John
   1980 *Paradigms Lost*. New York: Clarkson N. Potter.
Skeat, Walter W.
   1946 *An Etymological Dictionary of the English Language*. 4th rev. ed. Oxford: Clarendon Press.
Stewart, George R.
   1945 *Names on the Land*. New York: Random House.
Sturtevant, Edgar H.
   1917 *Linguistic Change*. Chicago: University of Chicago Press; and 1961, Phoenix Press.
Taylor, Isaac
   1925 *Words and Places*. Ed. by B.S. Snell. London: Thomas Nelson.
Vallins, George H.
   1949 *The Making and Meaning of Words*. London: A. and C. Black.
Wagner, L.
   1968 *Names and Their Meaning*. Detroit: Gale Research (reprint).
   1968 *More About Names*. Detroit: Gale Research (reprint).
Williams, Joseph M.
   1975 *Origins of the English Language*. New York: Free Press.

English words
from
Latin and Greek
elements

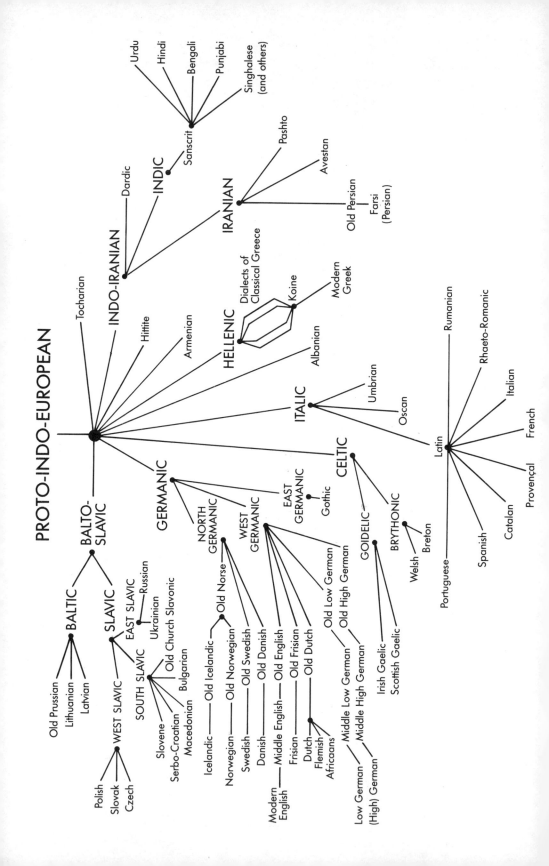

INTRODUCTION

THE INDO-EUROPEAN FAMILY OF LANGUAGES

Our English vocabulary is not something to be studied in isolation but is related in one way or another to many of the other languages of the world. The proper beginning for us, therefore, is to view the place of English in perspective, amid the many tongues of mankind.

Those students who have studied German have undoubtedly noticed a remarkable similarity between that language and their own. The German word *Milch* is very close in sound to the English *milk;* likewise, German *Wasser* and English *water, Brot* and *bread, Fleisch* and *flesh* closely resemble each other, not to mention a great many additional examples. This resemblance to English, moreover, is true not of German alone, but is also the case with other Northern European languages. Perhaps we can see this similarity best if we place side by side in systematic form the words for *mother, father,* and *brother* as they appear in various tongues.

ENGLISH	GERMAN	DUTCH	DANISH
mother	Mutter	moeder	moder
father	Vater	vader	fader
brother	Bruder	broeder	broder

While the spelling of these words makes their similarities obvious, we would be even more struck by their likeness if we heard them pronounced. For instance, a German "v" (as in *Vater*) sounds the same as an English "f." Also, a brief consideration of one's own speech will show that the sounds represented by "t," "th," and "d" are closely related. Compare the way we generally say "ladder" and "latter" in English, and how we pronounce "bottle." Also compare the following words, which all have the same meaning: *three* (English), 'tree' (as pronounced in Russian, Scandinavian, Sanskrit, Serbo-Croatian, and Irish English), *tres* (Latin, Spanish, and Portuguese), and *drei* (German).

At first glance we might conclude that the similarities among these languages are due to borrowing, that because these languages are spoken by people living relatively close to one another, such words were adopted from one of the languages by the others. This is not the

1

case, however, as we shall see later. For one thing, there is usually no need for languages to borrow such simple, fundamental words.

If we extend this table to cover a wider area, we shall find the same similarity, though not to so great a degree.

LATIN	GREEK	IRISH	SANSKRIT	PERSIAN
māter	mētēr	māthair	mātṛ	mādar
pater	patēr	athair	pitṛ	pidar
frāter	phrātēr	brāthair	bhrātṛ	birādar

Now we have already said that the similarities among these languages were not to be explained in terms of borrowing. Their resemblance can best be explained by the hypothesis that they are descendants of a single parent language, or proto-language. This proto-language does not exist in any recorded form and hence can be reconstructed only through comparison of the structures in recorded languages that reveal similarities of the sort examined above. Since such similarities can be demonstrated among most of the languages in Europe and languages even as far away as India, the proto-language has come to be called Proto-Indo-European, or, simply, Indo-European.

This Indo-European parent language, which became extinct long before written records existed, was spoken by a prehistoric people whose homeland was somewhere in southeastern Europe. The exact location of their origin, however, remains an unsolved problem. Tribes that settled in and near the Crimea during the fifth through the third millenia B.C. have been grouped together on the basis of the similarities of their archaeological remains. There is growing evidence that this Kurgan Culture is to be identified with the peoples who spoke the Proto-Indo-European language.

Sometime, beginning about 3500 B.C., successive waves of Indo-Europeans moved westward into Europe and southward into Persia and India. As various groups of Indo-Europeans became isolated from one another, consequently the language of each group began to evolve in its own peculiar fashion. Eventually a number of distinct dialects arose, and in the course of centuries there was no longer one common tongue, but a series of completely different languages, each of which in turn produced still more numerous descendants. The languages of these invaders for all practical purposes obliterated the languages of the earlier inhabitants in much the same way that, in the United States, English has displaced the languages of the American Indians.

Possibly the only survivor of the aboriginal languages of Europe is Basque, spoken in a mountainous corner of northern Spain, where the original inhabitants were able to maintain their way of life against the invaders.

In this way emerged the multitude of languages present today in Europe and southwest Asia. In diagrammatic form the relationship of the Indo-European languages resembles a family tree, some branches having died out, others having given rise to many descendants. A diagram of these relationships is found facing page 1. Languages related in this familial way and words within those languages related in the way examined above are called *cognates*.

1. Germanic (sometimes called Teutonic)

We should perhaps consider the Germanic branch first, for to it belongs English. The primitive Germanic, which antedates the earliest written records, eventually came to be divided geographically into three groups of languages: East, North, and West. The East Germanic languages did not survive into modern times, but we know their principal representative, Gothic, from early translations of the new Testament into that language. The language of the Vandals, the barbarian raiders who sacked Rome in A.D. 455, also belonged to this extinct group. The North Germanic languages are spoken today in the Scandinavian countries, Denmark, Norway, Sweden, and Iceland. West Germanic is represented principally by Modern German, Dutch, Flemish, and English.

2. Italic

When Rome was only a small village of rude huts on the banks of the Tiber, there were several Italic languages having equal status with Latin, but as Rome achieved a dominant position in the ancient world, these disappeared, and Latin alone remained. The modern descendants of Latin, usually called Romance languages, show by their geographical distribution something of the extent of the Roman Empire. In France and Spain the Roman Conquest resulted in the displacement of the earlier languages by Latin. So today French, Spanish, and Portuguese, as well as Italian, are classed as Romance languages. Far to the east, Romanian is likewise a descendant of the language of Roman colonists and soldiers. In the Provence region of southeast France, Provençal, the literary language of the troubadours, was once widely spoken and can still be heard today in a latter, modified form in some rural pockets. In northeast Spain, in and around Barcelona and spreading up into the Pyrenees, the Catalan language continues to be used by some six million people who to this day still fiercely resist assimilation. This is especially true in Andorra, where Catalan is the official language.

3. Hellenic

The Hellenic branch of the Indo-European family is today represented by Modern Greek, which is the descendant of the Classical Greek of Plato and Aristotle and the common Greek dialect of the Eastern Mediterranean area in which the New Testament was written.

4. Celtic

Over two thousand years ago the Celtic languages were spoken throughout a wide area of Western Europe, generally comprising France (or Gaul), part of Spain, and Great Britain. But, as we have seen, after the Roman conquest, Latin replaced the Celtic languages on the continent; and, as we shall see later, the West Germanic Anglo-Saxon largely replaced Celtic speech in Britain, in parts of which, however, where it was difficult for invaders to reach, Celtic languages still exist. Breton and Gaelic continue to be used in Brittany and (principally) Eire, respectively, while Welsh has enjoyed a sizeable renaissance in this century owing to a rise of nationalism in Wales.

5. Balto-Slavic

A. Numerous Slavic languages are spoken in the western regions of the U.S.S.R., and in Bulgaria, Yugoslavia, northern Greece (Macedonia), Poland, and Czechoslovakia.

B. Although spoken by dwindling numbers of people in the Baltic States of Lithuania, Latvia, and Estonia (annexed by the U.S.S.R. in 1940), the Baltic languages—Lithuanian and Latvian—are extremely important to the reconstruction and understanding of Indo-European. The classification of Balto-Slavic together as a single subdivision of Indo-European is regarded with skepticism by many modern linguists.

6. Indo-Iranian

A. The first term in the name Indo-European was determined by the fact that an Indian language, Sanskrit, is fundamental to the development of the science of historical linguistics. As early as 3000 B.C., sacred hymns began to be composed in this language; collections of these hymns, made much later, are called the Vedas. Sanskrit, however, is no longer spoken but, like Latin, has become a learned language.

From spoken dialects called Prakrits, which are related to the sacred dialect Sanskrit, came many of the languages of present-day India and Pakistan, such as Hindi (Hindu), Bengali, and Nepali, as well as Romany, the language of the Gypsies.

B. The sacred writings of ancient Persia were composed in a language closely related to the Indian dialects called Avestan. Farsi, the language of Iran (once Persia), contains an admixture of Arabic elements, but, at basis, it is a descendant of Old Persian, the Iranian dialect spoken by King Xerxes. Several other modern languages belonging to the Iranian group are spoken in small areas of Iran, Iraq, Afghanistan, and Pakistan.

C. Dardic comprises a group of related dialects spoken in the northernmost regions of India along the upper Indus Valley.

7. Armenian

Modern Armenian, the sole member of this group, is a language native to a small area east of the Black Sea, partly in Turkey and partly in the U.S.S.R.

8. Albanian

The only surviving representative of the Albanian branch is Modern Albanian, spoken in Albania, a country nestled between Greece and Yugoslavia on the Adriatic Sea.

9. Anatolian, Phrygian, Thracian, Illyrian, and Tocharian

These are historically confirmed languages belonging to the Indo-European family but without modern descendants.

Because all of these languages have come from a common ancestor, they are called cognate languages. The similarities among them, which are not confined merely to vocabulary but include elements of grammar as well, might be compared to the physical similarities which exist among brothers and sisters, or among cousins. We must remember, however, that the Indo-European is only one of a number of language families throughout the world. The other families have not been studied so thoroughly as Indo-European and consequently no universal agreement has been reached as to the exact extent of many of them.

THE DEVELOPMENT OF THE ENGLISH VOCABULARY

The fraternal relationship between English and its cognate relatives described above helps us to understand the grand parentage from which they all descended and classifies the casually noted similarities between English, German, and their other relatives near and far. But such study will not help us to comprehend the way in which most of our words have entered the English vocabulary. An examination of the words listed on a page in any good dictionary brings a surprising revelation: most of our "English" words are not native to English at all.

Most people borrow words from other nations with whom they have contact. Owing to the accidents of history, a few languages have been great repositories from which others have borrowed. On the other hand, some nations—such as France—are jealous of their language and have tried to maintain its purity untainted by foreign loan words. Yet others are less than careful about the adoption of foreign words and expressions. English has been both a great borrower and a great lender, and history has seen the English-speaking nations dominant at one time and subjugated at another. Hence the history of the English vocabulary is particularly complicated.

Romano-Celtic Period   50 B.C. to A.D. 410*

The location of most developments in the history of English was the British Isles, and for our purposes the earliest inhabitants of these islands were the British peoples who began to arrive there about 1000 B.C. bringing with them in their various incursions an Indo-

---

*All of these dates are only approximate. We do know that the Roman legions left England in A.D. 410. And A.D. 450 (or ca. 450) has been set, by many, as the opening of the Old English Period—but others set this date at A.D. 428, when the first Germanic tribes began invading Britain. All of this does not mean, of course, that the people stopped speaking Roman-Celtic on New Year's Eve, 410, and did not utter another word until they began speaking Old English on January 1, 428, or 450, or ca. 450. It took many years for the Germanic influence to spread through the islands, many more for it to overtake, overwhelm, and eventually supplant Roman-Celtic (which got shoved to the far western and northern extremes), and a great many more for the East Midland Dialect to root and become the standard. It took some three hundred years, in fact, for the large majority of English inflections to get clipped off, a continuing process which ran through almost the entire Middle English Period (p.10).

European language of Celtic affiliation. But numerous nations have occupied these islands since. The first "foreign" invaders who came in numbers were the Romans, who gradually established increasing control over the most southerly and easterly regions of the islands, from Julius Caesar's first invasion (55–54 B.C.), to the emperor Claudius' conquest (A.D. 43–48), until the greatest expansion in the time of the Antonine emperors (A.D. 180). Two earth-and-stone barriers built across the "waists" of Scotland demonstrate that the Romans were unable to subdue the whole island; yet their presence there was influential for centuries, long after the last centrally appointed official was withdrawn sometime about A.D. 410.

The nature of the Romano-British society which developed in Britain after A.D. 180 is difficult to know in detail. Latin was likely the language of the towns while various Celtic dialects were spoken by the agrarian population in the countryside. The rural areas were studded with villas (villages), where, no doubt, Latin and Celtic could be heard spoken together. This reconstructed picture derives partly from the pattern of the Romano-British vocabulary which comes into English. The place-name suffix -cester, -chester (Winchester), meaning "village," comes from the Latin castra, "camp," as do other words which have to do with town- and village-life, such as street from via strata, "paved road"; -wich (Greenwich) from vicus, "village"; cheap (the old meaning of which was "bargain") from caupo, "tavern-keeper," surviving in the London street Cheapside. But some placenames for geographical features and some words deriving from rustic life remain from Celtic: dunum, "hill-fort," survives as a suffix in some Romano-Celtic place-names including London and the pre-Roman capital Camulodunum (modern Colchester), while the names of the rivers Avon, Ouse, and Thames are of Celtic origin; also the words ass (a beast of burden), bannock (fried bread), and brock (badger, skunk), and a few other words have survived into English from the Celtic of that period.

Old English 450 to 1066

A group of three closely related tribes speaking a West Germanic dialect akin to Frisian (still spoken in the north of the Netherlands and in northwest Germany) and to the modern Saxon dialect (Low German) moved into this same geographical area (including the Danish peninsula) sometime about 350. Soon they began piratical raids upon the British coast and elsewhere. Movements of other Germanic tribes had induced the Romans to withdraw troops from Britain, and legend has it that the Romano-British inhabitants hired Germans to help keep out Germans and to ward off the Picts, who kept crossing the Roman walls in Scotland and making raids in the north. But when their employers failed to pay them, the Germans turned to conquest on their own. Thus (or in some other way) arose the first Germanic settlement in Britain; established about 450, it was called the Kingdom of Kent. This first incursion, by a tribes called the Jutes, was followed up by the Saxon settlements of Essex (East Saxony), Wessex (West Saxony), Sussex (South Saxony), and Middlesex (Middle Saxony—the London area), and by those of the Angles—Mercia and Anglia. The name *England* comes from this latter tribe.

Isolated from the other West Germanic tribes on the mainland, and in some measure from each other, these kingdoms soon began speaking distinct dialects. At this point we can say that English was born. Separately and together these kingdoms warred on each other and in their expansion drove the Romano-Celts back into the mountains of Wales and Cumberland. Wessex became the politically dominant kingdom, and consequently its dialect, to some extent, became standard by about 700, when its literature first began to appear. A considerable literature does survive, especially from the period of King Alfred the Great of Wessex (871-899): a compiled history called the *Anglo-Saxon Chronicles,* translations from religious classics, saints' lives, legal documents, medical remedies, riddles, and the transcription of an oral epic poem, *Beowulf.*

The English language has its foundation in these West Germanic dialects. From them derive native suffixes and prefixes which are used on words to denote special relationships: the adjective suffix *-y* as in *holy, mighty;* the suffix *-en,* indicating material composition as in *golden, silken;* the endings *-ish* and *-like* as in our words *mannish, childlike* (the suffix *-like* also gives us the adverbial suffix *-ly* —whence the unlikely inbred *likely,* which etymologically, though rather illogically, means "similar to something similar to"); *-ful* as in *bountiful* and *beautiful; -some* as in *handsome* and *winsome; -ward* as in *earthward, upward;* the noun suffixes *-hood* as in *childhood, womanhood; -dom* as in *kingdom, wisdom; -ship* as in *friendship, kinship; -ness* as in *wilderness, righteousness; -th* as in *strength, wealth, youth; -er* as in *writer, reader;* the prefixes *un-* as in *unpleasant, unhappy; for-* in *forgive* and *forget;* and *be-* as in *become, before,* and *beset.* The pronouns of modern English are essentially the same as those of Old English: *I, we, you, he, it, the, this, that, who, what, mine, your, each,* and *any.* Our numbers were their numbers too, including words such as *twin* (in part from OE *twa,* "two") and *other* (often meaning "the second" in OE), but which we no longer recognize as numbers Our system of comparison, in all its oddity, is ancient: *good, better, best,* and *evil, worse, worst* were Saxon. The way our verbs are conjugated comes from those dialects: *bid, bade, bidden; sing, sang, sung;* and some confusion over such series stems from the (incomplete) tendency to have regularized the many Old English conjugations into the one easiest to learn, the one ending in *-(e)d* and its variations with *-t.*

The basic vocabulary of modern English (including most of the unrepeatable words you know) comes through the ages unchanged from Old English: *love, say, live, have, own, do, be, will, bury, name, reach, long, strong, high, quick, sun, food, hand, finger, friend, brother, father, mother, stone, earth,* etc., etc. Also, from the poetics of that time, come many alliterative expressions still used today such as "still as a stone," "sticks and stones," "from top to toe," etc.

During Alfred's lifetime and later, during the 11th century, the Vikings made raids on the east coast of Britain—piratical at first, but in the end strategic. Alfred was forced to recognize the Vikings' possession in fact of some one-half of what we now call England, a district and rule termed the Danelaw. These as yet un-Christianized Danes were synonymous with "foreigner" and "wrongdoer." Still, a great number settled in Britain, and Scandinavian family names and place names (those ending in *-by, -thorpe, -beck,* and *-thwaite*) as well as Scandinavian loan words came into English. King Knut (Canute) achieved what no Saxon king had been able—to unify the land as one peaceful realm. (Knut was also king of both Denmark and Norway for a time.)

The language of these Danes was a North Germanic dialect. Numbers of its words were very similar to the West Germanic words of Old English so that the words merged as the people merged: *man, wife, father, folk, house, life, summer, winter, hear, see, bring, come,* etc., etc. Some dying words were given new life by the Danish infusion: *dale,* "valley" (used until recently only in Yorkshire, where the Danes settled); *barn* may well have disappeared from English entirely without the Danish revival as would the verb *blend.*

On the other hand, the phonetics of the two languages were different; for example, Scandinavian has *sk* where English has *sh.* Hence there are many pairs of words in English with these phonetic differences which originally had the same meaning: *skirt-shirt, hale-whole, nay-no, raise-rear, fro-from, screech-shriek,* etc. Sometimes the Scandinavian word entirely replaced the English one: *egg, sister, Thursday, kettle, give, gift, get,* and *guild* all had native counterparts which have disappeared. Sometimes the native word survived but with an imported meaning. In Old English *dream* meant "joy"—its modern meaning, was taken from the Vikings; *bread* meant "fragment" in Old

English; *dwell* meant "lead astray"; and *plow* meant "measure of land." Other common Scandinavian words simply enriched the deficient native vocabulary: *sky, skull, fellow, husband, skin, wing, haven, root, skill, anger, low, loose, odd, wrong, ill, ugly, rotten, happy, drown, hit, take, call, thrive,* etc.

Middle English   1066 to 1500

The battle of Hastings in 1066 reduced England to the status of a fiefdom, the lords of which were the French-speaking aristocracy of Normandy. Political subjugation leads to linguistic imperialism, which follows a predictable pattern. The overlords learn little of the native language, but the natives, once they have become bilingual, admit into their own language increasing numbers of words and phrases from the invading language. Had the French continued to dominate, this process might have been carried to completion; but since they did not, the result is a curious redundancy in the English vocabulary—pairs of synonyms, one French, the other native English: *hog, swine, pig, farrow, sow,* and *boar* are all native terms to do with raising pigs, but beside them we must place the French word *pork,* the word for pig meat cooked and ready for the lord's table. Other examples are *hut* (English) vs. *cottage* (from French), *bill* vs. *beak, clothe* vs. *dress, help* vs. *aid, deed* vs. *action, folk* vs. *people.* Both in spelling and in meaning many native words have been influenced by French words of similar appearance, sound, or meaning. (French itself had earlier borrowed many words of Germanic origin.) Hence *rich* owes allegiance both to OE *rice,* "powerful, rich" and to French *riche; main* both to OE *moegen,* "strength" (which was influenced by Scandinavian *megn,* "very") and to French *maine* (from Latin *magnus,* "great"), which itself may have been influenced by *main,* "hand" (from Latin *manus*). Most of our terms for government and law come from Norman French: *govern, state, realm, crown, country, nation, power, authority, parliament, people,* etc.

The ascendancy of a new aristocracy that centered in London undercut the standardization of Old English to the West Saxon dialect. With time and circumstances the Norman overlords ceased to be foreigners, and they began to adopt English as their everyday language. Since the Norman capital was London, the dialect adopted as standard was the East Midland which was spoken in the region of London. This was the language of the court, the bureaucracy, the universities, and the literature (for example, that of Chaucer). French was still the language of elevated discourse, and it continued to be taught. The Latin ancestry of French was strongly felt, and English education was infused with a great Latin component, an influence which spilled over into everyday language. It is often impossible to determine whether a Latinate word in English was borrowed from French or directly from Latin: *grave, gravity, solid, consolation,* etc. Sometimes a French loan word was later re-formed on Latin lines: *descrive* went to *describe; parfait* went to *perfect.* Then, too, the Latin genius had long been instilled into the English head, and some non-Latin words were invented to look as if they had been borrowed: *intensity* is older than French *intensité,* and a Latin prototype (*intensitas*) does not exist.

The invention of printing during this period considerably complicated the evolution of the language. French and Latin spelling influenced the orthography of native words. The result was that early Middle English enjoyed an almost phonetic spelling. Printing tended to preserve this spelling, but the pronunciation of English has undergone great changes since. The *k* and *gh* of *knight,* silent now, were pronounced by Chaucer whose spelling we maintain: the *i* in the same word was then pronounced as in "hit," but today we pronounce it as in "bite." William Caxton's printing press also made final the tendency toward the adoption of the East Midland dialect as the standard.

Modern English   1550 to Present

The career of Caxton (1476–90) is the event which arbitrarily marks the beginning of Modern English. Three great developments within this period have profoundly changed our language: 1) British colonialism, a **political** development which we might date to the defeat of the Spanish Armada in 1588; 2) an **intellectual** one—the revival of ancient learning and the reaction to that revival—Renaissance and Enlightenment; 3) an **economic** and **technical** development, the industrial and post-industrial revolutions and the development of modern science.

The merchant class, who exploited and settled the territories opened up by British explorers, pirates, and navy, did not belong to the aristocracy which spoke the London dialect. Hence New England was settled largely by speakers of the East Anglian dialect. Social struggles between the two dialect groups were an instrumental cause for the American Revolution and may have contributed to the radical shift in the pronunciation of English in modern times as described above. Two opposing forces still affect our speech patterns and our judgments of one another: the leveling influence that was brought about first by maritime commerce and by its extension via radio and television and, most of all, by printing (written words have no sound), which tends to unite us; and the social, class, and national dialects, which tend to keep us apart. Commercial expansion has had other effects as well: English has become an international language. Consequently, foreign words have been borrowed as our trading partners borrowed English. From Persian come *divan, khaki*, etc.; from the languages of India come *cot, punch* (the drink), *ginger, thug*, and *loot; kowtow, tea*, and *catsup* are Chinese. When the Netherlands and England shared a monarch (and during their allegiance against the Spanish) many Dutch words, having to do especially with sailing and art, came into our language: *yacht, yawl, schooner, deck, cruise, iceberg, freebooter*, and *easel, etch, sketch*, and *landscape*. From the period of Dutch and English competition in South Africa came a few others with their local (not their broader Dutch) connotations: *veld*, "open rangeland"; *trek*, "a colonial migration by oxcart"; *spoor*, "track of a wild animal"; etc. Dutch and English contact in New York-New Amsterdam has left *cookie* and *boss*. From Japan we borrowed a few words: *japan* (a verb) means "apply a glossy black lacquer," and through Japanese from Chinese comes *tycoon*. Competition with the Portuguese and with the Spanish in the New World and the Far East led English speakers to borrow a number of words: *armada, escapade, embargo, cargo, palaver*. From native Americans we have taken a number of words: *caucus, moccasin, jerky, chocolate, tomato, wampum, powwow, tomahawk, totem*, etc., as well as the names for plants and animals of species that are native to the Americas: *raccoon, skunk, coyote, hickory, peyote*. Place names from the American Indians are in abundance, including the names of half the states themselves. From our Spanish and French competitors in the Americas have come others: *prairie, butte, levee, bayou, picayune, mesa, siesta, ranch, canyon, stampede, rodeo, cafeteria, vigilante, marijuana*, etc.

We have also borrowed words for ethnic specialties from around the world: *sherry, patio, anchovy, matador, cordovan, lime*, and *don* from Spanish; *pasta, spaghetti, macaroni, balcony, sonnet, colonnade, corridor, grotto, opera, fresco, dilettante*, and *fascist* from Italian; *wurst, pretzel, delicatessen, kraut, kindergarten, hinterland, weltanschauung, lebensraum, noodle*, and *Nazi* from German; *steppe, samovar, podzol, vodka, sputnik*, and *Samoyed* from Russian; *sherbet, caraway, sash, alcove, hashish, harem, assassin, zero, algebra, alcohol, cipher, alchemy* (and *chemistry*), *elixir, nadir*, and *zenith* from Moorish and Arabic cultures; *boomerang* and *kangaroo* from native Australian languages; *mana, taboo, lanai, lei, hula*, and *Hawaii* from Polynesian languages; and many others.

The Renaissance opened the door for regiments of Latin and Greek words to march into our dictionary. Some seventy percent of the words encountered there give tribute to these languages as their source. Conversely, and more relevant to the point being made here, about ten percent of the Latin vocabulary has found its way directly into English without a French intermediary. At first, the words borrowed were those used in learned applications and in translating or writing about learned matters. Hence, Chaucer uses the French-derived *egal* in his poetry but the Latinate *equal* in his treatise, *The Astrolabe*. This results in a great many doublets*, one French, one Latin or Greek: *genie* (through French) vs. *genius* (from Latin); *complaisance* vs. *complacence; base* vs. *basis; certainty* vs. *certitude; critique* vs. *critic; colour* vs. *discoloration.* (The American spelling of such words as *color* has reverted to the Latin form while the British spelling *colour* keeps the French form.)

Later, words were coined on the basis of Latin precedent but without regard to the actual presence or absence of a direct Latin model. *Fragment* is a Latin word with a suffix dropped off, but *fragmentary, fragmental*, and *fragmentation*—and the back-formed *frag* (noun and verb) that came out of the Vietnam war—have no Latin originals. Since the need has arisen for new words to describe the discoveries of science and to name the innovations wrought by technology, Latin and Greek have come into the dictionary as an avalanche. Lexicographers cannot keep up with the flurry of new words formed from these languages, and indeed some words come into being and fall out of use before they are recorded in any dictionary.

Most of the words to be studied in this book entered English during the Renaissance or later, directly from Latin and Greek. Since they were generally borrowed or coined by scholars, they lend themselves to systematic treatment. But many of the words which came through French or some other intermediary do not show such regularity in form as to be readily analyzed. When such words contain a base which is important enough to be learned, the base will be listed separately from the Latin form.

ASSIGNMENT

I. Which of the following languages are cognate with English?

1. Hindi
2. Hungarian
3. Korean
4. Russian
5. Arabic
6. Portuguese

---

*See the discussion of doublets in Latin Lesson XXII.

II. To which branch of the Indo-European family does each of the following languages belong?

1. Bulgarian
2. Romanian
3. Sanskrit
4. Spanish
5. Greek
6. Welsh
7. Swedish

III. With the aid of a dictionary find the language from which each of the following is ultimately derived.

1. almanac
2. bizarre
3. boomerang
4. chair
5. cherub
6. chocolate
7. crag
8. dollar
9. galore
10. geyser
11. gingham
12. hominy
13. horde
14. hurricane
15. julep
16. khaki
17. magazine
18. mammoth
19. paradise
20. robot
21. sapphire
22. sherbet
23. swastika
24. tungsten

IV. With the aid of a dictionary trace the linguistic route of each of the following words into Modern English.

1. apricot
2. bishop
3. butter
4. car
5. chemist
6. orange

PART I

Word elements
from Latin

LESSON I

THE DICTIONARY

The most valuable tool in improving vocabulary is a good dictionary—and the word *good* here is not to be taken lightly, for there is gradation in quality among dictionaries as there is with most things in life. Available at the time this book was published, some of the better dictionaries, any one of which would be a good choice for this course, are the following:

> *Random House College Dictionary* (RHD)
> *Webster's New World Dictionary* (WNWD)
> *Webster's New Collegiate Dictionary* (WNCD)
> *Webster's Ninth New Collegiate Dictionary* (W9)
> *The American Heritage Dictionary* (AHD)

There are also various paperbacks out by some of the major dictionary publishers. The *Oxford American Dictionary* is to be especially avoided for this course as it does not record any etymology, and etymology plays a very large part in this course.

Because of the lengthy process of publishing a book, several months can pass between the time the final editorial work is accomplished and the time the book appears on the shelf. Students should therefore understand that recent coinages, abbreviations, blends, acronyms, loan words, clips, and so on, as well as current slang—all of which may have been seen recently in *Newsweek, Playboy,* or *New Woman*—may well not be in his or her brand-new dictionary.

New words may not be there for other reasons. Many factors, too detailed to mention here and some of which are even out of the editor's hands, contribute to the decision to or not to include particular words in an update. Simple economics, for example, often dictate that only so many words can be added to a new update as a result of space allowance dictated by the publisher, which in turn is dictated by pressure to keep the price competitive. It is often difficult to appreciate the compound problem here.

Students should also learn at some time to find their way around the unabridged dictionaries. The three most popular ones are the one-volume *Webster's Third New International Dictionary,* the thirteen-volume *Oxford English Dictionary* together with its updated *New Supplement,* and the *Random House Dictionary of the English Language, The Unabridged Edition.*

It might also be pointed out that there are now dictionaries for almost every subject one can think of, from architecture, musical terms, and pharmaceutical science, to machine tools, insurance technology, and barley, malting, and brewing. The current *Books in Print*, itself updated every year and available for reference in any good bookstore, will list all of these, which can be ordered if they are not on the shelves.

As politics over the years has produced the Democrats and their polar counterpart the Republicans, so dictionaries have had their prescriptivists (those who would *prescribe* the language, by dictating to people what they should and should not say or write) and its descriptivists (those who would *describe* the language, by simply recording what it is that people say and write without giving value judgments). The battle has raged for some two centuries, and prescriptivists were well in command in the early years. As early as 1697, Daniel Defoe proposed an academy that should be "sufficient authority for the usage of words, and sufficient also to expose the innovations of other men's fancies... and have liberty to correct and censure the exorbitance of writers." He allowed the academy should be the "judges of style and language, and no author would have the impudence to coin without their authority." Jonathan Swift was right behind him: "Some method should be thought on for ascertaining and fixing our language for ever....I see absolutely no reason why any language should be perpetually changing." Furthermore, "besides the grammar-part... they will observe many gross improprieties, which however authorized by practice, and grown familiar, ought to be discarded [and] utterly thrown out of our language."*

Similar proposals were being made in other countries, such as Italy and France. Against a constant wash of criticism, the French Academy, since its inception in the 1630s, continues to this day its adamant and conservative attitude toward the intrusion of foreign elements into the French language, determined as the Academy is to keep French "pure and eloquent" and cleanse it of impurities.

Throughout the years, purists and other self-appointed protectors of and commentators on the language have bristled against the liberals on matters of pronunciation, spelling, usage labels (discussed further in section VI, *Special Information* following), hybrids (see Lesson VII), taboo words and jargon (Lesson XVIII), clips (Lesson XX), blends

---

*Albert C. Baugh, *A History of the English Language*, 2nd ed., Appleton-Century-Crofts, New York, 1963, pp. 316 ff.

(Lesson XXI), and other aspects of the language. With modern contributions from Jacques Barzun, John Simon, Edwin Newman, T.S. Eliot, William Saffire, George Orwell, W.H. Auden, Kenneth Hudson, Ezra Pound, and other notables, controversy continues, although—at least in the making of dictionaries—descriptivism has won the day. Therefore, no amount of criticism will prevent "gross improprieties," "diseased English," "the exorbitance of writers," or other "impurities" from entering the language—and in due time, your dictionary, if the words live long enough, for it has already been said that some words come into being and fall out of use before they are recorded in any dictionary.

Noah Webster's 1806 *A Compendious Dictionary of the English Language* offers for the word *clock* "an instrument to show time, beetle, large insect, ornament, part of a stocking"; *genitals* "the parts of generation"; *generation* "an age, race, family, production"; *progeny* "an offspring race, issue, generation"; *offspring* "a propagation, generation, race, fruit"; *propagation* "generation, production, increase." Dictionaries have come a long way since then, and many people do not realize just how much information a modern dictionary contains. In looking up a word, they usually note only its definition and spelling, but a good abridged or desk dictionary will contain most—and, in some dictionaries, all—of the eight categories of information that follow.

I. Form of the Word

This includes not only the most commonly accepted spelling but also the more usual variant forms (e.g., *theater,* but also *theatre*). Also, the division of a word into syllables is shown; this indicates how a word should be divided when it is necessary to break it at the end of a line. Likewise, in the case of certain words, capitalization (compare, for example, the meanings of *Democratic* and *democratic*), the use of italics (for foreign words and phrases), hyphens (as in *white-headed*), and apostrophes (as in *fool's gold*) are indicated.

For the purposes of saving space, contemporary dictionaries universally do not define suffixed words with predictable definitions but add them on at the end of an entry—as *iteratively* and *iterativeness* are added on to the main-entry word *iterative* because their meanings can be determined by tacking the meaning of *-ly* and *-ness* onto the appropriate definition of *iterative. Hardly* and *hardness,* on the other hand, are given main-entry status since their respective meanings cannot be determined in this manner.

II. Pronunciation

The phonetic values of the individual letters in a word are indicated by a set of symbols (e.g., $\bar{a}$, $\ddot{a}$, $\dot{o}$, etc.) in parentheses after each entry. Many people unfortunately do not take the trouble to determine what sounds are represented by these symbols, which vary somewhat from dictionary to dictionary. This is not a difficult task, however, for at the bottom of the page, or on the inside of the covers, or in the introductory material there is a key which shows, by giving familiar words as examples, the pronunciation indicated by each of the symbols (e.g., $\bar{a}$, is pronounced as in *day;* $\ddot{a}$, as in *bother;* $\dot{o}$, as in *saw,* etc.). The syllable on which the accent or stress falls is marked, and in some instances a secondary accent is also indicated. Remember that your dictionary is not attempting to set the pronunciation of a word but is only describing how educated users generally pronounce it. In many cases, therefore, several different accepted pronunciations will be given.

However, do not expect consistency even here. Some dictionaries do considerably better than others, for example, in coverage of British pronunciation. AHD (1982), RHD (1984), WNCD (1981) all cover the British pronunciation of *clerk, schedule,* and *waistcoat,* but none of them cover *controversy, garage, geyser,* and *St. Bernard.* AHD further misses *quinine, reveille,* and the letter *Z.*

There is also inconsistency in the given pronunciation of loan words. Latin loan words are discussed in Lesson XXV; pronunciation exercises of words from Greek are in the first two lessons of Part Two; and further discussion of loan words from other languages opens Lesson VII of Part Two.

III. Grammatical Information

A dictionary will list the part of speech of the entry, whether noun, verb, etc. Of course, a word may serve as more than one part of speech, as, for instance, *travel,* which can be either a verb or a noun; in such a case the meanings are given for both uses. There will also be listed, *if irregular,* the past tense and participles of verbs (e.g., under the word *drive* are given *drove, driven,* and *driving*), the plural forms of nouns (e.g., *children* and *mice*), and the comparative and superlative forms of adjectives (e.g., under the word *much* are listed *more* and *most*).

IV. Etymology

We have already seen in the introductory exercise that a dictionary indicates the language(s) from which a word has come into modern

English. Some dictionaries will also give the meaning of the word in the original language(s) if the sense is different from that of the modern English word; and here, some dictionaries are more meticulous than others in offering, where possible, a meaning of the source word(s) that most closely fits the meaning of the modern English word that derives from it.

Also, in an effort to save space (and hence to keep the cost of the dictionary down), dictionaries usually do not offer the ultimate etymology, even where it is known, for many words. In the case of *irrepressibility,* for example, you must learn to clip off the prefixes and suffixes and get it down to the basic word, in this case *repress.* Also, especially in the case of etymologically related words, most dictionaries offer only the immediate derivation, with a note to the user that a complete etymology is given at the related word. You may have to look in three (or more) places to track down the ultimate etymology of some words. Some dictionaries do not offer ultimate etymologies for many words; you may even have to go to another—better, or larger—dictionary.

V. Definition

Besides giving modern meanings of words, most dictionaries also list older meanings, including those which have passed out of use. Dictionaries vary considerably in the manner in which they present the different meanings of a word. Some list the definitions in historical order; that is, the oldest one is first, and the most modern one(s) are at the end of the list. Others do the complete reverse—by starting with the commonly known definitions. Another arranges definitions according to a "semantic order," which is supposed to allow the reader to follow the logical development of the various meanings of a word. AHD arranges the various meanings of a word in what it calls "a psychologically meaningful order" so that "a complex word can to some extent be perceived as a structural unit. Senses are not arranged historically or by frequency of use. Rather, they are ordered analytically, according to central meaning clusters from which related subsenses and additional separate senses may evolve. Such a meaningful order is considered to be [although the editors do not say by whom] the most useful presentation for the general reader."

You must refer to the guide in the front of your dictionary to determine which of these patterns your dictionary follows.

VI. Special Information

The use of subject labels and geographical labels has remained fairly constant, and without much controversy, over the years. But the terms *slang, colloquial, informal,* and *dialect* have gone through some heavy weather, especially since the publication in 1961 of *Webster's Third New International Dictionary,* whose editors chose to delete hundreds of usage or status labels from words that had for many years carried them. This dictionary opened up a new chapter in the war between the conservatives of the language (who accused *W3* of serving "to reinforce the . . . disastrous . . . notion that good English is whatever is popular"*) and the liberals (or descriptivists, who claim "there are many different degrees of standard usage which cannot be distinguished by status labels"†). A spate of linguists, educators, administrators, journalists, and others took sides and joined the foray with a flood of books and newspaper and magazine articles. Questions like: What is good English? Who is to decide? What should be the standard, the spoken language or the written language? have all been argued for many years and will likely continue to be for many more.

With the increasing number of new dictionaries—for grade-school students, junior high, senior high, college, office, and for "general" use—that came onto the marketplace in the 1970s and 1980s, and with the inevitable commercial competition that ensued, each editor (or editorial board) set the standards for their own dictionary. If an editor thought a particular word was slang, it was labeled "slang." Not surprisingly, dictionaries vary in this area. For example, out of a random sampling of a few early- and mid-1980s contemporary dictionaries *psycho* appears as "slang" in five and not marked at all in three; *weirdo* and *frosh* (freshman) are "informal" in two, "slang" in two, and not recorded in two—as with *civvie, loonie,* and many other words. The label "informal" has generally replaced "colloquial" in American dictionaries.

Although dictionaries vary in the labeling of a word, the definitions of the labels themselves are reasonably standard. The following usage labels are often misunderstood:

Informal refers to words that are suitable to casual or familiar speech, or to letters or other creative writing, but are generally not considered appropriate to formal speech or writing.

Dialect is in common use in reference to a language considered as one of a group that have a common ancestor. Here we can say that Persian, German, Latin, and English are Proto-Indo-European dialects. *Dialect,* in the sense of its being a variety of a language used by a

---

*Editorial in *New York Times,* October 12, 1961.
†Rebuttal to the above *New York Times* editorial, by Philip B. Gove, Editor in Chief of *W3,* in *New York Times,* November 5, 1961.

group of speakers who are socially or geographically set off from the mainstream, has largely fallen into disuse. To many, dialect in this sense implies inferiority, and with the contemporary view that the grammar, phonology, and vocabulary of all speakers of a language are linguistically on an equal par, what used to be called a Scottish dialect, Southern dialect, Black dialect, and so on, are now generally referred to, at least on the formal level, as Southern U.S. English, etc.

Obsolete means that a word or a particular definition of a word has entirely disappeared from current usage as, for example, the meaning of *explode*, "to drive an actor off the stage by noisy disapproval."

Archaic means that a word or definition is generally obsolete but is still kept for certain special uses, as, for instance, *hath*, which is confined mainly to church ritual.

Students are advised to consult the guide in the front matter of their dictionaries in order to understand the types of labels (if any) and their application as determined by the editors.

VII. Synonyms

One of the most useful services performed by a dictionary is the listing of synonyms (and, to some extent, antonyms). Of course, there are special dictionaries devoted entirely to this, but a good abridged dictionary can give much useful information to a person trying to avoid repetitious use of the same word. Often, also, a paragraph is included explaining the varying shades in the meanings of synonyms. For example, if one is looking for the synonyms of *filthy*, he will be referred by the dictionary to the entry *dirty*, where he will find listed *dirty*, *filthy*, *foul*, *nasty*, *squalid*, and perhaps even others. Then the slight differences between these synonyms in meaning or usage will be described, such as that *filthy* suggests something both dirty and offensive, while *foul* implies something which is revoltingly offensive and is putrid or stinking.

VIII. Idiomatic Usage

An idiom is an expression whose meaning cannot be derived from the individual words in it, for example, *to turn over a new leaf*, meaning "to begin anew, to make a fresh start." Even *turn over* by itself has some seven different idiomatic meanings in current use, as in "to turn over your financial affairs to someone," "to turn over an idea in your mind," "to turn over (=sell) all the Christmas stock in your store," "to turn over your car engine on a cold morning," etc. These special verb + adverb expressions are often called phrasal verbs (as in AHD), as distinguished from verb phrases such as *was going* or *had been typing.* Sometimes a verb + adverb is an idiom, as in all the examples above, but many times the verb and adverb each retains its own meaning. In the sentences, "The cook turned over the pancakes," or "The baby turned over in his crib," *turn over* is not an idiom. Similarly, in "I looked up the chimney," *look up* is not idiomatic; but in "I looked up the word in my dictionary," it is.

There is a standard practice in the recording of idioms in dictionaries (except for AHD, which has its own system). If there is a noun in a phrase, the item will be entered under that noun (take to the *cleaners,* spill the *beans,* below the *belt*); under the first or most important noun if there is more than one noun (*nuts* and bolts, *lion's* share, a *shot* in the arm); under the verb if there is no noun (*bend* over backwards, *hem* and haw); if there is no noun or verb, the item will be under the first or most important word (out of the *blue; fair* and square, *every* now and then). But do not expect absolute consistency in all cases. For example, *bed of roses* is a main entry in some dictionaries but is entered under *rose* in others.

IX. Miscellaneous

For reasons that are determined by a dictionary's editor, dictionaries vary in what is commonly referred to as front matter and back matter. AHD has an appendix on *Biographical Entries*; RHD doesn't, which does have an appendix on *Signs and Symbols,* which AHD doesn't. The latest WNCD even provides an *Index,* as well as an appendix on *Foreign Words and Phrases* that neither AHD nor RHD has. Any of this could change, of course, with a new editor. Some dictionaries give a sketch of the history of the English language, articles on usage and acceptability, British English (and English as spoken in other parts of the world), given names, colleges and universities, a brief style manual, geographical entries, and other encyclopedic material.

Because many people are unfamiliar with the concise manner in which dictionaries are written, users often fail to get the full benefit from looking up a word, and sometimes even misinterpret the information that they do find. The exercises that follow are designed to familiarize the students with their respective dictionaries and give them practice in finding specific information.

ASSIGNMENT

I. Give the variant spellings of the following as listed in your dictionary. If there are geographical preferences, state such choices:

Example: *judgment*—preferred American; *judgement*—preferred British.

1. abridgment
2. adviser
3. archaeology
4. catchup
5. fulfill
6. movable

II. Find whether in your dictionary the following pairs of words remain separate, are hyphenated, or are written as one word:

1. anti Semitic
2. anti slavery
3. black list
4. black market
5. folk dance
6. folk rock
7. folk lore
8. good humored

III. Since pronunciation exercises are best done orally in class, be prepared to give the pronunciation of the following words. Give any geographical preferences, variants, or exclusive uses of any pronunciation:

1. chiropodist
2. schedule
3. forbade
4. perfect
5. frappé
6. forecastle
7. heinous
8. chauvinism
9. alumnae
10. creek

IV. Give the plural or plurals of the following. Indicate any preferences or exclusive uses of any plural:

1. analysis
2. antenna
3. appendix
4. grotto
5. goose
6. mongoose
7. moose
8. phenomenon
9. datum
10. news

V. Give all the past tenses and participles of the following verbs:

1. abide
2. awake
3. awaken
4. bid
5. cleave (to split)
6. dive
7. drag
8. dwell
9. plead
10. spit (to eject saliva)

VI. Describe the origin of each of the following:

1. amethyst
2. gerrymander
3. grog

4. guy (a person)
5. O.K.
6. paraphernalia

VII. Give the usage or status label (if any) of each of the following:

1. ain't
2. fake (counterfeit)
3. irregardless

4. lave (to wash)
5. phony
6. poke (sack)

VIII. Give the geographical label (if any) of each of the following:

1. agley
2. billabong
3. cayuse

4. pone
5. pub
6. pukka

IX. Give all the synonyms listed in your dictionary for each of the following:

1. claim
2. gentle
3. inert

4. monetary
5. paramount
6. sparkle

X. Distinguish between the following pairs of synonyms:

1. begin—commence
2. copious—ample
3. curious—inquisitive
4. fair—impartial
5. faithful—loyal
6. meaning—significance

7. riddle—enigma
8. specific—special
9. sudden—abrupt
10. timely—opportune
11. value—prize
12. vulgar—common

XI. Give the meaning(s) of each of the following idiomatic expressions:

1. do for
2. dog in the manger
3. let on
4. down at the heel

5. fill the bill
6. carry on
7. make away with
8. get over

DEFINITION

In most of the lessons in this book, students will be asked to define words, for the ability to define is one of the surest tests of a knowledge of word meanings. The easiest way to arrive at a definition is to look it up in a dictionary; but, if a person merely copies the dictionary wording in an unthinking fashion, he or she is not likely to retain any lasting memory of it. Rather, with the aid of a dictionary, one should try to define an unfamiliar term in his own words. To do this, however, it is necessary to know something of the requirements for an adequate definition.

I. *A definition should be equivalent to the term to be defined.*

In the first place, a definition should be neither too broad nor too narrow. To define a *saw* as "a tool" would be to define it too broadly, for there are many other kinds of tools besides saws. On the other hand, a definition such as "an instrument with teeth used for cutting wood" is too narrow, since some saws are used to cut metal. In the same way, the definition of *pen* as "a writing instrument" is too broad because it would include pencils, typewriters, and so on. But "a writing instrument with its own supply of ink" is too narrow a definition for it includes every type of pen except a quill pen.

In the second place, for a definition to be equivalent, a noun should be defined as a noun, a verb as a verb, and so on. In defining the noun *penury,* for example, do not say "poor" or "to be poor"; rather, use a noun or phrase, such as "want" or "lack of resources." When one defines a verb like *alleviate,* its meaning should be expressed not as an adjective, "less severe," but as a verb, "to make less severe." In the case of an adjective, one should use another adjective or adjective phrase. Thus *gregarious* does not mean "a herd" but "tending to gather in a herd."

II. *A definition should give the essential characteristics of the term to be defined and not merely make a statement about the term.*

Essential characteristics are rather elusive and relative, and they will vary with the purpose of the definition. But if, for instance, one defines *democracy* as "a type of government which has the interests of its citizens at heart," while this statement is no doubt true, he has provided no real explanation of the word. A more serviceable definition would be "government by the people." Likewise, to define a *traitor* as "a man whom everybody hates" does not tell much about the meaning of the word. Samuel Johnson, who compiled the first great English dictionary, occasionally yielded to his prejudices or to a spirit of playfulness in giving definitions, with the result that he has provided some famous examples of this type of shortcoming. Dr. Johnson, who cared little for the Scots, defined *oats* as "a grain, which in England is generally given to horses, but in Scotland supports the people."

III. *A definition should be simple and clear, and expressed if possible in terms more familiar than the one to be defined.*

Again, the classic example of failure to observe this rule is Dr. Johnson's definition of *network,* "anything reticulated or decussated, at equal distances, with interstices between the intersections."

Above all, a definition should not contain the term to be defined nor any derivative of it. Do not define *imperturbable,* for example, as "incapable of being perturbed."

IV. *A definition should not be expressed in negative terms where affirmative can be used.*

It is not very helpful to be told that a *sofa* is "neither a bed nor a chair," or that a *Protestant* is "a Christian who is not a Catholic." On the other hand, some terms like *imperturbable* and *improvident* have to be defined negatively.

LATIN BASES

As was indicated in the introduction, many of the longer and more difficult words of the English vocabulary are compounds formed from several individual elements. These elements are of three kinds, known as bases (sometimes called roots or stems),* prefixes, and suffixes,

---

*Technically, *root, stem,* and *base* are not synonymous, *root* being a much broader term than the other two. This book, since it is primarily concerned with these elements as they are to be found in English words and not as they appear in Latin or Greek, makes varying use of all three types in the exercises, whichever type seems in a particular instance more useful for the student. Since, however, in the great majority of cases it is the base that has been listed, I have used this term throughout. (See Oscar E. Nybakken, *Greek and Latin in Scientific Terminology,* Ames, Iowa, 1959, pp. 3–5.)

and a relatively small number of them have been used again and again in various combinations to form different words. In this lesson you will be introduced to Latin bases, that is, Latin words as they appear in English derivatives without the various characteristic Latin endings, *-us, -a, -um, -are,* etc. Throughout the book these bases will be printed in capital letters followed by a hyphen; e.g., FIRM-, GRAV-, MOD-. In later lessons we shall see how, by the addition of various prefixes and suffixes, many English words have been formed from a single base. For example:

con-FIRM-at-ion
in-FIRM-ity
in-FIRM-ary
FIRM-ament
re-af-FIRM-at-ion
af-FIRM-at-ive

Frequently, of course, Latin bases appear in English without the addition of any prefix or suffix.

I. Sometimes a base by itself forms an English word.

Latin Base	Meaning	English Derivative
FIRM-	firm, strong	firm
VERB-	word, verb	verb
FORT-	strong	fort

II. In other cases a final silent *e* is added in English. (This *e* is not a suffix and has no meaning.)

Latin Base	Meaning	English Derivative
GRAV-	heavy	grave
FIN-	end, limit	fine

Dictionaries, in describing the origin of an English word derived from Latin, will give the actual Latin word rather than the base; e.g., the word *verb* is listed as coming from the Latin *verbum.* In some cases, also, a dictionary will give two forms of a Latin word; e.g., our word *origin* is derived from the Latin *origo, originis* (the nominative and genitive cases). If one keeps in mind the English words, however, the roots, VERB- and ORIGIN,- will be readily apparent; in this book, bases as they appear in English will be our primary concern.

III. Sometimes a word was borrowed into English at different times and through different avenues. This happened when a Latin word passed through another language, usually French or Old French, before English picked it up, with the resulting new English word having a decidedly French twist. Then later on, the Latin word that whelped the French word we borrowed was itself borrowed into English. For example the English verb *grieve* came in from Old French, which borrowed it from the Latin base GRAV-, duly altering it on arrival to conform to the French sound system or spelling system, or (as in this case) both. Later, English lifted the Latin base GRAV-.

In all cases where this has happened to a Latin base being studied, the form(s) borrowed directly from Latin will be given first, and any forms that came in through French are shown in brackets. For example:

Latin Base	Meaning	English Derivatives
GRAV-, [GRIEV-]	heavy	grave, gravity, grievance
LINE-, [LIGN-]	line	line, align

IV. In some cases a Latin base is extended by the suffixed element *-at-* (sometimes *-it-*), which was a normal part of many Latin verb bases. (To this sometimes a silent *-e*, or other suffix, was added.) In these instances *-at(e)* merely represents a different form of the Latin verb and usually has little or no effect upon the meaning. Consider the base SPIR- "to breathe" with some of its possibilities:

a- SPIR-e
a- SPIR-at(e)
a- SPIR-at-ion
con- SPIR-e
con- SPIR-at(e)
con- SPIR-at-ion
ex- SPIR-e
ex- SPIR-at(e)
ex- SPIR-at-ion
in- SPIR-e
in- SPIR-at(e)
in- SPIR-at-ion
re- SPIR-e
re- SPIR-at(e)
re- SPIR-at-ion
per- SPIR-e
per- SPIR-at(e)
per- SPIR-at-ion
tran- SPIR-e
tran- SPIR-at(e)
tran- SPIR-at-ion

Aspire and *aspirate* are both alive and breathing, but have different meanings today—which is generally not the case. This is, however, now also true with *respire*, "to breathe in and out," which went solo until the late 1960s when it was joined by the verb *respirate*, "to subject to artificial respiration." *Conspirate* and *transpirate* have not arrived yet, and perhaps never will, although the *-at-* is required for most suffixes (*-ion, -ive, -ory*, etc.). *Expirate* (= *expire*) and *perspirate* (= *perspire*) both had short lives, but, again, the *-at-* is retained for additional suffixes. *Inspirate*, "to breathe in," also aborted early, but with the rather recent revival of Latinates ("Never use a familiar word where an unfamiliar one will do"), *inspirate* is coming around for a second time, thus inviting its obvious opposite *expirate*, "to breathe out," to join in the revival.

With *-it*, we *exhibit, inhibit, inhabit, audit,* and *credit,* rather than *exhibe, inhibe,* etc., although for a while in the seventeenth century we did *creed* "to believe." And today we *imbibe,* rather than *imbibit,* although we must retain the *-it-* for *imbibition* "the act of imbibing." The *-ite* form produces such as *expedite* (although we *impede,* and in Scotland they even *expede*) as well as *unite.*

We have said above that this *-at-* or *-it-* was the normal part of many Latin verb bases. It was, in fact, the past participle stem (the entire ending was *-atus, -itus*), as *-ed, -en,* etc., are past participle endings in English. We know that past participles in English can be part of a verb phrase (He *has broken* the window; They *have restored* the old mansion), or many of them can be adjectives (a *broken* window, a *stalled* car, a *restored* mansion). Similarly, these *-at-* and *-it-* forms produced adjectives in Latin, and when English borrowed words with this ending, these words naturally became adjectives in English, such as *explicit, apposite, opposite, illicit.* Some became both adjectives and verbs, as *separate* and *corporate/incorporate.* Some of the adjectives have included a noun use, as *requisite, composite.* Some do not have any adjective use but are today nouns and verbs, as *deposit* and *audit.* And English has further stretched some into adjectives, nouns, and verbs, such as *aggregate, duplicate, degenerate, subordinate.*

A similar suffix (*-ate* only) was used to form verbs from nouns, adjectives, and other verbs by a process of extending the base so that the English derivative ends in *-ate.* Here, the suffix means "to make," "to do something with," "to cause to be," "to do over and over," and so many other different senses that it is better in writing out the analysis of words to list it simply as "verbal suffix," as with the four examples below. When other suffixes are added to the verb, the final *e* is, of course, dropped, as *locate, location.*

Prefix	Base	Meaning			English Derivative
	LOC-	place	+	-ate	locate, location, locator
	NOMIN-	name	+	-ate	nominate, nomination, nominative
e- +	LIMIN-	threshold	+	-ate	eliminate, elimination, eliminable
	PULS-	to push	+	-ate	pulsate, pulsation pulsator, pulsational

Over the years, -ate has been suffixed with indiscriminate abandon—on Latin nouns and adjectives where the Latin verb derivative never existed, as *acidulate,* and *insulate,* and even on non-Latin words, as *camphorate, chlorinate,* and *calibrate.* (In Part Two, Lesson XV, we will see that the Greek suffix -*ize* has been performing a similar duty.)

The -*ate* (-*ite*) as an adjective suffix will be formally introduced at Lesson X. There is also a noun suffix -*ate,* which is discussed in Lesson XV.

ASSIGNMENT

I. Learn the following bases and their meanings. Study each base so that you can recognize it when it occurs in a long, compound word.

Latin Base	Meanings	English Derivatives
ALIEN-	of another	alien, alienation
ART-	art, skill	art, artifact
FIN-	end, limit	final, definite
FIRM-	firm, strong	firmament, confirm
FORT-	strong	fort, forte, comfort
GRAND-	great	grand, grandeur
GRAV-, [GRIEV-]	heavy	grave, grievance

(*Grief* is an orthographic variation of the form GRIEV-.)

LINE-, [LIGN-]	line	line, align
NIHIL-	nothing	annihilate, nihilism
NUL(L)-	nothing	null, annul
PART-	part	part, depart
VERB-	word, verb	verb, adverb, verbatim, proverb
VEST-	garment	vest, vestment

II. Some bases listed above appear as English words by themselves or with the addition of a final *e*; however, without using a dictionary, list as many other words formed from each of them as you can. For example, from the base GRAND- have come *grandee, grandiose, grandam, grandioso, grandiloquent, grandeur,* the combining form *grand-,* which appears in words such as *grandfather,* and the foreign proper names *Grand-Terre, Rio Grande, Grande Soufriere* as well as several borrowed foreign expressions such as *Grand Prix, grand tour,* and *Grand signior.* You must check your words in a dictionary to make sure that they actually contain the particular Latin base. For instance, *investigate* has nothing to do with VEST-, "garment," but is formed from another base VESTIG-, "trace." It will be found that the meanings given for the bases do not always exactly fit the definitions of the words containing them, for over the years various changes of meaning have occurred, some of which will be studied in later lessons. Nevertheless, in most cases, a connection between the meaning of the base and the modern definition can be seen.

III. List the base and its meaning in each of the following italicized words and define the word as it is used in the sentence or phrase.

Example: departure—PART- part: an act or instance of departing or leaving.

1. For an *infinitesimal* fraction of a second his fingers closed again on the small object.—Joseph Conrad

2. Even ill-health, though it *annihilated* several years of my life, has saved me from the distractions of society and amusement. —Charles Darwin

3. The fact that he sought the burgeoning countryside in ignorance of what he was doing, while I expose myself to the *aggravation* of hay, does not alter the case.—E.B. White

4. It was in the cards that he would never attain the Presidency; his reaction to flower dust *nullified* his qualities of leadership. —E.B. White

5. . . . they are endowed by their Creator with certain *unalienable* Rights.—Thomas Jefferson

6. His fluency betrayed him into *verbiage,* and his descriptions are more diffuse than vigorous.—John Addington Symonds

7. The *investiture* of Prince Charles as the Prince of Wales took place at Caernarvon Castle in northwest Wales.

8. He that is well practiced in his.art may write *verbatim* as fast as a man can...speak.—John Wilson, *The Art of Stenography*

9. Preaching, not teaching, was his *forte.*—William Allen White

10. An ambitious man might make his own *aggrandizement,* by the aid of a foreign power, the price of his treachery to his constituents.— *The Federalist*

11. The governments and society of Europe, for a year at least, regarded the Washington Government as dead, and its ministers as *nullities.*—Henry Adams

12. In his writings, Proust became famous for his extraordinary *particularization* of daily events.

13. Indeed, Titian's twelve-sheet print *The Submersion of Pharaoh's Army in the Red Sea,* in its tonal vigor and *grandeur* of notation, is to woodcut what the Sistine Chapel is to fresco. *—Time*

14. ...travelled for hours in those long thoroughfares that seemed to stretch away into *infinitude.*—W.H. Hudson

15. In the speech he gave a clear *affirmation* of his former pledge.

16. While he thus disgusted his subjects by his haughty deportment, he *alienated* their affections by the imposition of grievous taxes.—William Hickling Prescott

17. But he looked again, and the face and person seemed gradually to grow less strange, to change...into *lineaments* that were familiar.—Dickens

18. Religion by force, especially of the state, is a moral *travesty* and a contradiction in terms for modern man.—*Harper's Magazine*

19. Poor fellow, his brain slipped a cog and went out of *alignment* and he was taken off to the funny farm.—Bill Mark

20. How can one be objective about anything? I find it impossible to exhibit *impartiality* even to the smallest degree.—Allan Magee

IV. Describe what is wrong with each of the following definitions:

1. diffident: a person who lacks self-confidence

2. raceme: a simple inflorescence of the centripetal or indeter-
   minate type, in which the several or many flowers
   are borne on somewhat equal axillary pedicels
   along a relatively lengthened axis or rachis

3. supine: not standing upright

4. perjury: dishonesty

5. impervious: not pervious

6. dog: man's best friend

7. redundancy: quality of being redundant

8. mutton: a kind of meat

9. carnivorous: eating human flesh

10. benign: not harmful

11. chemist: a scientist

12. vigilance: to watch carefully

13. poultry: a collective term for chickens

14. magnanimous: greatness of mind

15. uncle: the brother of one's father

16. introvert: a quiet person

17. calumny: an accusation

18. drunkenness: habitual inebriety

19. patriotism: the last refuge of a scoundrel

20. improvident: when a person lacks foresight or thrift

LESSON III

ASSIMILATION OF PREFIXES

More often than not the Latin bases which will be studied appear in English with the addition of prefixes, that is, elements placed in front of the bases to modify their meanings. Most of these elements were originally Latin prepositions or adverbs. Thus:

ab-	from	+	DUCT-	to	lead	abduct
con-	with	+	DUCT-			conduct
de-	off	+	DUCT-			deduct

This, of course, is not something confined to words of Latin derivation. There are a number of native English prefixes, seen in words like *by•stander, off•spring, fore•arm,* and *with•stand.*

An English word may contain more than one prefix, as in *dis•af•fected, non•con•ductor,* and *re•pro•duction.*

There are two special points which must be kept in mind in learning to recognize prefixes.

I. When a prefix is used before certain consonants, its basic form often undergoes phonetic change. For example, the basic form of the Latin prefix meaning "not" is *in-,* as in *inglorious.* If words were only written and not spoken, we could accordingly expect *inpossible,* which is not inpossible to say—when we concentrate on what we are saying. But we do not often really think about speech while we are talking, and it is then that certain sounds blend together into neighboring sounds, to which they become identical or similar. This process is called assimilation, and when the second sound (as the *p* in *possible*) affects the sound just before it (as the *n* in the prefix *in-*), the process is called retrogressive assimilation; that is, the sound moves backwards. In the word *impossible,* the closed lips and nonpositioned tongue in forming the letter *p* make us more apt to put an *m* (also formed with closed lips and nonpositioned tongue) in front rather than an *n* (open lips and positioned tongue). Therefore, it is easier to say *impossible* than *inpossible* because there is less movement in and of the mouth, and it is human nature to do something the easiest way. In the word *inglorious,* it was not found necessary to assimilate any sounds since the stage setting of the tongue and mouth required for pronouncing *g* is very similar to that required for an *n*. So, long before Rome was burning (A.D. 64) and Nero Claudius Caesar Drusus Germanicus was fiddling, the Romans had been prolifically assimilating wherever it felt right; for it was indeed in the Latin language that all of these assimilated spellings were formed.

The following words are also formed by assimilation. Take time to notice in each instance how much easier the assimilated form is to pronounce than the unassimilated *prefix* + BASE would have been.

ad-	to	+ GRAV-	heavy	+ *-ate*	aggravate
ad-		+ SIMIL-	like	+ *-ation*	assimilation
con-	together	+ LECT-	to gather		collect
dis-	apart	+ FER-	to bring		differ
ex-	from	+ FECT-	to make		effect
in-	not	+ LEG-	law	+ *-al*	illegal
ob-	toward	+ FER-	to bring		offer
sub-	under	+ CUMB-	to lie		succumb

You will find that a knowledge of prefixes and an awareness of the process of assimilation will help you spell more correctly, for double consonants are one of the sources of spelling difficulty in English. When you realize that assimilation has taken place in the case of words like *ag•gression, as•sist, col•lide, oc•cur,* etc., errors in writing one consonant when there should be two will be less likely to occur.

II. Another point to remember in connection with prefixes is that occasionally the base itself exhibits slight changes in form when a prefix is added. The general rule is that *a* went to *e,* and *e* went to *i.*

Latin Base	*Meaning*	*English Derivatives*
SACR-	holy	sacred, sacrament, but also conSECRate, deSECRate
APT-	to fit	apt, aptitude, but also inEPT
FAC-, FACT-*	to make	factory, manufacture, but also afFECT, deFECT, and efFICient
SED-	to sit	sedentary, but also preSIDe

---

*Latin verbs have several different forms, two of which are often found in English words derived from these verbs. Since these forms are not easily predicted one from the other, it is best to memorize them all.

Such changes are difficult to categorize and to predict with certainty. Therefore, in the case of bases subject to this process, such variant forms will be given in parentheses:

FAC-, (FIC-),   to make
  FACT-, (FECT-)
SED-, (SID-)   to sit
SACR-, (SECR-)   holy

ASSIGNMENT

I. Learn the following **prefixes** and their meanings. (The first form given for each prefix is the basic or most usual one.)

Prefix	*Meanings*	*Examples*
ab-, a-, abs-	away, from	abduct, abnormal, avert, abstract
(This prefix is never assimilated, so do not confuse it with *a* followed by a double consonant, which is from *ad-*.)		
ad-, ac-, etc.	to, toward	adopt, admire, access, aggression, attract, allocate, ascend
(Occasionally this prefix appears simply as *a-*, usually before *-sc-*, *-sp-*, and *-st-*; e.g., *aspire, ascribe*. When in doubt, however, assume that the prefix *a-* is a form of *ab-*, "away.")		
ambi-	both, around	ambidextrous
ante-	before, in front of	anteroom, antecedent
(Do not confuse this with *anti-*, a Greek prefix meaning "against.")		
circum-	around	circumference, circumscribe
con-, com-, co-, etc.	with, together, very	connect, conduct, compose, compress, collect, correspond, co-operate

contra-, contro-, counter-	against	contradict, controversy, counteract
de-	down, off, thoroughly	descend, dejected
dis-, di-, dif-	apart, in different directions, not	dispute, disable, divert, divorce, differ

These prefixes can be found listed in a good abridged dictionary, where they are generally more fully discussed.

II. Learn the following bases and their meanings:

Latin Base	*Meanings*	*English Derivatives*
CED-, CESS-	to go, yield	concede, precede, excess, procession
DUC-, DUCT-	to lead	induce, transducer, conduct, reduction
JUDIC-	judgment	judicial, adjudicate
JUR-, JUST-	right, law; take an oath, form an opinion	jury, conjure, just, justify
LEV-	light (in weight); to lift	levity, elevate
LOQU-, LOCUT-	to speak	colloquial, eloquent, elocution, interlocutor
LUD-, LUS-	to play, mock	interlude, delude, illusion
PREC-	to request, beg; prayer	imprecate, precarious

(*Pray* and *prayer* also come from this verb, through French.)

TRUD-, TRUS-	to push, thrust	protrude, intrusion, unobtrusive
VEN-, VENT-, [VENU-]	to come	intervene, invention, avenue, venue

III. List the prefix and base, together with their meanings, in each of the following italicized words. Define each word as it is used in the sentence or phrase. In this and similar exercises the bases contained in the italicized words are ones assigned in the lesson or in previous lessons. If you cannot remember the meaning of a particular base, however, refer to the section at the end of Part I, where are listed all bases which you are expected to learn.

Example: adjuration—ad- to + JUR- to swear: a solemn entreaty.

1. How could he *abjure* the faith that was intertwined with the dearest affections of his heart?—William Hickling Prescott

2. Russia, historically desirous of dominating the Balkans, will use Soviet policy to stimulate rather than *alleviate* Greek troubles.—*Harper's Magazine*

3. Into this jungle of *abstruse* learning Pico plunged with all the ardor of his powerful intellect.—John Addington Symonds

4. Synonyms in English often result from borrowing both a Greek word and the translation of it into Latin made by the Romans—for example, periphrasis and *circumlocution.*

5. . . . the noise and nerve-numbing will continue—and get worse with the *advent* of supersonic commercial traffic.—*Time*

6. I shall now proceed to *delineate* dangers of a different and, perhaps, still more alarming kind.—*The Federalist*

7. . . . whenever a particular statute *contravenes* the Constitution, it will be the duty of the judicial tribunals to adhere to the latter and disregard the former.—*The Federalist*

8. Friendship takes place between those who have an *affinity* for one another.—Thoreau

9. Congress *convened* in August for a special session.

10. Since his *accession* to the Crown, Charles the Fifth had been chiefly engrossed in the politics of Europe.—William Hickling Prescott

11. Here, in the twinkling of an eye, he *divested* himself of his coat.—Dickens

12. . . . evidence, mainly negative in kind, has been *adduced* to prove the story of it a fabrication.—Francis Parkman

13. The right inherent in society, to ward off crimes against itself by *antecedent* precautions. . . .—John Stuart Mill

14. There is no need to dwell here on the evils of *collusion* . . . to fix prices and to restrict production.—*Harper's Magazine*

15. And now, hopelessly out of condition, our sedentary executive still *deludes* himself into thinking he is the suave and sexy lady-killer that he also thought he was thirty years ago. —Michael Jacobs

16. By a powerfully welded chain of *deductive* evidence, the guilt of the robbery and apparent murder had been fixed on Clifford.—Hawthorne

17. How, it was asked on the other side, can the fundamental laws of a monarchy be *annulled* by any authority but that of the supreme legislature?—Macauley

18. But the life I lead. . .is not *conducive* to health.—Dickens

19. Thus, for a third time, Beatrix's ambitious hopes were *circumvented.*—Thackeray

20. . . .I should *deprecate* strongly the overemphasizing of party differences now, and recommend that we all bind ourselves with unflagging energy and unbroken union to the national task.—Sir Winston Churchill

IV. Form words by combining the following elements, changing the spelling of the prefix where necessary.

Example: con- + lusion: collusion.

1. *ad-*	+	lusion	6. *ob-*	+	clusion
2. *sub-*	+	fuse	7. *in-*	+	ruption
3. *ad-*	+	rogate	8. *ad-*	+	monition
4. *dis-*	+	tract	9. *ob-*	+	trusive
5. *ex-*	+	fusive	10. *con-*	+	rosive

LESSON IV

ABBREVIATIONS AND ACRONYMS

With the glut of abbreviations that have poured into the language, especially since the 1960s, it is not surprising that there are entire books devoted to abbreviations. Contemporary updates of dictionaries cannot hope to (nor do they even try to) keep up with any more than just a fraction of them. Apart from the old standbys (B.S., M.A., M.B.E., Conn., RFD, C.O.D., Feb., and a few hundred others), most dictionaries try to stay within certain limits—for example, governmental (FMCS, FNMA, FCC, USDA), political (GDR, DDR, OECD, SALT, SHAPE, NATO), sports (NBA, NHL, rbi), educational (CEEB, SAT, NEA), scientific- and medical/hospital-related (iRNA, DOA, GeV, ICU, EKG), computer-related (ROM, COM, VDT, GIGO), and a few other important fields—including a few unclassifiables (BYOB, BMOC = big man on campus, TAS = telephone answering service, TDN = total digestible nutrients). Many abbreviations of organizations and those from the commercial world are avoided simply because there are too many of them. Heavyweights, like NBC, BBC, ASPCA, ACLU, FFA, NAACP, and other such are, however, usually listed.

Since the middle 1940s, acronyms have become a fixed feature of the English language. Sometimes there is a fine line between what is an abbreviation and what is an acronym. Strictly speaking, an acronym is a word that is formed from the initial letter (or letters) of other words. From the above paragraph then, SALT, SHAPE, and NATO are acronyms since we pronounce them as words—and to computer hounds, so is GIGO (Garbage In, Garbage Out)—whereas SAT, as utterable as a word as anything in English could ever be is not, simply because we call it out letter by letter. During World War II, the U.S. armed forces built a *duck* (also D.U.K.W.), a combination of factory serial letters—*D* for boat, *U* for truck body, and *KW* for the truck chassis, that is, an amphibious vehicle. And there is a new *guppy,* which is not a fish but a streamlined and snorkel-equipped submarine (from *g*reater *u*nderwater *p*ropulsive *p*ower + *y*). Some acronyms are constructed so as to resemble words we consider humorous, derisive, or negative, or having some other desired effect, such as CREEP (*C*ommittee to *Re*elect the *P*resident), MAD (*m*utual *a*ssured *d*estruction), MADD (*M*others *A*gainst *D*runk *D*rivers), HOWL (*H*elp *O*ur *W*olves *L*ive—a Minnesota group); SCADS (*S*outh *C*entral *A*merican *D*ialect *S*ociety); GASP (*G*roup *A*gainst *S*mokers' *P*ollution).

Since an acronym can be pronounced like a word, it was probably inevitable that certain of them would assume the grammar of a standard word. We cannot say NATOs since there is only one such organization, nor can we say MADs, SHAPEs, or even M*A*S*Hes (from the movie and the TV series) since MASH carried a number, such as 4077. But with WASP (*w*hite *A*nglo-*S*axon *P*rotestant), since it is a person, we inflect it with an -*s* and have WASPs, and even create an adjective WASPish, an adverb WASPily, and the abstract noun WASPishness. Similarly, we expand MIRV to its logical plural MIRVs, and also add an -*ed* to give MIRVed.

Some abbreviations can become pluralized, too. We have had C.O.D.'s for many years, as well as M.D.'s and Ph.D.'s; and d.t.'s (and D.T.'s) has long been an alternate form of d.t. (in the sense *d*elirium *t*remens). Notice that an apostrophe is usually used for plural when the abbreviation has periods or is in small letters.

PREFIXES

It will be seen that most of these Latin prefixes in Lessons III, IV, and V are "living" English prefixes that are used freely in making new English words. Consider *extra-sensory, extra-special, extraterrestrial* (we have more *extra-* coinages in English today than the Romans ever dreamed of), *interfaith, interagency, interface, intergroup, pre-schooler,* and *preregister. Ex-, non-, super-,* and *intra-* are so popular that they have combined with hundreds of words in modern English, as *ex-friend, nonswinging,* and *Superman,* who is, of course, just *super-duper.* Some of the suffixes can even stand alone as separate words; such as one's *ex* (=ex-spouse or ex-lover), the *pros* and *cons,* a *super* meal, *super* (as a clipped form of *superintendent* of a building), *pro* (a clip for professional), *ultra* (a person who holds extreme views), and *sub* (=substitute; submarine; substratum). In 1985 the Spanish word *contra* as a noun, meaning "an anti-government rebel, a revolutionary," slipped into English in reference to military activity in Latin America. The Latin *contra* also produced the English *country:* in Late Latin it was a phrase, *contrata regio,* meaning "region lying against," and the noun (here, *region*) is the part that fell away, curiously enough, with the remaining part of the phrase entering Old French as *contree.* Other prefixes also became suffixed and turned into nouns, such as *outrage* (from *ultra,* "beyond"), and *soprano* (from *supra,* "above").

Although most of the words studied in Part One of this book were borrowed directly from existing Latin words, including prefixed words, no distinction has been made between these words and words which have been pieced together in modern times, such as *extrapunitive* or *introscope,* both of which are twentieth-century coinages.

ASSIGNMENT

I. Learn the following **prefixes** and their meanings:

Prefix	Meanings	Examples
ex-, e-, ef-, etc.	out, from, completely	expel, exasperate, eloquent, evade, efficient

In English, when *ex-* precedes a base beginning with *s,* the *s* is dropped.

ex-	+	SPECT-	to look	=	expect
ex-	+	SECUT-	to follow	=	execute

extra-, extro-	outside, beyond	extraordinary, extrovert
in-, im-, etc., *ig-* before *n*	not	ineffective, imminent, immoral, impartial, illegal, irresponsible, ignoble, ignore

(This prefix is related to the native English negative prefix *un-*. The two prefixes are so similar in spelling and meaning that they are often interchanged. Thomas Jefferson, for example, wrote of "unalienable rights," whereas *inalienable* is now the standard form. In general, the Latin prefix is used with words of Latin origin and vice versa, but there are many exceptions.)

in-, im-, etc., [*en-*], [*em-*]	in, into, against	inject, impose, impel, illuminate, irrigate, endure, embrace

(This prefix and the preceding one are the same in form only. The word *inflammable,* which used to be written on gasoline cans, is a good illustration of the necessity for keeping these two prefixes distinct: the word does not mean that the liquid will "*not* burn" (non-flammable), but that it will burst "*into* flame.")

infra-	below, beneath	infrared
inter-	between, among	interrupt, intercept
intra-, intro-	within	intramural, intravenous, introduce
non-	not	nonresident

(This prefix is less emphatic than *in-* or the native English *un-*; compare *nonreligious* and *irreligious, non-American* and *un-American*.)

ob-	toward, against, face-to-face, completely	obstruct, obstacle, occur, offer, oppress

(In many words it is difficult to see the force of the foregoing prefix.)

per-	through, wrongly, completely	permeate, persecute, perfect, perjury

II. Learn the following bases and their meanings:

Latin Base	Meanings	English Derivatives
CRUC-	cross	crucify, crux
GREG-	flock, herd	congregate, segregate
HAB-, AB-, (HIB-)	to have, hold as customary	habit, dishabille, able, inability, inhibit
PED-	foot	pedal, impediment, pedestrian
PUNG-, PUNCT-	to prick; point	puncture, punctual
SACR-, (SECR-)	sacred	sacrament, desecrate
SANCT-	holy	sanctify, sanctimonious
SENT-, SENS-	to feel, think	sentiment, consent, sensation
TURB-	disturb	perturb, turbulence

(*Trouble* also derives from this base through French.)

Latin Base	Meanings	English Derivatives
VERT-, VERS-	to turn	revert, aversion
VI(A)-	way, road	via, previous

III. List the prefixes and bases, together with their meanings, in the following italicized words. Define each word as it is used in the sentence or phrase.

1. The bishop may order the priest from the pulpit; but he can't force the steeltown *congregation* to abandon its complaint.

2. I should not *obtrude* my affairs so much on the notice of my readers if very particular inquiries had not been made by my townsmen concerning my mode of life.—Thoreau

3. ...and if the assertion were proved to be false or the pledge to have been broken, he should be liable to the penalties of *perjury.*—John Stuart Mill

4. . . .and rejects only those who brave the *obloquy* of publicly confessing a detested creed.—John Stuart Mill

5. With incredible endurance and *incessant* practice, Krickstein at age seventeen became the youngest winner of a men's Grand Prix event in tennis history.

6. . . .a *perverse* will that indulged children invariably acquire.—Emily Brontë

7. . . .a small, frosty lady *imperturbable* even in the face of a severe automobile accident sustained last summer at the age of ninety-four. . . .—*Harper's Magazine*

8. The adjustment should amount to whatever it takes to eliminate the slice and *align* the racquet perpendicular to the floor. —*Racquetball*

9. *Injustice* was built into the system owing to a badly written constitution.

10. He came so close to dismissal that only the indignant *intercession* of his mother saved him.—*Time*

11. In the second edition of his treatise he *expunged* or modified the passages which had given the manager offence.—Washington Irving

12. They cursed their fate, condemned their life, and wasted their breath in deadly *imprecations* upon one another.—Joseph Conrad

13. "I won't answer for it that he would know me," Strether's *interlocutress* pursued; "but I should be delighted to see him."—Henry James

14. . . .we cannot dedicate, we cannot *consecrate*, we cannot hallow this ground. The brave men living and dead, who struggled here, have consecrated it far above our power to add or detract.—Abraham Lincoln

15. . . .it was as if she demanded more than ever the recognition of her dignity as the last Grierson; as if it had wanted that touch of earthiness to reaffirm her *imperviousness.*—William Faulkner

16. No wonder that by the Nazoreans he was vilified and *execrated* continually.—Hugh J. Schonfield

17. A woman who has *inadvertently* parked her car in a loading zone may have to wait in court nearly all day. . . .—*Harper's Magazine*

18. He had been at pains to transcribe the whole book, with blottings, *interlineations*, and corrections.—James Boswell

19. He knew...that the social cost in aimless defection from society, like that of the beasts, or *insensate* anger against it, like that of the delinquents, was growing.—Arthur M. Schlesinger

20. ...I began to arouse myself from the stupefaction which a day's motor journey *induces*.—E.B. White

IV. By adding one of the following prefixes, *counter-, de-, dis-, in-, non-,* and also the native English *un-,* make negatives of the following words or reverse their meaning. Consult your dictionary to make sure that the word which you form actually exists.

Example: resident—nonresident

1. persuasive
2. militarize
3. enfranchise
4. resistance
5. resistible
6. combustible
7. inclination
8. clockwise
9. sensitize
10. audible

V. Give the meanings of the following abbreviations:

1. D.D.S.
2. F.R.S.
3. Skt.
4. v.t.
5. KGB
6. q.
7. a.m.
8. ca.
9. cf.
10. e.g.
11. i.e.
12. lb.

VI. Give the meanings of the following acronyms:

1. flak
2. laser
3. loran
4. radar
5. rem
6. SEATO

LESSON V

BACK FORMATIONS, APHERESIS, AND APHESIS

We are seeing, in Lessons III, IV, and this one, how a prefix—or two, or three—can be added to a word to change its meaning. The

Latin verb *calare* (giving us the base CAL- and CIL-) meant "to call, to summon." To this the Romans added the prefix *con-* (Lesson III) and came up with a new verb *conciliare* which meant "to unite, to connect" (that is "to summon" + "together")—which gives us the English words *conciliate* and *conciliator*. Then, to this *conciliare* the Romans added the prefix *re-* (meaning "again"—in Lesson V), producing *reconciliare* with the meaning "to restore, to repair" (that is, "to unite" or "connect" + "again")—which gives us the English *reconcile*. And, of course, if we can *reconcile,* we can *not reconcile;* whence the additional prefix *ir-* (=*in-* "not"—last lesson), to produce, with a couple of suffixes, the English concoction *ir•re•con•CIL•abil•ity,* with the base CIL- being the nucleus of the word.

This is by far the most common way of giving new meanings and new parts of speech to existing bases or words—by adding prefixes and suffixes respectively. But sometimes a reverse process takes place, and rather than adding elements, elements get dropped.

A back formation is the creation of one word from another by the clipping off of a suffix. The new word carries the same meaning as the parent word but, with this clipping, becomes a different part of speech. Many of these creations (but by no means all) are clipped forms from abstract nouns ending in *-ion,* as *absciss* (from *abscission*), *ablute* (*ablution*), and *accrete* (*accretion*). Some back formations take on a special sense, as the verb *formate* (from *formation*) meaning "to fly in formation"; and *respirate* (from artificial *respirator*) meaning to "subject one to an artificial respirator." Other back formations come from *-er, -or,* and *-ar* nouns: *escalate* (from *escalator*), *typewrite* (*typewriter*), *burgle* (*burglar*). Other backforms are *laze* from *lazy, sidle* from *sideling.*

Apheresis (from Greek, meaning essentially "a taking away") means the removal of a letter or syllable at the beginning of a word. *Account* was clipped to *count, esquire* to *squire,* and *most* when it means *almost.* The article + noun *an adder* was originally *a nadder,* as *an apron* was originally *a napron.* (The reverse process was taking place in the 1980s with *another,* as in the sentence, "But that's a whole nuther topic.") *Before* gets shortened to *'fore, because* to *'cause,* and *cantankerous* to *tankerous. Mushrooms* has its own glorious alteration in the underground *shrooms,* which contain a psychedelic ingredient that your old supermarket mushrooms would not dare to carry. As an extended form of this front-clipping, we have *cab* from *taxicab, phone* from *telephone,* and other such, as well as the proper names *Topher* from *Christopher, Zander* from *Alexander, Beth* from *Elizabeth,* and *Sandra* from *Alexandra.* These last examples are blending into the area of so-called 'clips' which are discussed further in Lesson XX.

An unaccented vowel at the beginning of a word was frequently quick to fall off, a process call aphesis (from a Greek word meaning "a letting go"). *Down* (adverb and preposition) was reduced from the Old English *adune,* which was itself a blending of *of dune,* meaning "off [the] hill," an instance where both forms *down* and *adown* lived side by side until near the end of the nineteenth century, when *adown* fell away, at least in prose. In other cases, both the original form and the aphetic form are still going, such as *mid* from *amid,* and *possum* from *oppossum. Bishop,* apart from the rest of its history, is an aphetic form of *episcopal.* In recent time the two words apheresis and aphesis have become synonymous to some writers.

ASSIGNMENT

I. Learn the following **prefixes** and their meanings:

Prefix	*Meanings*	*Examples*
post-	after, behind	postpone, postscript
pre-	before, in front of	prevent, predict
pro-	forward, in front of, for	promote, produce
re-, red- (before vowels)	back, again	renew, recede, recall, redemption
retro-	backward, behind	retroactive
se-, sed- (before vowels)	aside, away	secede, segregate, sedition
sub-, sus-, suc-, etc.	under, up from under, secretly	submerge, submarine, suspend, sustain, succumb, suffer, support
super-, [*sur-*]	above, over	superhuman, super-fluous, surreal, surcease
trans-, tran-, tra-	across, through	transfer, transparent, transcend, transcribe, traverse, travesty
ultra-	beyond, exceedingly	ultraviolet, ultramodern

There are several other Latin prefixes which occur so rarely that it is not worthwhile to learn them. These are: *juxta-,* "beside," "near to," seen mainly in the word *juxtaposition; preter-,* "beyond," in *preternatural;* and *subter-,* "below," "secretly," in *subterfuge.*

II. Learn the following bases and their meanings:

Latin Base	Meanings	English Derivatives
CLUD-, CLUS-, [CLOS-]	to shut	exclude, include, disclose
CUR(R)-, CURS-, [COURS-], [COR(S)-]	to run, go	recur, current, excursion, concourse, succor
GRAD-, GRESS	to step, go	gradual (literally, by steps), progress, aggression
PEND-, PENS-	to hang, weigh, pay	dependent, suspend, dispense, expense

(*Poise* and *ponder* also come from this base through French.)

PLE-, PLET-, PLEN-	to fill; full	implement, complete, deplete, plenary
SPEC-, (SPIC-), SPECT-	to look	specimen, conspicuous, inspect, respect
UND-, [OUND-]	wave	abundant, undulate, abound, redound
VID-, VIS-, [VIEW-]	to see	evident, provide, visual, provision, review
VOC-, VOK-	voice; to call	vocal, invoke, invocation, provoke, revoke

(*Voice* also comes from this base through French.)

III. List the prefixes (if any) and bases, together with their meanings, in the following italicized words. Define each word as it is used in the sentence or phrase.

1. ...a brevity which excludes everything that is *redundant* and nothing that is significant.... —Lytton Strachey

2. ...the gorilla infant will, in the course of time, develop an enormously powerful and *protrusive* muzzle.—*Harper's Magazine*

3. This tendency represents a *regression* to a more primitive stage of religion.

4. Though not of a *retrospective* turn, he made the best effort he could to send his mind back into the past.—Hawthorne

5. "You keep stayin' up late watchin' them top forty midnight *video* things and yo' brain, honey, is gonna turn to oatmeal." —Brian Levin

6. This is only one of many such *compendia,* and we know of at least one other handbook.—Kurt Weitzman

7. The sierra was so precipitous that it seemed to *preclude* all further progress.—Prescott

8. It was now evident that instant retreat was necessary; and the command being issued to that effect, the men. . . slowly began their *retrograde* movement.—Francis Parkman

9. All concerned. . . should be asked to report on the measures which they are taking to *implement* these instructions. . . . —Sir Winston Churchill

10. I have not the sense of perfect *seclusion* which has always been essential to my power of producing anything.—Hawthorne

11. The beginning of the universe seems to present *insuperable** difficulties.—*Omni*

12. . . . the *propensity* of mankind to exalt the past, and to depreciate the present.—Edward Gibbon

13. By sampling the usage of social extremes, a broad *conspectus* of cultivated, middle class, and folk speech is secured. . . . —Hans Kurath

14. . . . their country was vanquished simply because its *transgressions* against civilized behavior aroused the organized anger of most of humanity.—*Harper's Magazine*

15. Once more he bent his footsteps towards the scene of his living martyrdom, saddened with a deep *presentiment* that he was advancing to his death.—Francis Parkman

16. One lone person cannot count on the *succor* of public opinion. . . . —James Q. Wilson

---

*The word *super* was as flexible in Latin as it is in English. Several nouns, verbs, and adjectives sprang from it. Here, *super* comes from a verb base which meant "to rise above, surmount, project, conquer."

17. His teacher said, "When I speak, you're allowcd to *concur,* not offer opinions."

18. . . .cunning, ambitious, and unprincipled men will be enabled to *subvert* the power of the people, and to usurp for themselves the reigns of government.—Washington

19. He was obliged to pause and decide whether he would surrender and obey, or whether he would give the refusal that must carry *irrevocable* consequences.—George Eliot

20. It may be added that without this *supplemental* provision, the great and essential power of regulating foreign commcrce would have been incomplete and ineffectual.—*The Federalist*

IV. By changing the prefix, form the antonym of each of the following words.

Example: exhale — inhale

1. assent
2. supersonic
3. prelude
4. depreciate
5. associate
6. ante-bellum
7. converge
8. persuade
9. discord
10. inflate
11. retrogress
12. accelerate

V. Using your dictionary, find the original word from which each of the following has been back-formed.

1. spectate
2. emote
3. execute
4. scavenge
5. enthuse
6. vaccinate
7. pea
8. edit
9. surreal
10. preempt

VI. Using your dictionary, find the original word from which each of the following aphetic or apheretic forms derived.

1. lone
2. mend
3. state
4. auger
5. umpire
6. spite

LESSON VI

COMBINATIONS OF BASES

The Romans were fond of forming words by combining, and the English have carried on the tradition. Sometimes a connecting vowel, usually *i*, has been inserted between the bases in order to make the pronunciation easier. This *i* was in so many Latin words that it was natural it should become the standard connecting vowel. For example:

OMN-	all	+ *i* + POT-	power	+ *-ent*	omnipotent
MULT-	many	+ *i* + LATER-	side	+ *-al*	multilateral
CRUC-	cross	+ *i* + FER-	to carry		crucifer
FLOR-	flower	+ *i* + CULT-	to till	+ *-ure*	floriculture

Sometimes an *i* was used when there was never an *i* in the Latin base, as in the following examples. Sometimes other vowels were used as connectors, either because it was the vowel that ended the first base, or the vowel that began the second base, or for some other special reason as with *sacrosanct* (see footnote for sentence 9 below). For example:

BENE-	good	+ FIC-	to make	+ *-ial*	beneficial
AQU-	water	+ *i* + FER-	to carry		aquifer
QUADR-	four	+ *u* + PED-	foot		quadruped
TERR-	land	+ AQU-	water	+ *-eous*	terraqueous
TERR-	land	+ *e* + PLEIN-	full		terreplein
TERR-	land	+ *i* + GEN-	to produce	+ *-ous*	terrigenous
SACR-	sacred	+ *a*		+ *-ment*	sacrament
SACR-	sacred	+ *i* + FIC-	to make		sacrifice
SACR-	sacred	+ *o* + SANCT-	holy		sacrosanct

In some cases there is no connecting letter, usually because the two connecting consonants blend easily in speech. For example:

| FAC- | to make | + SIMIL- | | | facsimile |
| NOMEN- | name | + CLAT- | to call | + *-ure* | nomenclature |

52

Both the /ks/ (the *c* + *s* of the first example of the above two) and the /nk/ (*n* + *c* of the second example) are common consonant clusters in English. The Latin *prima rosa* (= first rose), when it came into English, even lost its internal *a* when the two words eventually came together, giving us the word *primrose*.

As will be seen in this lesson, bases which denote numbers are frequently found in combination with other bases.

ASSIGNMENT

I. Learn the following numerical bases and their meanings:

SEMI-	half, partly	semiannual
UN-	one	uniform, unanimous
PRIM-	first	primary, primitive
DU-	two	duet, dual
BI-, BIN- (before vowels)	two; twice	bicycle, binoculars
TRI-	three	tricycle, triangle
QUADR(U)-	four	quadrangle, quadruple
QUART-	fourth	quarter
QUINT-	fifth	quintuplet, quintet
SEXT-	six; sixth	sextet
SEPT(EM)-	seven	septet, September*
OCT-	eight	octet
OCTAV-	eighth	octave
DECI(M)-	tenth	deciliter, decimal
CENT-	hundred	century, centennial
MILL-	thousand	millimeter, mill

This list does not contain all the bases for the sequence from one to ten. Some have been omitted since they appear in few English words or only in very technical terms. These are: SESQUI-, "one and a half times," SECOND-, "second," TERTI-, "third," QUINQUE-, "five," SEX-, "six," SEPTIM-, "seventh," NOVEM-, "nine," NON-, "ninth," and DECEM-, "ten."

It is useful to learn the suffixed element -(*u*)*ple* "-fold" along with the bases given above: *triple,* "threefold," *quadruple,* "fourfold,"

---

*Originally the Romans began their new year on March 1; thus, September was the seventh month, October, the eighth, and so on. When the beginning of the year was put back to January 1, the names of the months were left unchanged.

etc. This element appears in extended form in the words *triplets, quadruplets,* etc.

As with some other bases that have been studied, such as with most of those in Lesson II, by adding a letter we can form a free-standing word, such as *octave* and *prime. Cent, mill,* and *quart* need no addition. Sometimes longer words are clipped down so that they resemble bases, as *bi* (=bisexual), *tri* (=trimaran), *quad* (=quadrangle; quadruplet; quadrate), *quint* (=quintuplet), *semi* (=semitrailer; semifinal; and the British semi-detached house). Some of these can admit a plural, such as *octaves, quads, quints, semis, cents, mills, quarts.*

Roman Numerals

While we are studying the Latin bases for numbers, we might also consider Roman numerals, which are used to indicate volume numbers of periodicals, dates such as those on buildings and motion pictures, the introductory pages and chapter numbers of books, and for various other purposes. Most students have probably studied Roman numerals before, so this part of the lesson will be largely a review, but a worthwhile review nonetheless, for these symbols occur just often enough to be troublesome but not often enough to make one accustomed to their use.

The symbols which are chiefly used are:

I = 1	X = 10	D = 500
V = 5	L = 50	M = 1000
	C = 100	

If a smaller numeral follows a larger one, the two are added (e.g., XI = 10 plus 1 = 11); if a larger numeral follows a smaller one, the smaller is subtracted from the larger (e.g., IX = 10 minus 1 = 9). If a numeral stands between two larger numerals, it is subtracted from the second, and the remainder is added to the first (e.g., XIX = 10 plus 9 = 19). The introductory pages of a book will often use lower-case numerals: i, v, x, l, c, d, m.

Examples:

III	(or iii)	3	IX	9	MDCCCLXIII	1863
IV	(or iv)	4	XII	12	MCMLIX	1959
VII	(or vii)	7	XXVII	27	MMI	2001
VIII	(or viii)	8	XLIV	44		

II. List the prefixes (if any) and bases in the following italicized words. Define each word as it is used in the sentence or phrase.

Example: semiconductor—SEMI- half + <u>con</u>- together + DUCT- to lead: a mineral substance that conducts electricity with an efficiency between that of a metal and an insulator.

1. Some...with many legs, even to the number of an hundred,...or such as are termed *centipedes.*—Sir Thomas Browne

2. I have ventured to suggest a hint for such a structure as may support the road..., rather calling it a *Via-duct** than a bridge.—Repton

3. During the last three months an element of baffling *dualism* has complicated every problem of policy and administration. We had to plan for peace and war at the same time.—Sir Winston Churchill

4. ...because of the city's [Berlin's] *quadripartite* occupational status.—*Time*

5. Fertility hormones have produced a rash of -uplets from twins to *sextuplets.*

6. ...another voice shouted occasional replies; and this *interlocutor* seemed to be on the other side of the hedge. —Thomas Hardy

7. The president of the university addressed the *convocation.*

8. The long, narrow plain was interrupted in places by *transverse* canals.

9. Let them establish your fundamental rights by a *sacrosanct*† declaration.—Thomas Jefferson

10. This is an extremity to which no government will of choice *accede.*—*The Federalist*

11. Any system of compulsory wage arbitration would have to be *tripartite,* with representatives of the workers, employers, and the public making up the tribunal.—*Harper's Magazine*

---

*So far as it is known, Repton was the first to use the word (*O.E.D.* 1816). Today it is spelled *viaduct.*

†The *o* in this word is an inflectional ending in the original Latin phrase *sacro sanctus* and was retained when the two words blended together—like the possessive-case *s* in the English *doomsday* (day of doom) and *Wednesday* (Woden's day). Call this *o* "an inflection."

12. . . .the wall which had been constructed by the ancient kings of Assyria to secure their dominions from the *incursions* of the Medes.—Edward Gibbon

13. A *centigrade* thermometer. . . .

14. All they had hitherto suffered, the *desecration* of their temples, the imprisonment of their sovereign. . . .—William Hickling Prescott

15. He managed five wins in the tournament (a record for him) but was defeated in the *semifinals.*

16. This outpost settlement had had its membership *decimated* during the Arab riots.—*Harper's Magazine*

17. Victory is traditionally *elusive.* Accidents happen. Mistakes are made.—Sir Winston Churchill

18. I heard her sigh low. She was *pensive* a few minutes, then rousing herself, she said cheerfully. . . .—Charlotte Brontë

19. . . .let it be named from the fishes that swim in it, the wild fowl or *quadrupeds* which frequent it. . . .—Thoreau

20. (a) The colonies. . .of the gibbons and perhaps of other *primates* not far away from the line of human descent. . . . —*Harper's Magazine*

    (b). . .the election of a new Archbishop of Athens (who is also *primate* of the country) is a matter of high national interest.—*Time*

III. With the aid of a dictionary explain the connection between the numerical bases which were presented in this lesson and the following words.

Example: *primate* — (a) one who occupies the "first" rank; (b) one of the highest or "first" order of mammals, including man and the apes.

1. unicorn
2. primer
3. primeval
4. biscuit
5. trivial
6. trillion
7. Septuagint
8. octogenarian
9. centurion
10. mile

IV. Write the following in Arabic numerals:

1. XVIII
2. xlix
3. CVII
4. DCLX
5. DCCCXLIV
6. MDCCXXXIX
7. xxxii
8. LVII
9. CCXIV
10. MMXX
11. lxvii
12. xcvi

LESSON VII

HYBRIDS

In the previous lesson, words formed by combining two bases were considered. Usually such combinations are made up of elements that have been taken from the same language, but sometimes words are formed composed of bases from different languages. For example:

Word/Base	Source Language	+ Word/Base	Source Language	= Hybrid
battle	Latin	+ ax	English	= battleax
crest	Latin	+ fallen	English	= crestfallen
contra-	Latin	+ band	Germanic	= contraband
GEN- ("race")	Greek	+ CID- ("kill")	Latin	= genocide*
MON- ("one")	Greek	+ LINGU- ("tongue")	Latin	= monolingual

The word *type* was really promiscuous:

type	Greek	+ cast	Scandinavian	= typecast
type		+ face	Latin	= typeface
type		+ phenomenon	Greek	= type-phe-nomenon
type		+ script	Latin	= typescript
type		+ write(r)	English	= typewrite(r)

Many times when a word was borrowed into English, it seemed the natural thing to do to attach a native English prefix or suffix to it. For example:

English Prefix	Word	Source Language	English Suffix	= Hybrid
by-	pass	Latin		= by-pass
off-	ramp	French		= off-ramp

---

*Although *genocide* is a word that could have been coined two thousand years ago (for example, by such as Gaius Valerius Catullus, first century B.C. poet, who missed his chance in his phrase *caesi acervi,* "heaps of the slain"), the word was, in fact, first recorded in 1944 in reference to the "destruction of a nation or of an ethnic group." The following year the "United Nations' indictment of the 24 Nazi leaders has brought a new word into the language—genocide . . . namely, the extermination of racial and national groups . . . ." (*O.E.D.* 1972). Since the mid 1960s, however, *the Holocaust* (from the Greek meaning "burnt whole") has become the standard term applied specifically to the destruction of the Jews during World War II.

English Prefix	Word	Source Language	English Suffix	= Hybrid
fore-	close	Latin		= foreclose
fore-	court	French		= forecourt
un-	gracious	Latin		= ungracious
un-	faith	Latin	*-ful*	= unfaithful
	cash	Latin	*-less*	= cashless
	eager	Latin	*-ly*	= eagerly
	boor	Dutch	*-ish*	= boorish

ASSIGNMENT

I. Learn the following bases and their meanings:

ANIM-	mind, feeling, life	animal, animated
ANN(U)-, (ENNI-)	year	annals, annual, perennial
BENE-, BON-	well, good	benefactor, benefit, benign, bonus
CANT-, (CENT-), [CHANT-]	to sing	canorous, incantation, incentive, enchant
CUR-	cure, care	sinecure, secure
EQU-, (IQU-)	equal, even	equal, equidistant, iniquity
FER-	to bear, carry	refer, transfer, conference
LAT-	to bear, carry	elate, relate, translation
MAGN-	great	magnitude, magnify
MAL(E)-	bad	maladjusted, malicious, malignant
MULT-	many	multitude, multiply
OPTIM-	best	optimum
PLIC-, PLEX-, [PLY-]	to fold, tangle, interweave	complicate, implicate, implicit, complex, imply, multiply

II. List the prefixes (if any) and bases, together with their meanings, in the following italicized words. Define each word as it is used in the sentence or phrase.

1. Not long afterwards he made a *magnanimous* public gesture of reconciliation towards German men of learning and letters. —*Atlantic Monthly*

2. In 1970 a young man does not accept an *iniquitous* condition with fatalism.—Ward Just

3. *Malice* hath a strong memory.—Thomas Fuller

4. Miss Miller was...hurried in gait and action, like one who had always a *multiplicity* of tasks on hand.—Charlotte Brontë

5. Despite her elegant dress, you could tell by hearing her talk that she was not brought up on *bonbons.*

6. The *inanimate* objects were not changed, but the living things had altered past recognition.—Charlotte Brontë

7. (a)...it is most remarkable to find no record of its existence prior to the second *millennium* B.C.—*Harper's Magazine*

    (b) It seemed, in fact, as if the *millennium* were dawning upon the land; for the sword was beaten into a ploughshare, and the spear into a pruning-hook.—Washington Irving

8. He was *aggrieved* at the accusation that he had cheated on the test, an activity in which he had not indulged in this particular class.

9. After spreading the contents of the garbage can around the kitchen, my dog invariably exhibited *compunction*—which I was invariably convinced was purely fake.

10. The answer was evasive—I should have liked something clearer; but Mrs. Fairfax either could not, or would not, give me more *explicit* information.—Charlotte Brontë

11. The fat boy waited to be asked his name in turn, but this *proffer* of acquaintance was not made.—William Golding

12. It is a work based on much reading and *correlation* of data in biology, psychology, aesthetics, literature, and the fine arts. —*Harper's Magazine*

13. Religious symbols and *incantations* are sometimes used in magic, and magic sometimes has a sacred aspect.—*Cultural Anthropology*

14. After the crushing defeat of the Turk at Lepanto, Venice had no challengers of any size left in the Mediterranean. Its empire, *secured* by an invincible fleet of galleys, ran from the northern Adriatic to Crete....—*Time*

15. The inexorable political calendar provides for (a) *biennial* congressional elections and (b) *quadrennial* presidential elections at stated dates, regardless of when wars end.—*Harper's Magazine*

16. ...[the book] became common unto many, and was by transcription *successively* corrupted until it arrived in a most depraved copy at the press.—Sir Thomas Browne

17. As our common *complexities* increase, any tale of individual simplicity (and yours is the best written and the cockiest) acquires a new fascination.—E.B. White

18. Liberal internationalism is a passion for democratic principles, and for bold *interventionist* Government to carry them out.—*Time*

19. Nothing seems to make an impression on their minds; nothing short of being knocked down by a porter, or run over by a cab, will disturb their *equanimity.*—Dickens

20. Don't you know that good grades will *optimize* your chances for getting a scholarship?

III. With the aid of a dictionary, determine the languages from which the elements in each of the following hybrids have been drawn.

1. television
2. anteroom
3. megaton
4. ill-tempered
5. automobile
6. speedometer
7. monorail
8. antibody
9. aqualung
10. monaural

LESSON VIII

SUFFIXES

Along with bases and prefixes, suffixes have often been used in word formation. Suffixes are word elements attached to the end of a base, and, as with prefixes, most of us are familiar with them in the case of native English words. For example:

kind	+	*-ness*	quality of	kindness
care	+	*-less*	without	careless
boy	+	*-ish*	like	boyish

In the same way, many English words of Latin origin have been formed by the addition of suffixes. For example:

FIN-	end	+	*-al*	pertaining to	final
NUMER-	number	+	*-ous*	full of	numerous
POPUL-	people	+	*-ar*	pertaining to	popular

It should be mentioned here that direct translations of suffixes are impossible: Latin *numerosus* became English *numerous,* with NUMER- meaning "number," and *-osus* becoming "-ous"—and that was that. The meanings "full of," "pertaining to," etc., supplied by dictionaries (and this text), are merely practical efforts at paraphrasing and given only for the sake of example.

Like prefixes, some suffixes can also change the meaning of a base, but the basic function of a suffix is to form a different part of speech. In the case of the previous examples, adjectival suffixes were attached to noun bases to form adjectives. We shall be dealing with three types of suffixes: adjective-forming, noun-forming, and verb-forming. In some instances, however, a suffix normally classed as adjective-forming will actually be found to form a noun. This is because of a tendency, present in most languages, for adjectives to be used as nouns. Thus, in English *good* is generally an adjective, but in the sentence, "The good die young," it is used to mean "good people." Similarly, the words *numeral* (NUMER-, "number" + *-al,* "pertaining to") and *pedal* (PED-, "foot" + *-al*) usually occur as nouns despite the fact that *-al* is classed as an adjective-forming suffix.

More than one suffix is sometimes found in a single word. For example:

CLASS- class, rank+*-ic* belonging to + *-al* pertaining to classical
EQU-　　equal　　　+*-al* pertaining to + *-ity* state of　　　equality
POPUL-people　　　+*-ar* pertaining to + *-ity*　　　　　　popularity

When a suffix which ends in *e* is followed by an additional suffix, the *e* is generally dropped. For example:

VERB- word + *-ose* full of　　　　+ *-ity* quality of　verbosity
URB-　city + *-ane* pertaining to + *-ity*　　　　　　urbanity

ASSIGNMENT

I. Learn the following **adjective-forming suffixes** and their meanings:

-al (-ial, -eal), "pertaining to," "like," "belonging to," "having the character of"

VOC-	voice	+	*-al*	vocal
VERB-	word	+	*-al*	verbal
EQU-	equal	+	*-al*	equal

-ane, -(e)an, -ian, [-ain], same meanings as the preceding

VETER-	old	+ -an	veteran
MUND-	world	+ -ane	mundane
MOUNT-	mountain	+ -ain	mountain

The suffix *-an* (*-ian*) frequently forms words which are used as nouns and so comes to mean "one connected with."

| LIBR- | book | + -ary place for | + -an | librarian |
| BARBAR- | foreign + | | + -ian | barbarian |

-ar, "pertaining to," "like," "belonging to," "having the character of"

POPUL-	people	+ -ar	popular
REGUL-	rule	+ -ar	regular
FAMILI-	family, household	+ -ar	familiar

-ose (-iose), "full of"

| GRAND(i)- | great | + -ose | grandiose |
| COMAT- | lethargy | + -ose | comatose |

-ous (-ious, -eous), "full of," "having the character of," "like"

FAM-	fame, report	+ -ous	famous
POPUL-	people	+ -ous	populous
VARI-	varied	+ -ous	various

Both the "i" and the "e" in these suffixes are connecting vowels, as discussed in Lesson VI. As will be seen in lessons that follow, several suffixes have a connecting vowel.

The various suffixes that you will study in this book can be found, with very few exceptions, in a good dictionary, where they are generally discussed more fully than in this book. You will find sometimes that a meaning for a suffix as found in a dictionary may fit more comfortably the definition of a word than any of the meanings offered in this book. Sometimes the ones in the book will fit very well. To define *corporal* in sentence No. 9 below as "pertaining to the body" would serve, but to define *verbose* as "full of words"—no banana. My terrific essay can be full of words, but that is not what *verbose* means. On the other hand, to define it as "expressed in or characterized by the use of many or too many words" seems unnecessarily wordy. In all your definitions, conciseness is to be considered, but never at the expense of precision.

II. Learn the following bases and their meanings:

AQU(A)-	water	aquatic, aqueduct
CORPOR-, CORP(US)-	body	incorporate, corpuscle, corpse
OMN-	all	omnipresent, omnivorous
REG-, (RIG-), RECT-	right, straight; to rule, stiffen, straighten	regular, rigid, rectify
SIMIL-, SIMUL-	like, similar	simulate, simile
TEMPER-, TEMPOR-	time, due season; to set bounds	temperate, temperature, temporary
TEN-, (TIN-), TENT-, [TAIN-]	to hold	tenant, continue, content, contain
TEND-, TENT-, TENS-	to stretch, strive	tendon, tense, tent, distend, pretense
TENU-	stretched, thin	tenuous, attenuate

(The last three bases are related both in form and meaning.)

III. List the prefixes, bases, and suffixes, together with their meanings, in the following italicized words. Define each word as it is used in the sentence or phrase.

Example: interlinear—<u>inter</u>- between + LINE- line + -<u>ar</u> pertaining to: between lines.

1. But they greeted first with disbelief and then with dismay the disclosures of the *devious* bypaths into which resentment... had led their senior Senator.—*Harper's Magazine*

2. ...a speech that was plain, straight, and pungent, enriched by a meaty, homely, and *colloquial* metaphor, a concrete descriptive power that made use of the good straight words of common speech.—Thomas Wolfe

3. At the mere push of two buttons, their duplicating machine would make twelve copies of fifty pages and *collate* the whole all by itself.

4. It took the hot-air balloon half an hour to *distend* before it rose from the ground.

5. . . .the separation between spiritual and *temporal* authority (which placed the direction of men's consciences in other hands than those which controlled their worldly affairs). —John Stuart Mill

6. . . .Malaya is run by a coalition Alliance Party, which has established a *tenuous* racial harmony among Malaya's 6,500,000 polyglot population.—*Time*

7. *Continual* complaining about your work in this class will be construed by this teacher as a blatant excuse for laziness.

8. But his type of *verbose* and overornamental oratory was becoming outmoded.—Samuel Hopkins Adams

9. Rosie had not attempted to inflict *corporal* punishment beyond an occasional punch or slap.—W.H. Hudson

10. He had *aqueous* gray eyes, and a sallow bumpy skin. —Thomas Wolfe

11. An English ruin is more beautiful often in its decay than even it was in its *primal* strength.—Hawthorne

12. Governments of *dissimilar* principles and forms have been found less adapted to a federal coalition of any sort.—*The Federalist*

13. . . .the *crucial* need for economic stability.

14. The artillery, also, was so *injudiciously* placed as to be entirely worthless.—Washington Irving

15. One of New England's *perennial* chores, as perennial as winding the clock and putting out the cat, is adjusting to the mutable American economy.—*Harper's Magazine*

16. Under *pretense* of going to the library to study, he headed off for the party—only to discover it had been canceled.

17. And in what way does your ingenious little fairy tale *pertain* to a single thing we are talking about here in class?

18. The special-effects monster, it seems, was *incorporeal:* a booming, bass voice used for stuffing out a hideous, bloated outfit.

19. In proportion as each succeeding ray has less force, it is driven out of its *rectilinear* direction.—Oliver Goldsmith

20. The presidency of Dwight Eisenhower was *contemporaneous* with the onset of the space age.

IV. Distinguish in meaning the following pairs of words. These pairs have the same bases but different suffixes.

1. official—officious
2. aquatic—aqueous
3. equal—equable
4. continuous—continual
5. urban—urbane

6. judicial—judicious
7. imperial—imperious
8. funeral—funereal
9. human—humane
10. military—militant

LESSON IX

WORD ANALYSIS: ETYMOLOGICAL DEFINITION

Now that you have been introduced to the three elements used in word formation—bases, prefixes, and suffixes—you will be able to separate the words in the exercises into their component parts. From here on, when asked to analyze a word, list its elements and their meanings, as in exercise III of the previous lesson. By developing this technique of word analysis you will acquire a valuable method for attacking unfamiliar words of Latin or Greek origin. When you first encounter a new word, if you break it down into base, prefix, and suffix, it will seem less strange and puzzling, and in many cases its meaning can be guessed with the help of the context, that is, the rest of the sentence or phrase in which it is used. Even if you can recognize only some of the elements that a word contains, this technique will be useful. Furthermore, after analyzing unfamiliar words, you will find them much easier to remember, because the various bases, prefixes, and suffixes which will be studied are excellent mnemonic devices; it will be of considerable aid to the memory if you can link the unfamiliar with the familiar, if, for example, you are aware that *perturbation* contains the same base as *disturb*.

Word analysis, however, is not an infallible method of determining the meanings of words. It must be used with care and intelligence. A good dictionary will still be indispensable; you should always verify your guesses made on the basis of analysis and context. There are in particular two areas of difficulty in analyzing words. In the first place, confusion can sometimes arise because two or more Latin bases are spelled the same way. To cite an extreme instance of this, *transparent, parent,* and *preparation* contain three different bases, each spelled alike but with separate meanings, PAR-, "to appear," PAR-, "to give birth," and PAR-, "to make ready." Sometimes, also, a word may seem to contain a familiar Latin base and yet not come from Latin at all. *Artichoke* has nothing to do with ART-, "skill," but is apparently of Arabic origin.

In the second place, the combined meaning of base, prefix, and suffix, which is called the *etymological meaning,* is frequently not the same as the current meaning. For instance, the etymological meaning of *precarious,* "pertaining to prayer" (PREC-, "prayer"), seems at first glance rather remote from its usual meaning of "hazardous, insecure." It is not likely that one could deduce the current meaning simply by using a knowledge of word elements. Only by comparing the etymological meaning with the current meaning does one come to realize that a "precarious" situation was originally one completely out of human control, dependent only upon prayer and entreaty. Again, on the basis of the meanings of its elements, *transgressor* is "one who steps across" (*trans-,* "across" + GRED-, GRESS-, "to step," "to go," + *-or,* "one who"). The connection with its current meaning "sinner" is not readily apparent until one sees that originally the sense of the word was "one who steps across the bounds of righteousness." The verb *decimate,* as we saw from its root, would seem to have something to do with "tenth," yet it normally refers to the destruction of a large part of a group, as in the sentence, "The enemy troops were *decimated* by machine gunfire." Not until we learn that at one time the word referred to the practice of punishing mutinous soldiers by executing every tenth man and that it came to be used loosely, can we connect the two senses. Thus, in many cases, a student must be careful to distinguish the current meaning from the etymological meaning.

Such differences between current meanings and etymological meanings offer many problems in connection with word analysis. But there is a positive side to this. As was mentioned earlier, one of the most effective ways of improving vocabulary is to become "word-conscious," to develop an interest in words for their own sake. The words which you will find most interesting are not those which can be analyzed in a more or less cut and dried fashion, but those which have changed their meanings in the course of centuries, and so present a problem which challenges the imagination. When you find a word which is capable of analysis but which means something quite different from the sum of its parts, plug in your curiosity and try to determine how its present sense developed.

Usually a dictionary will be of help in this, and often you will find an interesting explanation for such a development, an explanation which may reflect some custom or belief or event of the past, or some characteristically human way of looking at things. For instance, *lunatic* contains the base meaning "moon" (also found in *lunar),* reminding us that insanity was once thought to be caused by the influence of the moon. The etymological meaning of *candidate* is "clad in white," a word arising from the practice of Roman politicians who, when campaigning for office, wore artificially whitened togas as a symbol of personal purity.

Note that the analysis of words into prefixes, bases, and suffixes frequently does not correspond to their division into syllables. Thus, *bellicose* is made up of the elements *bell-*, "war," *-ic*, "pertaining to," and *-ose*, "full of," but is divided into syllables *bel-li-cose*.

ASSIGNMENT

I. Learn the following **adjective-forming suffixes** and their meanings:

-(u)lent, -(o)lent, "full of," "disposed to"

| FRAUD- | deceit | + | -(u)lent | fraudulent |
| VI- | force | + | -(o)lent | violent |

-ic, -tic, "pertaining to," "like"

CIV-	citizen	+	-ic	civic
CLASS-	class, rank	+	-ic	classic
RUS-	country	+	-tic	rustic

-ary, "pertaining to," "connected with," "having the character of"

LITER-	letter, literature	+	-ary	literary
MILIT-	soldier	+	-ary	military
TEMPOR-	time	+	-ary	temporary

If this suffix is followed by an additional element, the final *y* appears as *i*.

| PREC- | prayer | + -ary | + -ous | precarious |
| ANTIQU- | old | + -ary | + -an | antiquarian |

The suffix *-ary* frequently forms words which are used as nouns and so comes to mean "one connected with."

| ANTIQU- | old | + -ary | antiquary |
| DIGNIT- | worth | + -ary | dignitary |

-ile, -il, "pertaining to," "like," "belonging to," "having the character of"

JUVEN-	youth	+ -ile	juvenile
HOST-	enemy	+ -ile	hostile
CIV-	citizen	+ -il	civil

II. Learn the following bases and their meanings:

DOM(IN)-	house, master	dome, predominant
FLAG(R)-, FLAM(M)-	to burn; flame	flagrant, conflagrant, inflammation
FLAT-	to blow	inflate, flatulent, conflation
GEN-, GENER-	race, kind, origin	general, genus, generous
GEN-	to give birth to, produce	genital, ingenious, ingenuity

(These two bases are related. The basic stem *gen-* in Latin, meaning "to beget, bear, bring forth," itself begot upward of thirty words in Latin, which, in turn, have offered a wide variety of words and meanings as these Latin words were borrowed into English.)

LATER-	side	equilateral, laterally
LUC-, LUMIN-	to shine; light	lucid, illuminate
PAR-	to ready, bring forth, provide	prepare, separate
SEN-	old	senate, senior
SERV-	to serve, save	servant, service, preserve, conservation

III. Analyze the following italicized words and define them as they are used in the sentence or phrase.

Example: collateral*—<u>col</u>- together + LATER- side + -<u>al</u> pertaining to: situated or running side by side; parallel.

1. The principal doctor was lost in the imbecilities of a *senile* optimism.—Lytton Strachey

2. Ian Smith and his proclamation of UDI (*unilateral* declaration of independence) for the British territory of Rhodesia in 1965 gave Prime Minister Wilson and the British government a relentless barrage of headaches.

3. Try as he might, he could not *generate* any enthusiasm among his fellow councilmen for the issuing of bonds to raise money for new street lights.

4. An intimacy with Dr. Johnson, the great literary *luminary* of the day, was the crowning object of his aspiring and somewhat ludicrous ambition.—Washington Irving

---

*As in the phrase "...the collateral mountain ridges enclosing the Shenandoah Valley of Virginia."

5. The *turbulent* multitude continued roaming and shouting and howling about the city during the day and a part of the night.—Washington Irving

6. *Aquatic* sports are always popular on Florida's lakes.

7. He was generally clad in a long, patched livery coat...which bagged loosely around him, having evidently belonged to some *corpulent* predecessor.—Dickens

8. The peace we have with us today is as *precarious* and unsatisfactory as the form of a strip artist with peritonitis.—E.B. White

9. Please don't *invoke* your petty little dogmas in discussion with me; when you think them through, come back and we can have a conversation instead of a button-pushing session.

10. I want you to draw me two *quadrilaterals*—one a rhombus and one a trapezoid.

11. Though this *gregarious* man is an inveterate joiner and belongs to "every fraternal order in Muncie...."—*Harper's Magazine*

12. She *deflated* his ego, at least momentarily, by announcing—to everyone within a ten-mile radius—that he had the intellectual range of a baked potato.

13. He *retained* the best lawyer in the state but still lost his case.

14. Religions differ so much in their accidents that in discussing the religious question we must make it very *generic* and broad.—William James

15. She was so hooked that even the very thought of him *inflamed* her passions.

16. ...the flickering brightness from the inside shining up the chimney and making a *luminous* mist of the emerging smoke.—Thomas Hardy

17. They had not learned the noble dialects of Greece and Rome ... and they prized instead a cheap *contemporary* literature.—Thoreau

18. The will of the monarch produced a false and *servile* unanimity, and no more than two patriots had courage to speak their own sentiments, and those of their country.—Edward Gibbon

19. It would be a gross exaggeration to suggest that I was even for a moment *enchanted* by our illustrious guest of honor, a pompous ass if I ever met one.

20. You may *infer* by my painful facial expressions that I consider your horrid rock music to have all the acoustical properties of a major industrial accident.

IV. Divide each of the following words (a) into prefixes, bases, and suffixes; and then (b), with the help of your dictionary, divide them into syllables.

Example: incorrigible— (a) in-cor-rig-ible, (b) in-cor-ri-gi-ble

1. luminary
2. aqueous
3. precarious
4. contemporaneous
5. gregarious
6. unilateral

LESSON X

DISSIMILATION AND OTHER SOUND CHANGES

We have seen in Lesson III how, through the process called assimilation, a sound became similar or identical to a neighboring sound. A reverse process also took place—and also during Roman times—called dissimilation, a nineteenth-century coinage (*dis-* "not" + SIMIL- "similar") defined* as a process "by which two identical sounds are made unlike, or two similar sounds are made to diverge." Most dissimilated situations concerned words that contained *r—r* or *l—l*. For example, the Latin stem *peregrin-* (a blend of *per-* "through" + *ager* "the field") dissimilated the first *r* to *l*, in its travels through French to English, giving us our *pilgrim* ("one who wanders"). English, in this case, also picked up the undissimilated original, giving our words *peregrine, peregrine* falcon, and *peregrinate* ("to travel, especially on foot"). Similarly, from *Pales* (goddess of herds and shepherds) comes the derived Latin adjective *Parilis*, which coexisted with the original adjective *Palilis*. The Latin *turtur* ("a turtle dove") ended up in English as *turtle*; the French *marbre* came into English as *marble*; *bramble* emerged from *brimbrum*—in each case the second *r* dissimilating to an *l*. In speech, many speakers completely drop the first *r* in *library* and *governor* by saying 'liberry' and 'guvner' or 'guv-ə-ner.'

---

*Here, and presumably for the first time, by the English grammarian Henry Sweet.

The suffixes *-al* and *-ar* (Lesson VIII) are in fact one and the same suffix and a good example of dissimilation. When the base had an *r* in it, the suffix got the *l*. When the base had an *l* in it, the suffix got the *r*. When neither an *r* nor an *l* was in the base, the suffix used the *l* form. Consider the examples offered at these two suffixes in Lesson VIII: *popular, regular, familiar; verbal* (also *regal, royal, natural, parental*); and *vocal, equal.*

Vowels also dissimilated, one of the most frequent instances being an *ii*, with the second *i* dissimilating to *e* in derivatives. For example, what in Latin would have been *piitas* (derived from *pius, pii*) went instead to *pietas*—giving both *piety* and *pious* to English. Similarly, the Latin *societas* evolved from *socius, socii*—supplying English with both *society* and *social*; and *varietas* from *varius, varii*—from which we have both *variety* and *various.*

There were several sound changes that were standard features of Latin and which account for there being two different forms for some Latin bases. Several of these bases you have already studied. In the examples below, *-tum* is the regular form of the past-participle suffix.

dt or *tt* before a vowel often went to *ss* or *s*:

VID-   + *-tum* = *vidtum* > *visum*   ——producing VID-, VIS-
MITT- + *-tum* = *mittum* > *missum*——producing MITT-, MISS-
VERT- + *-tum* = *verttum* > *versum* ——producing VERT-, VERS-
SENT- + *-tum* = *senttum* > *sensum* ——producing SENT-, SENS-
CLUD- + *-tum* > *cludtum* > *clusum* ——producing CLUD-, CLUS-
LUD-   + *-tum* = *ludtum* > *lusum*   ——producing LUD-, LUS-

(The forms *vidtum, mittum*, etc., have never been found in any Latin text, as with *verrtum, scribtum*, etc., following.)

rrt went to *rs*:

VERR-"to drag" + *-tum* = *verrtum* > *versum* ——VERR-, VERS-
CURR-   + *-tum* = *currtum* > *cursum* ——CURR-, CURS-

before *s* or *t*, *b* went to *p* and *g* went to *c*:

SCRIB-   + *-tum* = *scribtum* > *scriptum* ——SCRIB-, SCRIPT-
REG-   + *-tum* = *regtum*   > *rectum*   ——REG-, RECT-
FRANG- + *-tum* = *frangtum* > *fractum* ——FRANG, FRACT-

None of these sound changes were hit or miss, nor were they thought out; they were completely natural. They are the result of things that take place in our mouths when we talk. For example, it is easier to pronounce two voiceless consonants together, like the *-pt-* in SCRIPT- and the *-ct-* in RECT-, than it is to pronounce a voiced consonant with a voiceless consonant, the *-bt-* and *-gt-*. Similarly, we are more inclined to say /bodl/ for the word "bottle" rather than /botl/, simply because the voiced *l* makes us want to use the voiced *d* in front rather than the voiceless *t*.

These are only three of the several sound changes that occurred in Latin, but they will help to explain some of the variety in many of the Latin bases you are studying.

ASSIGNMENT

I.   Learn the following **adjective-forming suffixes** and their meanings:

-ine, "pertaining to," "like," "of"

FEMIN-   woman   +   *-ine* feminine
CAN-   dog   +   *-ine* canine

(There are a number of adjectives formed by means of this suffix from the names of various living creatures; for example, FEL-, "cat," *feline;* ASIN-, "ass," *asinine;* BOV-, "cow," *bovine;* AQUIL-, "eagle," *aquiline,* etc.)

-ate, -it(e), "possessing," "being," etc. This is often equivalent to the English past participle ending *-ed,* and is the same *-at-/-it-* element that is discussed in Lesson II.

ad- + CUR-   care   + *-ate* accurate
ad- + EQU-   equal   + *-ate* adequate (literally, made equal to)
FAVOR-   favor   + *-ite* favorite
ex- + PLIC-   to fold   + *-it* explicit

-ant, -ent (-ient), equivalent to the English present participle ending *-ing*

URG-   to press   + *-ent* urgent (literally, pressing)
ad- + PAR-   to appear   + *-ent* apparent (literally, appearing)
VIGIL-   to watch   + *-ant* vigilant (literally, watching)

This suffix frequently forms words which are used as nouns, and so it comes to mean "person who," or "that which."

AG-   to do   + *-ent* agent (literally, person doing)
in- + HABIT-   to live   + *-ant* inhabitant (literally, person living in)
ad- + HER-   to stick   + *-ent* adherent (literally, person sticking to)
SERV-   to serve   + *-ant* servant (literally, person serving)

II. Learn the following bases and their meanings:

CUMB-, CUB-	to lie down	succumb, incubator
FEDER-	league, treaty	confederate
FID-	faith	confident
FIDEL-	faithful	infidelity
HER-, HES-	to stick	adhere, adhesive
ORD(IN)-	to put in order, arrange	order, ordinary
POT-, POSS-	to be able, have power	potent, possible
SAL-, (SIL-), SALT-, SULT-	to leap	salient, resilient, saltatorial, insult
SED-, (SID-), SESS-	to sit, settle	sediment, insidious, session
TERR-	land, earth	terrestrial, territory

III. Analyze the following italicized words and define them as they are used in the sentence or phrase.

1. He was too *diffident* to do justice to himself; but when his natural shyness was overcome, his behaviour gave every indication of an open affectionate heart.—Jane Austen

2. This intention of abandoning Astoria was, however, kept secret from the men, lest they should at once give up all labor, and become restless and *insubordinate.*—Washington Irving

3. The slaves were chiefly women, employed as servants, wool-processors, or *concubines.*—Edward McNall Burns, *Western Civilization*

4. It was expected that newspeak would have finally *superseded* oldspeak (or Standard English, as we should call it) by the year 2050.—George Orwell

5. Superficial observers will speak of the paganism of the Renaissance, its unblushing license, its worldliness...as though these qualities were not *inherent* in human nature, ready at any moment to emerge.—Symonds

6. What will be singled out as the *salient* event of our time by future historians, centuries hence...?—*Harper's Magazine*

7. To man he is a divine ambassador, a minister *plenipotentiary,* the Creator's special representative.—Mark Twain

8. Elsewhere metropolitan America has adopted a diet proper to

the *sedentary* life, but the Western city dweller eats a cowhand's meal.—*Harper's Magazine*

9. The *subsidiary* theme in the correspondence is one urging me to Manhattan.—John Kennedy Toole

10. ...the ideally best form of government is that in which the sovereignty...is vested in the entire *aggregate* of the community.—John Stuart Mill

11. ...viewed in the same light and from the same *terrain* from which they view it themselves.—Thomas Lister

12. The *pungent,* acrid smell of rotting leaves, of flowers, of blossoms and plants dying in the poisonous and cruel gloom. —Joseph Conrad

13. He has seen but half the *universe* who never has been shewn the house of Pain.—Emerson

14. How complex, sensitive, *resilient* is the society we have evolved over centuries, and how capable of withstanding the most unexpected strain!—Sir Winston Churchill

15. His *inordinate* desire for immediate fame and fortune ultimately brought him considerably more pain than pleasure.

16. The unprovoked act of terrorism was a *flagrant* violation of the recent truce between the two countries.

17. The [Roman] senate was thus made *omnipotent* and irresponsible.—James A. Froude

18. No one who has sworn to support the Constitution can conscientiously vote for what he understands to be an unconstitutional measure, however *expedient* he may think it. —Abraham Lincoln

19. ...the necessity that is *incumbent* on every writer to form some plan or design before he enter on any discourse or narration.—David Hume

20. Died...[of] a *congenital* heart condition....—*Time*

IV. The following words contain bases which have been studied previously. With the aid of a dictionary, by consulting the etymology and the various meanings given for the word, explain the connection between the meaning of the base and the current meaning of the word.

1. annals	9. jury
2. ordinance	10. magnate
3. confinement	11. obvious
4. impediment	12. prejudice
5. impend	13. punctuate
6. incorporate	14. segregate
7. incubate	15. senate
8. invent	16. travesty

LESSON XI

SEMANTIC CHANGE

The vocabulary of a language describes the things and activities which the speakers of that language have come to consider important. The interplay between these cultural facts and the vocabulary used to describe them is extremely complex, and a total analysis of their inter-relationships would prove impossible. Nonetheless, the attempt to ar-rive at such an analysis is interesting to the professional linguist and yields results useful even to the layman.

Consider the array of cultural facts to be a huge world or universe. We might then subdivide the total area into territories peculiar to a definable set of activities and facts. For example, *food-preparation* would constitute such a territory, and all the artifacts and activities related to food-preparation would be grouped together. Then the vocabulary used to describe these things and activities would form a related set (called by linguists a semantic field). These sets could be further subdivided again and again down to the level of an indi-vidual thing or activity. *Cook,* for example, belongs to the territory *food-preparation,* and *cook* itself can be further subdivided into indi-vidually named activities: *boil, steam, braise, roast, fry, grill, bake, sauté,* etc.

But notice that some of these verbs, originally restricted to the ter-ritory *food-preparation,* do duty in other territories as well. *Boil* can be used to refer to the "heat" of a person's anger. *Fry* is used cruelly to describe the effects of an electric chair, and *roast* to refer to one's discomfort on a hot day, and also to ridicule or criticize severely (although sometimes, as on a television show, all in good fun). Words which do such double duty are in the process of semantic change.

This avenue of approach to the subject of semantic change suggests a method by which we can categorize the various kinds of semantic change. Words which do duty in several territories have grown in the breadth of their application by a process we will call *similitude*. *Boil* is applied to the phenomenon of anger because the emotion causes a hot flushing sensation similar to the feeling and redness caused by mild scalding. You might hear someone say "I'm roasting" on a hot day because the environment feels similar to an oven from which escape is impossible.

Similitude can itself be subdivided into subcategories: based upon function, upon structure, upon appearance, and so on. The use of the word *horse* in *sawhorse* is based upon structure (it has four legs) and upon function (it bears a load), as with the *pommel horse* (in gymnastics) and *clotheshorse*. The *eye* of a needle is based upon appearance only, in resembling the shape of a human eye, as opposed to the *eyepiece* of a telescope, which is based through similitude on its function (you look through it to see things) as well as upon structure (it has lenses). The *head* and *foot* of a bed are based on relative location only, that is, the *head* is where the *top* is, which is where the *headboard* is and where the pillow goes, but not necessarily where your own head has to go. You can sleep with your head at the *foot* of the bed if you want to, which is at the other end, or the *bottom,* which is where the *footboard* is.

We might here add several other subcategories of change effected through similitude: **emotional, operational**, and **symbolic**. The verb *nag* originally meant "bite" when it was imported into English from a Nordic dialect. But the territory *bite* was already covered by the native English word *bite*. Hence the imported word came to be applied to the territory *criticism* on the basis of similitude—the biting **emotional** effect felt by someone who is subject to constant prompting, complaint, or criticism. The word *write* belonged originally to the territory *scratch,* but when the new technology of making meaningful scratches on paper (or bark, rather) came into vogue, *write* was adopted as the word for the newly created territory on the basis of the similarity between the **operations** of writing and of scratching. This left the old territory to be covered only by the word *score,* "notch, a count of twenty notches," until later the word *scratch* was created by blending (see Lesson XXI) two separate words *cratch* and *scrat,* both of which referred to wounding by nail and claw.

In change based upon **symbolic** similitude, an item is described by a word thought to epitomize or symbolize that item. The word *jugger-*

naut is a good example. Originally an image (called *Juggernaut*) of the Hindu deity Krishna that was annually worshipped in a procession and that was drawn on a wagon so immense that it was unstoppable even when worshippers threw themselves in its path, the word has taken on new meanings through this symbolism: (1) a belief or institution that elicits blind or destructive devotion; (2) any overwhelming or irresistible force or movement; (3) (in England) a large trailer truck that transports goods by road throughout Europe, which would surely wipe out anything in its path. Also, consider the symbolic implications in the word *bulldozer*.

A pretty girl's appearance is so stunning that she is described as if she were good-looks in the flesh: "she is a beauty." A person is so intelligent that he functions as if he were gray matter pure and simple: "he's a brain." One part of an operation comes to stand for the whole: "*book* that person for murder." Conversely, a word for the whole structure comes to be applied to its most significant part: *clock* referred originally to a bell-tower, then to the striking mechanism which rang the bell, then to the machinery which kept the striking mechanism on time, and finally to any mechanism which keeps the time whether it strikes the hours or not.

We can see from the examples above that symbolic change often changes the part of speech of a word, as when *book* is used as a verb (see Functional Change in Lesson XIII). Also, there is often a change in the quality of a word from abstract to concrete and vice versa, as when a girl is described as a beauty (see Lesson XV).

The last and perhaps most important kind of semantic change based upon similitude is ***metaphorical*** change. Here, as usual with change based upon similitude, a word is made to do duty in two different territories. But in metaphorical change the total ambience of the word in its original territory is used to clarify or illustrate the new territory. Let us take as an example the declaration "the meeting was a circus." *Circus,* a word from the territory of entertainment, has been transferred to the territory of business. But along with the word comes its total ambience, all of its connotations: the **operation** of the meeting was like that of a circus—seemingly disorganized; the **function** of the meeting broke down and became sheer entertainment—it was a joke; the **appearance** of the meeting was like that of a circus—a hubbub of sounds, a kaleidoscope of sights; the **emotions** raised at the meeting were those more appropriate to a circus than a business affair—childish confusion and delight without adult purpose.

Metaphors are powerful motivators of semantic change, and they often acquire an immediate vogue that can last for years or even centuries. However, because of the voguish or faddish nature of metaphors in general, many fall by the wayside and are forgotten in a few months or a couple of years. Conservative dictionary editors are often skeptical of fashionable words ("Why include a word if no one is going to be using it next year?" one editor asked), which is why a lot of metaphorical usage is slow to enter contemporary dictionaries. On the other hand, the word *circus,* in the sense of a place or an activity displaying rowdy or noisy behavior, has been around for more than a hundred years.

Metaphors that pass out of use are referred to as "dead." The word *rehearse,* for example, originally belonged to the territory of farming. It referred to the operation of harrowing, or the breaking up of the clods of earth with an animal-drawn sledge (called *disking* by modern American farmers). To be effective, the operation had to be repeated over and over again—to *re-hearse,* that is, "to harrow again." The word was then extended to any similar operation which needed tedious repetition for success. The current meaning of the word, however, is restricted to the latter sense in an even more narrow application: a practice repetition to prepare for public performance. The original territory of the word, that of farming, has long since been forgotten, and the metaphor is dead.

Besides change resulting from similitude, we must consider by contrast the kind of change which takes place when the change of meaning occurs without the involvement of territories other than the one native to the word. For example, the word *liquor* has always been, and still is, confined to the field of words which is used to describe fluids and their motion. A near relative, *liquid,* has retained this broad, general application to the whole field while *liquor* has shrunk in the range of its application to be almost totally confined to a narrow subdivision of *fluid,* namely intoxicating drink. This semantic shift began to affect the word *liquor* early on, when Roman poets favored this word to refer to wine. The French word *liqueur,* as adopted into English, has an even narrower field of application: liquor flavored with an aromatic substance.

We shall refer to this latter type of change by the term **modulation**, the other major subdivision of semantic change. Here, as with similitude, there are subdivisions: a word which narrows its range of application (as with *liquor* above) is said to have undergone **specialization**; a word that does the opposite—that is, goes from a narrow meaning to a broader, general meaning—is said to have undergone **generalization**. Both of these subdivisions are discussed in the next lesson.

A particular type of modulation, called **radiation**, occurs when a word of very broad meaning fans out, or radiates, into several specific meanings, all of which, nevertheless, keep the same basic meaning of the word. The word *action,* for example, from the base ACT- (Lesson XVIII), which has the broad, primary meaning "doing," has spawned upwards of twenty different and specific meanings that are in current use, such as the sequence of events in a play or movie, the movements of a mechanism (such as a watch), a legal proceeding, combat between military forces, and so on. The words *prime* and *primary* also offer prime examples of semantic change through radiation.

Often words undergo change through similitude and modulation simultaneously, complex changes that are difficult to trace—and which desk dictionaries make no effort to trace. This task is left to the *Oxford English Dictionary,* which arranges its material according to the semantic history of each word and is the best source for studying semantic and linguistic change.

Certain words have undergone complex changes along paths so closely parallel that it is useful to attach labels to the patterns they exhibit: *degeneration* and *elevation* will be taken up in Lesson XIV, *weakening* in Lesson XVI, change due to *changing concepts* in Lesson XVII, and *euphemism* and *taboo-deformation* in Lesson XVIII. Other linguistic changes which involve phonetics more than semantics will be taken up in Lessons XIX – XXII.

ASSIGNMENT

I. Learn the following **adjective-forming suffixes** and their meanings:

-able, -ible, "able to be," "able to," "tending to"

	PORT-	to carry	+ -able	portable
ad- +	APT-	fit	+ -able	adaptable
	FLEX-	to bend	+ -ible	flexible

If this suffix is followed by an additional element, it becomes *-abil-, -ibil-.*

ad- +	APT-	fit	+ -able	+ -ity	adaptability
	FLEX-	to bend	+ -ible	+ -ity	flexibility

The suffix *-ability* (*-ibility, -bility*), meaning "inclination, suitability, capacity, or tendency to act or be acted upon in a (specified) way," is also found in most dictionaries, with *teachability* and *capability* as examples. More importantly it covers such words as *ensilability* and *roadability,* where there is no (or not yet) *ensilable* or *roadable.*

-ile, "able to be," "able to," "tending to"

AG-   to do   + *-ile*   agile
VOLAT- to fly   + *-ile*   volatile
REPT-   to creep + *-ile*   reptile

This suffix is distinguished from *-ile, -il,* "pertaining to," etc. (see Lesson IX) by the fact that it is normally attached to verbal bases.

-acious, "tending to," "inclined to"

AUD- to dare + *-acious*   audacious
TEN- to hold + *-acious*   tenacious

II. Learn the following bases and their meanings:

CRED-	to believe, trust	credential, creditor, discredit
DOC-, DOCT-	to teach	document, doctor, indoctrinate
FA(B)-, FAT-, FESS-, FAM-	to speak, reveal	affable, infant, preface, confess, fame, fabulous
FALL-, FALS-, [FAIL-], [FAULT-]	to deceive	fallacy, false, failure, default
MOD-	measure	modicum, modest, modern, modify
MUT-	to change	mutant, mutation
TANG-, (TING-), TACT-	to touch	tangent, contingent, contact, intact
TRACT-	to drag	tractor, traction, detract

III. Analyze the following italicized words and define them as they are used in the sentence or phrase.

1. The soldier who fell in battle was transported at once to the region of *ineffable* bliss in the bright mansions of the Sun. —William Hickling Prescott

2. She had the pathetic failing of refusing to *credit* herself in some particular without calling up a minus somewhere else.

3. The comet is not dead, but *transmuted*. . . [and] glorious in its agony.—Larry Niven

4. The *Fates* have spoken.

5. . . . for while everyone well knows himself to be *fallible,* few think it necessary to take any precautions against their own fallibility.—John Stuart Mill

6. The fact narrated must correspond to something in me to be *credible* or intelligible.—Emerson

7. ...a stronghold of privateers, the home of a race whose *intractable* and defiant independence neither time nor change has subdued.—Francis Parkman

8. General Grant's plan for defeating Lee and bringing the South to its knees was *contingent* upon the Federals taking Richmond.

9. The more clinical "*genitally* contracted" has slowly been gaining ground over the old romantic "venereal,"* with the contraction "V.D." consequently fading out. If only the diseases could be got rid of so easily!

10. The true harvest of my daily life is somewhat *intangible* and indescribable as the tints of morning or evening. It is a little star-dust caught, a segment of a rainbow which I have clutched.—Thoreau

11. This did not appear the worst nor by any means a *despicable* alternative.—Thoreau

12. In the United States are more than two million, the least *assimilable* of immigrants.—*Harper's Magazine*

13. The republicans hold, as a fixed *incontrovertible* principle, that sovereignty resides in the great mass of the people. —Thomas Paine

14. You would darkly slander him whom you cannot openly *defame.*—E. Bulwer-Lytton

15. Nothing in the whole adventure, not even the upset, had disturbed the calm and *equable* current of Mr. Pickwick's temper.—Dickens

16. ...notions based on such patently *fallacious* ideas that even the economists had abandoned them before Mr. Berenson began to write.—*Harper's Magazine*

17. It was set down many years past, and was the sense of my conceptions at that time, not an *immutable* law....—Sir Thomas Browne

18. Some of them are unmannered, rough, intractable, as well as ignorant; but others are *docile,* have a wish to learn, and evince a disposition that pleases me.—Charlotte Brontë

---

*The word comes from the Latin base VENER- "to love," a base that has also produced the English *venerable, venerate,* and *Venus* (=Roman goddess of spring and beauty, identified with Aphrodite, the Greek goddess of love and beauty); hence, here a disease that was born out of love.

19. . . . the related argument that increased consumer purchasing power is an infallible remedy for unemployment is hardly *tenable. —Harper's Magazine*

20. Even at twenty-nine he is still *obsessed* with the image of adolescent virility, which has retarded his development.

IV. Using your dictionary, give the original or etymological meanings of the following words which have undergone semantic change through similitude.

1. cancer	7. insult
2. eradicate	8. muscle
3. flourish	9. pastor
4. focus	10. remorse
5. gladiolus	11. scruple
6. gland	12. seminary

LESSON XII

SPECIALIZATION AND GENERALIZATION OF MEANING

Specialization is a process whereby the meaning of a word shifts from the general to the specific. Thus, *undertaker* originally meant "one who undertakes to do anything," but now has come to mean "one who undertakes the special task of preparing bodies for burial." *Disease,* as can be seen by analyzing the word, once referred to any "discomfort," but now has the narrower meaning of "illness," that is, a particular type of discomfort. *Deer* in Shakespeare's time meant any animal but now is applicable to only one specific type.

The following are some examples of specialization of meaning which have already been encountered in earlier lessons:

The base VERB- originally meant "word" and still does in *verbose* and *verbatim,* but in the case of *verb,* a particular type of word denoting action, it has narrowed its meaning.

Diffident once meant "not trusting," and Milton speaks of "diffidence of God"; but now it has acquired the more specific meaning of not trusting oneself, lacking self-confidence.

The base VEST- as a Latin word referred to any garment; now, however, *vest* is applied to a special type of clothing.

Sometimes just the opposite process takes place and the meaning of a word becomes broader. This type of semantic change is known as generalization. Thus, *decimate* (DECIM-, "tenth") originally referred to the destruction of one tenth of a military unit; now it refers to the destruction of any large part. The word *vaccine* comes from the Latin *vacca*, "cow," coined because the first such immunizing substance was obtained from cowpox. Though the name *vaccine* is still used, it is no longer applied only to material from cows, however, but to other substances as well, such as Salk vaccine (used against poliomyelitis), which is produced from monkey kidneys.

In its evolution a word may show both specialization and generalization. *Assassin* is a word which entered the languages of Europe during the Crusades, when the members of a certain Mohammedan sect, having vowed the killing of Christian leaders, made use of the narcotic hashish to work themselves into a state of frenzy sufficient for the dangerous task. *Assassin* (Arabic, *hashshashin*) consequently first meant "eater of hashish," then a special group of "hashish-eating terrorists" and finally any "treacherous murderer" whether under the influence of drugs or not.

Very often semantic change is complex in nature as in these examples:

Expedite (*ex-*, "from" + PED-, "foot"), as we have seen, originally meant "to free one caught by the foot," but now refers to the removal of any sort of difficulty.

From the sentence, "He was divested of his authority," it is obvious that *divest* (*di-*, "apart" + VEST-, "garment") is used to signify not just the taking off of clothing but the removal of other things as well.

Excruciate (CRUC-, "cross") once referred to the torture of crucifixion, but is now used in reference to any kind of pain.

As can be seen from the previous examples, when metaphorical usage occurs, a certain amount of generalization is involved as well.

ASSIGNMENT

I. Learn the following **adjective-forming suffixes** and their meanings:

-itious, "tending to," "characterized by"

FICT-	to invent	+ *-itious*	fictitious
ex- + PED-	foot	+ *-itious*	expeditious

-id, "tending to," "inclined to"

FRIG-	to be cold	+ *-id*	frigid
RAP-	to seize	+ *-id*	rapid
HUM-	to be wet	+ *-id*	humid

-ulous, "tending to," "inclined to"

GARR-	to chatter	+ *-ulous*	garrulous
TREM-	to tremble	+ *-ulous*	tremulous

II. Learn the following bases and their meanings:

AC(U)-, ACR-, ACET-	sharp, bitter	acid, acute, acetic acid
CAD-, (CID-), CAS-	to fall, befall	cadence, accident, incident, casual, occasion
CAP-, (CIP-), CAPT-, (CEPT-), [CEIV-]	to take, seize	incapacitate, recipient, capture, except, reception, receive
FAC-, (FIC-), FACT-, (FECT-)	to do, make	faculty, efficient, manufacture, effective

(Also connected with this base are *defeat* and *feasible,* which came in through French.)

FLOR-	flower	florist, floral, Florida (through Spanish)

(Also connected with this base are *flour* and *flower,* which came in through French.)

FLU-, FLUX-, FLUV-, FLUOR(O)-	to flow; a flow	fluid, flux, effluvia, fluoroscope
FOLI-, [FOIL-]	leaf	folio, defoliant, tinfoil
NOC-, NOX-, NIC-, NEC-	to harm, kill	innocent, obnoxious, pernicious, internecine

| NOV- | new | novel, novice, innovative |

III. Analyze the following italicized words and define them as they are used in the sentence or phrase.

1. No matter how *incredulous* we really are about monsters, ghosts, and creatures from outer space, we love being frightened out of our wits by a scary movie.

2. The drama was condemned to trivialities which only too faithfully reflected the political stagnation and the literary trifling of a *decadent* civilization.—John Addington Symonds

3. Knowing where he had come from was something of a *distracting* comfort at a time when he was not awfully sure where he was going.

4. His teacher made a superhuman effort to *elevate* him to the dizzying heights of mediocrity.

5. It is even more graceful than the weeping willow or any *pendulous* trees which dip their branches in the stream instead of being buoyed up by it.—Thoreau

6. In his general deportment he was pompous and important, affecting a species of *florid* elocution, which often became ridiculous.—Sir Walter Scott

7. Today's visitor thinks of the city as a tottery invalid, preserved by the skin of the teeth from the ravages of tide, *effluent,* mass sightseeing, and economic slump.—*Time*

8. All anemias are *pernicious,* so why was one poor little type singled out for this insulting name?

9. The girls admitted they trusted his suggestive attitude and *factitious* smile less than they would a half-crazed, starved, charging rhinoceros.

10. Your scheme just doesn't seem *feasible* to me. How is it you plan to get around those five nasty German Shepherd attack dogs?

11. The Colorado and the Green rivers are *confluent.*

12. For many hotels, though, the most immediate way to reach the upper crust is to *renovate* one or two floors.—*Time*

13. I thought he was just a crummy actor, but he's *versatile*—he's crummy at a lot of things.—*Punch*

14. The enemy continued to conceal themselves in the supposedly *defoliated* jungle while agent orange continued its insidious work upon all who came into contact with it.

15. What is more difficult than to *perceive* the real designs of an evil genius?

16. When sometimes a frying-pan caught fire...and the old man was seen backing out of the doorway, swearing and coughing violently in the *acrid* cloud of smoke....—Joseph Conrad

17. Someone with a positive manner, perhaps a detective, used the expression "madman" as he bent over Wilson's body that afternoon, and the *adventitious* authority of his voice set the key for the newspaper reports next morning.—F. Scott Fitzgerald

18. To understand all mysteries, to have all knowledge, to be able to comprehend with all the saints, is a great work; enough to crush the spirit, and to stretch the strings of the most *capacious,* widened soul that breatheth on this side of glory. —John Bunyan

19. ...to provide *efficacious* securities against this evil.—John Stuart Mill

20. One considerable advantage is...its subservience to the easy and the humane...which can never attain a sufficient degree of exactness in its sentiment, *precepts,* or reasonings.—David Hume

---

LESSON XIII

FUNCTIONAL CHANGE

One type of semantic change, a variety of which has already been mentioned in passing (see Lesson VIII), is functional change, the process whereby a word, without change of form, that is, without the addition of suffixes, comes to be used as a different part of speech. Thus, words which were originally adjectives appear as nouns, nouns become verbs, verbs become nouns, and so on. This is so common an occurrence that usually we are not aware of it, but this type of shift is frequently encountered in the case of words brought from Latin into English, and it explains why, for instance, suffixes which are normally used to form adjectives are often found in words now used as nouns; for example, *reptile, agent, inhabitant.*

It would be pointless to run through all the various changes of this type, but we might mention a few of the more interesting ones. The colors, which are generally adjectives, are often used as nouns as, for example, a *red,* referring to a Communist, or a *pink,* referring to a Communist sympathizer, the *whites* of a person's eyes, the *blues,* the *greens* of a golf course. Another frequently encountered variety of such change occurs when nouns are used as verbs; so we say, "to *book* a criminal," "to *knife* a person," "to *iron* a shirt," and sports announcers can describe a referee as "positioning" the football instead of "placing" it on a particular yard line.

Thousands of other words underwent a similar process. For example, *screen, race, monitor, stomach,* and *load* were originally nouns which we use freely today as verbs. Likewise *permit, shake,* and *sink* were originally verbs which we also use today as nouns.

ASSIGNMENT

I. Learn the following **adjective-forming suffixes** and their meanings:

-ive, "tending to," "inclined to"

	ACT-	to do	+ *-ive*	active
ad- +	TRACT-	to draw	+ *-ive*	attractive
ex- +	FECT-	to do	+ *-ive*	effective

-uous, "tending to," "inclined to"

| *con-* + | TIN- | to hold | + *-uous* | continuous |
| *con-* + | SPIC- | to look | + *-uous* | conspicuous |

-ory, "tending to," "serving for"

intro- +	DUCT-	to lead	+ *-ory*	introductory
con- +	PULS-	to drive	+ *-ory*	compulsory
contra- +	DICT-	to speak	+ *-ory*	contradictory

II. Learn the following bases and their meanings:

CERN-, CRET-, [CERT-]	to separate, distinguish	discernment, secret, excrete, ascertain
DUR-	hard; to last	duration, endurable
FUND-, FUS-, [FOUND-]	to pour, melt	refund, fusion, confusion, foundry
NASC-, NAT-	to be born	nascent, native, prenatal, nature, natural

PEL(L)-, PULS- to drive, push   propel, compelling, impulsive, repulsive

PON-, POSIT-,   to place, put   component, deposit,
[POUND-]   position, compound, compose, oppose

([POSE-], though historically derived from a different verb, was confused in meaning with PON- so long ago that we will find it useful to consider it here.)

TORT-   to twist   torture, distort

III. Analyze the following italicized words and define them as they are used in the sentence or phrase.

    1. Yet he read a great deal in a *desultory* manner, without any scheme of study, as chance threw books in his way and inclination directed him through them.—James Boswell

    2. Night, that strange personality which within walls brings ominous *introspectiveness* and self-distrust, but under the open sky banishes such subjective anxieties. . . .—Thomas Hardy

    3. The *prefatory* chapters, which in most cases introduce the special subject of each history, contain a series of retrospective surveys over the whole history of Florence.—John Addington Symonds

    4. The conversation was varied and *discursive,* the king shifting from subject to subject according to his wont.—Macaulay

    5. His grandparents always went to Florida *during* the winter.

    6. *Conservative*: A statesman who is enamored of existing evils, as distinguished from the Liberal who wishes to replace them with others.—Ambrose Bierce, *The Devil's Dictionary*

    7. . . .the shiny and stagnant water in its *tortuous* windings amongst the everlasting and invincible shadows.—Joseph Conrad

    8. Haunting Hess's mind was a *compulsive* fear and hatred of Communist Russia.—*Time*

    9. Once inside, the expression of his face was no more *discernible* by reason of the increasing dusk of the evening. —Thomas Hardy

   10. The same *assiduous* cultivation was bestowed. . .to improve the minds of the sons and nephews of Constantine.—Edward Gibbon

11. All art has a *sensuous* element, colour, form, sound....
    —John A. Symonds

12. What people therefore saw of her in a *cursory* view was very little.—Thomas Hardy

13. His manner was not *effusive*. It seldom was; but he was glad, I think, to see me.—A. Conan Doyle

14. ...recommendation: that the colleges give each prospective law student an examination in *expository* writing at the end of his junior year to see if he needs extra work.—*Time*

15. The child's *obdurate* refusal to name his attacker obviously stemmed from overwhelming fear.

16. ...that moment of astonishment and *nascent* arrogance when a beginning author discovers that he is a good writer.—*Time*

17. We love characters in proportion as they are *impulsive* and spontaneous.—Emerson

18. The effect of Locke's forcible and *perspicuous* reasoning is greatly heightened by his evident anxiety to get at the truth. —Macaulay

19. While the river margin was richly fringed with trees of *deciduous* foliage, the rough uplands were crowned by majestic pines and firs of gigantic size.—Washington Irving

20. Its subject is probably the most *repulsive* in the classical lexicon: the vain Apollo has beaten the satyr Marsyas in a music contest.—*Time*

IV. Originally, what part of speech were the following italicized words and what part of speech are they as used in the sentence or phrase?

   1. to *stone* to death

   2. the *front* part of the house

   3. first *down* and ten to go

   4. He *steeled* himself against misfortune.

   5. The third *out* was made by the pitcher.

   6. He *blacked* the other boy's eye.

   7. He reported his *find* to the authorities.

   8. The crowd uttered *oh's* of delight at the sight of the fireworks.

   9. The deal is *off.*

  10. The coach *mothered* the younger members of the team.

V. Give some examples of your own of this type of change.

LESSON XIV

DEGENERATION AND ELEVATION OF MEANING

A number of words in English have undergone degeneration of meaning, a type of semantic change whereby a word which originally had a good, or at least a neutral, meaning has come to indicate or suggest something objectionable, low, or unpleasant. *Villain,* for instance, at one time signified merely "farm laborer," that is, one attached to a villa or country estate. Gradually, however, the word came to refer to one who had all the bad qualities which in an aristocratic age the gentry attributed to the lower classes. The same snobbish attitude is reflected by the evolution of the word *vulgar,* the etymological meaning of which (as distinct from the current meaning) is "pertaining to the common people" (compare *divulge,* literally, "to spread among the common people"). *Hussy,* a term for a woman of low moral character, is a contraction of *housewife,* its original meaning. *Homely,* literally "home-like," has retained its pleasant flavor in Britain, where it means "warm in manner or appearance," but has degenerated in the United States to mean "plain" or "ugly." *Amateur* once was a complimentary term; it means literally "one who loves" and referred to a person who engaged in an activity for its own sake, not out of an ungentlemanly desire for pay. In our more commercial age, however, the word *amateur* is frequently applied to an inept person, a dabbler, one who cannot keep up with the well-trained professional. This degeneration is well illustrated by the story of a college football coach who, disgusted by a particularly poor performance on the part of his players, remarked in a moment of forgetfulness that his team had played "like a bunch of amateurs."

Some instances of degeneration of meaning in words occurring in the previous exercises are the following:

Senile (SEN-, "old") has come to take into account only the worst characteristics of old age, especially feeble-mindedness. *Senate,* on the other hand, though formed from the same root, is associated with the best characteristics, wisdom and mature judgement.

Verbose, literally "full of words," now indicates a tiresome excess of language.

As with specialization, an opposite process sometimes occurs whereby a word comes to mean something more pleasing or dignified than it did originally. This is called elevation of meaning; it takes place less often than degeneration, however, for, as in most instances, it is easier to tear down than to rebuild.

A good example of elevation is *fame,* which originally signified any report, good or bad. Now, of course, it refers only to good report. Many titles of rank and office show elevation. *Lord* is a contraction of two Anglo-Saxon words meaning "loaf" and "guard," in other words, "bread keeper," a rather humble beginning for so exalted a title. *Constable* began as "chief groom of the stable" and rose to the point where, in the Middle Ages, it became the title of the highest military officer of France. Since then it has descended from its high station and now usually designates a minor official of the law. *Chancellor* once referred to an usher in a law court, the person stationed at the *cancelli,* the latticework separating the public from the judges.

An example of elevation with which you are already familiar is *urbane,* which was once a synonym for *urban,* "pertaining to a city." Sometime during its history the former rose in standing and acquired the meaning of "polite and polished," denoting the qualities which city dwellers like to think they possess; *urban,* however, kept its original meaning.

ASSIGNMENT

I. The next six suffixes are equivalent to the native English suffixes used to form abstract nouns, -*ness* (*heaviness, newness*), -*hood,* (*childhood, manhood*), and -*dom* (*boredom, freedom*). Learn the following **noun-forming suffixes** and their meanings:

-*ity (-ety, -ty),* "quality of," "state of"

GRAV-	heavy	+ -*ity*			gravity
SAN-	healthy	+ -*ity*			sanity
SOCI-	associate	+ -*ety*			society
NOV-	new	+ -*el*	+ -*ty*		novelty

If this is followed by an additional suffix, the final *y* disappears.

GRAV-	heavy	+ -*ity*	+ -*ate*	gravitate
SAN-	healthy	+ -*ity*	+ -*ary*	sanitary
DIGN-	worthy	+ -*ity*	+ -*ary*	dignitary

-(i)tude, "quality of," "state of"

LONG-	long	+	-(i)*tude*	longitude
MULT-	many	+	-(i)*tude*	multitude
MAGN-	large	+	-(i)*tude*	magnitude

If this is followed by an additional suffix, it becomes -(i)*tudin-.*

LONG-	long	+	-(i)*tude*	+	-al	longitudinal
MULT-	many	+	-(i)*tude*	+	-ous	multitudinous

-acy, "quality or state of being or having"

ac-		+ CUR-	care	+ -*acy*	accuracy
in-	+ ad-	+ EQU-	equal	+ -*acy*	inadequacy
con-		+ FEDER-	league	+ -*acy*	confederacy

This is generally the noun form of the adjectival suffix *-ate,* "possessing," "being" (see Lesson X).

II. Learn the following bases and their meanings:

AM-	to love	amorous, amatory
DE-, DIV-	god	deify, divine
[JOURN-]	day	journal
OR-	to speak formally, plead	oracle, oration, peroration
PROB-, [PROV-]	good; to test	probe, probity, approve
RAP-, RAPT-, (REPT-)	to seize	rapid, rape, rapture
STRING-, STRICT-, [STRAIN-]	to draw tight	stringent, strict, restrict, restrain
VER-	true	veritable, aver, very

III. Analyze the following italicized words and define them as they are used in the sentence or phrase.

    1. . . .the rapture of a worshiper on his knees before his *deity.* —*Time*

    2. Nor was his *rectitude* altogether proof against the temptations to which it was exposed in that splendid and polite, but deeply corrupted society.—Macaulay

    3. Among these men there was a *stringent* code of honour, any infringement of which was punished by death.—A. Conan Doyle

4. He had a sudden moment of *lucidity*—of that cruel lucidity that comes once in life to the most benighted. He seemed to see what went on within him, and was horrified at the strange sight.—Joseph Conrad

5. The fog had by this time become more *translucent,* and the position of the sun could be seen through it.—Thomas Hardy

6. ...the *inequity* of the struggle smothers the tragic sense, which demands a more equal conflict.—*Time*

7. Merely corroborative detail, intended to give artistic *verisimilitude* to a bald and unconvincing narrative.—W.S. Gilbert

8. The effort to preserve the present *inexorably* drives one into an embrace with the status quo.—William A. Williams

9. The beautiful fables of the Greeks, being proper creations of the imagination and not of the fancy, are universal *verities.*
—Emerson

10. Bear with unflinching *fortitude* whatever evils and blows we may receive.—Sir Winston Churchill

11. The historic interests of France in Syria, and the *primacy* of those interests over the interests of other European nations, are preserved.—Sir Winston Churchill

12. He was in high repute not only for piety but for *probity* and honor.—Francis Parkman

13. Meanwhile, start a *surreptitious* campaign to round up all other women in similar circumstances.—Betty Harragan

14. ...a test of visual *acuity.*

15. To the *efficacy* and permanency of your union a government for the whole is indispensable.—George Washington

16. He would sometimes pass me haughtily and coldly, just acknowledging my presence by a distant nod or a cool glance, and sometimes bow low and smile with gentlemanlike *affability.*—Charlotte Brontë

17. He showed, at the same time, his implacable *animosity* towards the Christians, by commanding that everyone taken within his dominions should be...sacrificed with all the barbarous ceremonies.—William Hickling Prescott

18. It was a *rapacious* achievement whose scope and speed had not been equaled in all history.—Frank Waters

19. She would have cried for assistance, but age and *infirmity* had long ago deprived her of the power of screaming.—Dickens

20. ...the obligation...to maintain inviolate the relations of peace and *amity* towards other nations.—George Washington

IV. By comparing the various meanings listed in your dictionary, including the etymological meaning, show how each of the following words has undergone degeneration of meaning.

Example: blackguard: (once) servants in charge of pots and pans; (now) villain.

1. artificial
2. boor
3. churl
4. egregious
5. gossip

6. grandiose
7. knave
8. sensual
9. slave

V. In the same way, show how each of the following words has undergone elevation of meaning.

1. frank
2. marshal
3. minister

4. nice
5. shrewd
6. sturdy

LESSON XV

CHANGE FROM ABSTRACT TO CONCRETE, AND VICE VERSA

A further type of semantic change is that whereby a meaning shifts from the abstract to the concrete. In this and the previous lessons, suffixes have been considered which form abstract nouns, but one can see at once that sometimes these are found in words which do not refer to qualities but to things. Most of us find it difficult to think for very long at a time in abstract terms; we prefer concrete, down-to-earth realities. As a consequence, a word which originally referred to a state or quality may come to signify an object or act exhibiting that quality.

Thus, when we speak about "the *multitude* who attended the concert," we are referring to actual people, not to "the state of being many." In the sentence, "His room was full of curiosities from all parts of the world," *curiosity* here indicates a concrete object, not a quality. An unruly child is often spoken of as a *terror,* and a beautiful woman is called a *beauty.*

The word *curiosity* was then later clipped (for clips see Lesson XX) to *curio,* which has taken on the exclusive, concrete meaning, "an object valued as a curiosity," whereas *curiosity* has four possibilities, and can be abstract or concrete. If I tell you about "the curiosities I have encountered in my life," I'm going to be talking about some weird stuff—some of which may be abstract (an odd, unusual, or interesting quality) and some of which may be concrete (a strange, rare, or novel object).

Occasionally a word shifts from a concrete to an abstract meaning. *Tragedy* first signified a play; then, in the sentence, "His life was full of tragedy," it has come to mean the quality exhibited by the play. *Tongue* refers not only to an actual organ of the body, but also to language, as in the phrase, "the gift of tongues." The word *brains* is often used for "intelligence," and *heart* for "courage."

As for me, I don't have the *guts* (= courage) to go parachuting, nor the *stomach* (= desire, liking) for horror movies, although I do have a good *head* (= intelligence, understanding) for mathematics, a good *nose* for sifting gossip from truth, and a good *ear* for jazz well performed.

ASSIGNMENT

I. Learn the following **noun-forming suffixes** and their meanings:

-(i)mony, "quality of," "state of"

TEST-	witness	+ -(i)mony	testimony
MATR-	mother	+ -(i)mony	matrimony

If this is followed by an additional suffix, the final *y* appears as *i.*

TEST-	witness	+ -(i)mony	+ -al	testimonial
MATR-	mother	+ -(i)mony	+ -al	matrimonial

-acity, "quality of being inclined to"

AUD-	to dare	+ -acity	audacity
CAP-	to take	+ -acity	capacity
RAP-	to seize	+ -acity	rapacity

This is the usual noun form of the adjective *-acious,* "tending to," "inclined to" (see Lesson XI).

-y, "quality of," "state of," "act of," "result of"

		CUSTOD-	guard	+ -*y*	custody
per-	+	JUR-	to swear	+ -*y*	perjury
contro-	+	VERS-	to turn	+ -*y*	controversy

If this is followed by an additional suffix, it appears as *i.*

		CUSTOD-	guard	+ -*y* + -*al*	custodial
contro-	+	VERS-	to turn	+ -*y* + -*al*	controversial

-ate, "office of," "holder(s) of the office of"

	SEN-	old	+ -*ate*	senate
	MAGISTR-	officer, master	+ -*ate*	magistrate
e- +	LECT-	to choose	+ -*or* + -*ate*	electorate

II. Learn the following bases and their meanings:

CID-, CIS-	to kill, cut	insecticide, fratricide, incision, precise
MATR-, MATERN-	mother	matron, maternity
PATR-, PATERN-	father	patrimony, paternity
PATRI-	fatherland, country	repatriate
PATRON-	protector	patronize
SEQU-, SECUT-	to follow	sequence, consequence, prosecute, consecutive
SOL-	alone	solitude, desolation
VIV-	to live	vivid, revive

III. Analyze the following italicized words and define them as they are used in the sentence or phrase.

1. He betrayed the leader whom he most affected to serve. His whole career was treachery to his own government. His life was one long *perfidy.*—William Hickling Prescott

2. Such is the *tenacity* of my imagination that the image formed in it continued in all its power and freshness.—Washington Irving

3. He looked up, however, and when aware of her presence a deep flush of shame *suffused* his handsome countenance.—Sir Walter Scott

4. . . . and first of the holy angels, who constitute a large part of this city, and indeed the more blessed part, since they have

never been *expatriated.*—St. Augustine

5. With the invention of high *fidelity* and the long-playing record, music in the world became revolutionized.

6. ...send three meals...by a waiter—an *obsequious* one if possible.—O. Henry

7. When an Inca died...his *obsequies* were celebrated with great pomp and solemnity.—William Hickling Prescott

8. While at anchor at this place, much ceremonious visiting and long conferences took place between the *potentate* of the island and the partners of the company.—Washington Irving

9. Pythagoras *averred* that the universe is made up of numbers, not as mere principles but as physical entities.

10. The sights, the air, the music, and the excitement...had quickened her blood and made her eyes sparkle with *vivacity.*—Thomas Hardy

11. Since then, Freeman has earned a national reputation as the caustic and *incisive* interviewer of the known and the renowned.—*Time*

12. "He's his own man!" the girl said proudly about her new boyfriend. "Who else would have him?" was her mother's *retort.*

13. But, if they determine to try the chance of war, they will, if they are wise, entrust to their chief that *plenary* authority without which war cannot be well conducted.—Macaulay

14. With the *Confederacy* having crumbled, General Lee surrendered to General Grant and then gave his Farewell Address to his army.

15. He points out how Ferdinand...used the pretext of religious zeal in order to achieve the conquest of Granada...and how his perfidies in Italy, his perjuries in France, were colored with a *sanctimonious* decency.—John Addington Symonds

16. Suddenly the *acrimony,* the conflict, was gone from their voices.—William Faulkner

17. In 1872 occurred the first execution in Cleveland's term, the climax of a sensational case of *matricide.*—Alan Nevins

18. By courtesy of his creditors, there still remained in his possession a small remnant of his *patrimony.*—Edgar Allan Poe

19. But the *veracity* of the narrative has never been questioned. —*Atlantic Monthly*

20. A *retentive* memory is a good thing, but the ability to forget is the true token of greatness.—Elbert Hubbard

IV. Use each of the following words in two sentences of your own making, the first expressing (a) an *abstract* meaning for the word, and the second (b) a *concrete* meaning.

Example: <u>delicacy</u>—(a) She handled the situation with great delicacy. (b) The table was loaded with delicacies.

1. authority
2. scholarship
3. impurity
4. novelty
5. justice
6. favor
7. divinity
8. likeness
9. brotherhood
10. inheritance

LESSON XVI

WEAKENING AND HYPERBOLE

As mentioned in Lesson XI there are different avenues down which a word undergoing semantic change may travel. Hyperbole (Greek: *hyper-* "excessive" + BOL- "to throw, put"), or exaggeration, is a path that leads to a process called weakening, by which the overused word becomes less forceful and vivid. *Awful* once meant "inspiring awe," but it is hard to find much of this meaning left in a sentence like, "You've been gone an awfully long time." The word *awesome,* on the other hand, never experienced this kind of change. *Wonderful* (literally, "exciting wonder") and *nice* (strictly, "exhibiting careful discrimination"), as they are ordinarily used in contemporary English, are also examples of weakening. Indeed, *nice,* by covering so much territory, is considered by many speakers to be so weak that it is scrupulously avoided. How many of us have had "weak word," or something similar, written next to *nice, cute,* and other such words in our grade-school and junior-high-school compositions? Consider also *gigantic* (basketball player), *terrible* (weather, attitude, typewriter, soup), *colossal* (sunset, dancing partner, evening), and *deadly* (dull).

Hyperbole can also be used in expressions, as in "I almost froze to death when I walked out into the yard to get the paper," "I almost killed myself when I tripped over the tennis ball," "I was bored to death in class today." Hyperbole is also often humorously applied to incongruous situations so as to enhance the exaggeration, as in, "I'm so hungry I could eat a horse," "He has enough energy to burn up city blocks," "She has a whoopee cushion for a brain," "He has the genes of a vacuum cleaner."

Examples of weakening are to be found in words derived from some of the bases that have been studied. When we say, "He is a man of infinite wisdom," *infinite* (*in-,* "not" + FIN-, "end," "limit"; literally "endless") is probably an exaggeration. The original meaning of the base CUR(R)-, CURS-, is "to run," but in most of its derivatives its sense has been weakened simply to "go," as in *excursion, concur,* and *recur.*

ASSIGNMENT

I. Learn the following **noun-forming suffixes** and their meanings:

-ion, "act of," "state of," "result of"

com-	+ PLET-	to fill	+ -*ion*	completion
pre-	+ VENT-	to come	+ -*ion*	prevention
pro-	+ DUCT-	to lead	+ -*ion*	production

-ment, "result of," "means of," "act of," "state of"
Various connective vowels usually precede this suffix.

ex- + CIT-	to arouse	+ -*(e)ment*	excitement
LIG-	to bind	+ -*(a)ment*	ligament
MON-	to warn, to advise	+ -*(u)ment*	monument
REG-	to rule	+ -*(i)ment*	regiment

-men, "result of," "means of," "act of," "state of"
Various connective vowels usually precede this suffix.

SPEC- to look + -*(i)men* specimen

II. Learn the following bases and their meanings:

CRE-, CRESC-, CRET-	to grow	crescent, excrescence, concrete
I-, IT-	to go	transient, ambient, initial, transition
JUG-, JUNCT-, [JOIN-], [JOINT-]	a yoke; to join	jugular, juncture, join, rejoinder, conjointly

LEG-, (LIG-), LECT-	to choose, pick out, read	legible, legend, eligible, elect, selective
MON-	to warn, advise	admonish, monument, monitor, premonition
SOLV-, SOLUT-	to free, loosen	solve, absolve, solution, absolute

III. Analyze the following italicized words and define them as they are used in the sentence or phrase.

1. A *predilection* for historical problems...is the justification offered for this practice.—Hans Kurath

2. ...sometimes read my unspoken thoughts with an *acumen* to me incomprehensible.—Charlotte Brontë

3. A work of such difficulty in itself did well deserve the *conjunction* of many heads.—Sir Thomas Browne

4. Nor have I scrupled, in so flagrant a case, to allow myself a severity of *animadversion* little congenial with the general spirit of these papers.—*The Federalist*

5. One ground for dismissing tenured faculty is *improbity.*

6. The mass would be likely to remain nearly the same, assimilating constantly to itself its gradual *accretions.*—*The Federalist*

7. Hunger is always the cause of tumults and *sedition.*—Lord Chesterfield

8. If at any time a shade of sadness stole across his brow, it was but *transient,* like a summer cloud, which soon goes by.—Washington Irving

9. The test of a first-rate intelligence is the *capacity* to hold two conflicting opinions at the same time and still retain the ability to function.—F. Scott Fitzgerald

10. Director John Dexter has paced the play to move one *resolute* step at a time, and encouraged the actors to deliver their lines with clarion force.—*Time*

11. As this *admonition* was accompanied with a threatening gesture and uttered with a savage aspect, the little boy rubbed his face harder, as if to keep the tears back.—Dickens

12. The trouble is, the times are out of joint. World War II's air-raid sirens have a way of going off in the middle of the old boy's *soliloquies.*—*Time*

13. She was wrapped in a white robe of some kind, whilst down her shoulders fell a twining *profusion* of marvellously rich hair.—Thomas Hardy

14. ...to pour into the pockets of the investing classes, especially in the East, a heavy unearned *increment.*—Allan Nevins

15. It was the richest, the most socially *coherent,* and the most formidably armed state south of the Alps.—*Time*

16. ...the Socratic philosophy rose like the sun in heaven, and spread its illumination over the whole intellectual *firmament.* —John Stuart Mill

17. At the same time it must not be supposed that the Renaissance burst suddenly upon the world in the fifteenth century without *premonitory* symptoms.—Symonds

18. An inveterate lighter and chewer of cigars, which he uses as *adjuncts* to conversation. . . .—*Time*

19. ...*ambition,* that ultimately political word which derives from the Roman candidates' practice of canvassing support on foot.

20. He had not yet got his *complement* of men, nor of vessels; and was very inadequately provided with supplies of any kind. —William Hickling Prescott

IV. Distinguish in meaning between the following pairs of words which are often confused.

1. adverse—averse
2. compulsive—compulsory
3. congenital—congenial
4. discrete—discreet
5. illicit—elicit
6. imminent—immanent
7. ingenious—ingenuous
8. lurid—livid
9. presumptuous—presumptive
10. sensuous—sensual
11. tortuous—torturous
12. turbid—turgid

LESSON XVII

CHANGE OF MEANING DUE TO CHANGING CONCEPTS

Some of the most interesting differences between etymological and current meanings have resulted from the influence on our language of discarded scientific ideas. The word *quintessence* is an example of this. The ancient Greeks believed that there were four basic substances which composed the universe: earth, air, fire, and water. In addition to these, Aristotle postulated a fifth element, which was so much lighter and subtler than the others that it was difficult to classify and so was termed simply "fifth being." This name entered our language as *quintessence* (QUINT-, "fifth," and *essence*). In the Middle Ages the fifth element came to be regarded by the alchemists as the most essential part of any substance. With the advance of scientific knowledge the idea of five elements was discarded, but the word *quintessence* remained, having lost its older significance of "fifth element" and keeping only the meaning of "the concentrated essence of anything" or, by extension, "the most perfect manifestation of some quality," as in the expression, "He is the quintessence of conceit."

One outmoded concept which has given rise to a whole series of such changes is known as the humoral theory of physiology. For over two thousand years the prevailing medical view was that soundness of mind and body depended on the proper mixture of four liquids or humors, as they were called, for the original meaning of humor is "liquid" (related to *humid*). These four "humors" were blood, phlegm, yellow bile, often simply termed bile, and black bile. Individual psychological differences were thought to be determined by the predominance of one or another of these fluids, and a person who had a proper mixture of them was supposedly pleasant and cheerful, in other words, good-humored. A person who behaved in an absurd or fantastic fashion was supposed to be suffering from an excess of some one of these fluids and so was termed "humorous." Eccentricity is, of course, likely to arouse laughter, and so *humor* acquired its modern meaning of "quality which excites amusement."

If we examine their derivations, we find that some other very common words reflect this concept that a mixture of humors causes a particular state of mind or body. A person's *temperament* (Latin, *temperare*, "to mix in due proportion") was the special combination of these fluids which resulted in his own individual personality. *Temper* was originally a synonym of *temperament*, but it has generally acquired the more specialized meaning of proneness to anger. In connection with metal the suggestion of a mixture formerly carried by this word comes out more clearly; the temper of steel refers to the blending of carbon, iron, etc. *Distemper*, which means literally "a disturbance of the proper mixture," likewise became specialized, describing a physical illness in animals rather than a psychological state. *Complexion* (Latin, "combination," from *con-* and *plectere*, "to weave") was also once synonymous with *temperament;* its current meaning arose from the belief that the special blend of the different humors was shown in the color of the face. *Idiosyncrasy*, which now means "quirk," has the etymological meaning "private mixture," that is, individual temperament.

The different kinds of temperament were designated by the name of the particular humor which predominated. An excess of blood (SANGUIN-, "blood") made a person *sanguine*, and thus of a cheerful, hopeful disposition, which is the current meaning of the word. A preponderance of phlegm made one stolid and unemotional, and so the term *phlegmatic* came to have this meaning. The Greek term for bile is *chole;* since this humor was thought to bring about an angry nature, a quick-tempered person is now sometimes termed *choleric*. The cause of melancholy (Greek, *melas*, "black," and *chole*, "bile") was held to be the presence of too much black bile.

Another equally outmoded notion which influenced the meanings of a number of words was astrology, with its basic assumption that the stars and other heavenly bodies control earthly affairs. *Disaster* means literally "ill-starred" (from Latin, *dis-*, and Greek, *aster*, "star," found in such words as *astronomy* and *astrology*). According to astrological teachings, the stars influenced not only events but human nature as well. An individual born under the planet Jupiter, or Jove, was supposedly *jovial*. Saturn, it was felt, caused men to be serious and gloomy, a temperament called *saturnine;* while the planet Mercury produced a *mercurial*, that is, volatile, personality. The heavenly bodies were thought also to affect the health of human beings; consequently, *lunatic* means literally "moonstruck" (from Latin, *luna*, "moon"), while *influenza* is simply Italian for "influence," reflecting the notion that some influence emanating from evil stars caused this disease.

ASSIGNMENT

I. The following are diminutive suffixes, that is, suffixes that denote something small or young. They have the same function as the native English suffixes -*kin* (in *lambkin* and *manikin*), -*let* (in *booklet* and *leaflet*), and -*ling* (in *duckling* and *darling*). Learn the following **diminutive suffixes** and their meanings:

-*(i)cule* (often -*cle* or -*icle* since the -*u*- is sometimes suppressed), "little"

MOLE-	mass	+ -*cule*	molecule
MUS-	mouse	+ -*cle*	muscle (but musc*u*lar)
PART-	part	+ -*(i)cle*	particle (but partic*u*lar)

-el, "little"

NOV-	new	+ *-el*	novel
MORS-	bite	+ *-el*	morsel
PAN(N)-	cloth	+ *-el*	panel

-il, "little"

| PUP- | boy, girl | + *-il* | pupil |
| CODIC- | book, document | + *-il* | codicil |

-ole, -ule (often *-le,* since the *-u-* is sometimes suppressed), "little"

VACU-	empty	+ *-ole*	vacuole
AURE-	golden	+ *-ole*	aureole
CAPS-	box	+ *-ule*	capsule
GLOB-	ball	+ *-ule*	globule
SCRUP-	sharp stone	+ *-le*	scruple (but scrup*u*lous)
CIRC-	ring	+ *-le*	circle (but circ*u*lar)

Diminutive suffixes in their original Latin form appear in many common English words.

FORM-	form	+ *-ula*	formula
CUP-	tub	+ *-ola*	cupola
CALC-	limestone, pebble	+ *-ulus*	calculus
GLADI-	sword	+ *-olus*	gladiolus
CEREB(R)-	brain	+ *-ellum*	cerebellum

II. Learn the following bases and their meanings:

FERV-	to boil, bubble	fervent, fervidity
FRANG-, (FRING-), FRACT-	to break	frangible, fraction
GRAN-	grain	granary, granite, granola
MINOR-, MINUS-, MINUT-	small, smaller	minority, minute, diminutive
PATI-, PASS-	to endure, suffer	patient, passive, passion
QUIR-, QUISIT-, QUEST-	to ask, seek	inquire, inquisition, question, inquest
SEC-, SEG-, SECT-	to cut	secant, segment, bisect, section

III. Analyze the following italicized words and define them as they are used in the sentence or phrase.

1. ...where the lake bottom contains little vegetation and the water little or no plankton or the *minuscule* animal life which provides the major part of the diet of many varieties of fish. —*Atlantic Monthly*

2. His *exquisite* timing would make a Swiss watch blush.

3. *Transection* of the brain along the midline into two hemispheres does not produce the devastating results one might think; only specially devised tests reveal a change in thinking strategies.

4. I was the most *incorrigible* kid on my block, and I must tell you that I reveled in that fact.—Michael Jacobs

5. The *refraction* of light that gives a diamond its fire is based on certain mathematical laws.—*New Yorker*

6. The *requisition* for medical supplies for the troops was phoned in three weeks ago but nothing has arrived yet.

7. "You have a very *commodious* bathroom," he said to his hostess with a sly grin as he returned to the party. "I am flushed with pleasure," she retorted.—Bart DeWolf

8. Spread like a fan around the new lumber mill, a *progeny* of flimsy, cigar-box houses sprang up almost overnight.

9. The government wanted to raise the import duty on foreign cars, not so much for the *revenue* it would bring, but as an effort to stem the high tide of foreign cars entering the country.

10. Emma was very *compassionate;* and the distresses of the poor were as sure of relief from her personal attention and kindness, her counsel and her patience, as from her purse.—Jane Austen

11. But critic Nathan—though the day had passed when he could kill a play with a quip—remained an acute and *acidulous* observer of the theater.—*Time*

12. Thus his morning *canticle* he sung "Awake, my Love...." —Alexander Pope

13. We ask advice, but we mean *approbation.*—Charles C. Colton

14. Instead of any *diminution,* there is need of great increase of disinterested exertion to promote the good of others.—John Stuart Mill

15. Apply leeches...unto the *jugular* veins in the neck.—John Steer, translator of Fabricius's *Experiments in Chyrurgie**

16. Court will *adjourn* for the day.

17. The convexity of the *curette†* is to be placed against the edge of the cornea.—Wells, *Diseases of the Eye*

18. Unfortunately, the only computer at our disposal was *incompatible* with the software we were given to work with.

19. The liberal-minded churchman put a room at his disposal, and allowed him to *dissect* dead bodies.—John Addington Symonds

20. ...an enchanted forest, bearing the spell of an *infrangible* silence.—Howitt

IV. Distinguish in meaning between the following pairs of words:

1. choler—cholera
2. jovial—Jovian
3. mercurial—mercuric
4. sanguine—sanguinary
5. saturnine—saturnalia

LESSON XVIII

EUPHEMISM, TABOO DEFORMATION, AND CIRCUMLOCUTION

As we shall see in Lessons XVIII-XXII, some processes of change affect the phonetic shape of a word as well as altering its meaning. Among certain people, the uttering of a word is believed to invoke unseen powers. Hence, in some tribes no one is called by his real name for fear that an eavesdropping sorcerer might use the name in a witchcraft to harm the person. In other cultures, a chance word or phrase is thought to be ominous, especially during the performance of a prescribed ritual. In Greek custom, only the celebrant could utter the formulas; other participants were to maintain ritual silence. *Euphemein*

---

*Chyrurgie is an old form, from Greek, of the modern word *surgery*.

†This French suffix is the feminine form of the diminutive suffix *-et* (*islet, owlet, plummet, tablet, bullet, turret*—in some of which the diminutive force has obviously long been lost). The *-ette* is not only a diminutive (*dinette, kitchenette, cigarette*), but has come to mean, sometimes humorously, "female" (*usherette, farmerette, coquette, majorette, suffragette*), and also "imitation," as in the tradename *Leatherette*.

was the command, "Hush!" (the etymology of which means "use words of good omen"), from which we derive the English word *euphemism*. This practice goes beyond ritual. The superstitious try to avert evil by charming it with a lucky name. The Greeks called the treacherous Black Sea "Kindly-to-Strangers" (Euxine) in the hopes that it would so become. In a similar way, the frigid Greenland (larger than Mexico) was so named in the hopes of attracting settlers there, a venture which even the Danes would probably admit has rather failed in that its population is about 1/10th of 1 percent of that of Mexico.

In our less superstitious society, the practice of substituting a less direct phrase for a direct term goes by the name *euphemism*. *Sweat* is called by a Latin borrowing, *perspiration*. *Gravedigger* and *dead-burier* were the original terms for an unpleasant task. As burial became more complicated, the upper classes negotiated with a contractor to undertake the whole operation, whence the term *undertaker*. But even this vague term has become offensive. Now we use *funeral director* or *mortician* as euphemisms, just as some people prefer to *pass away* rather than to *die*. (At the other end, English is not without its black humor and slang even here. When you *conk, croak, bite the dust, turn up your toes,* or *give up the ghost* on land you can get *planted* in a *boneyard*. But if you *kick the bucket* at sea, you get a *deep six*.)

The etymological meanings of some words of Latin derivation show that they were originally euphemisms. The substitution of "depart" for "die" is seen in *obituary* (*ob-* and 1-, IT-,"to go"), *perish* (*per-*, "completely" and I-, IT-), and *decease* (*de-* "off," and CED-, CESS-, "to go"). *Expire* (*ex-*, "out," and SPIR-, "to breathe") meant originally "to breathe one's last." *Casualty* (CAD-, CAS-, "to befall") was formerly "a happening," as was *accident* (cf. the expression, "if anything happens to me," used instead of "if I die"). *Insane* (*in-*, "not" and SAN-, "healthy") also was probably once a euphemism, just as today in certain circles *sick* means "mentally ill."

Other examples of euphemism show themselves in the activities of toilet and sex. Our notorious, earthy quadriliterals ("four-letter words"), which up through about the seventeenth century enjoyed a respectable reputation in the common vocabulary of English, had to go underground in shame, to be replaced by such as the Latin *excreta* ("things sifted out or separated") and *defecation* ("the act of cleansing or refining"), which are additional examples of euphemism in etymology. Even *bathroom* and *toilet* are avoided in certain circles. Instead we *go powder our noses,* in the *restroom,* or *washroom,* or *little boys'* (or *little girls'*) *room,* etc. Even in the early grades in school we were taught to ask, "May I be excused, please?" And what goes through the pipes is called *effluent,* (a "flowing out of"), again Latin. But the rebellious 1960s changed all this at various social levels by reintroducing the so-called "taboo" or "vulgar" words into both the spoken and written language, which opened up whole new chapters in censorship—and the lifting of it, as in live theater and the big screen.

Euphemisms for *sex* also come and go. In the 1940s and 1950s, most people were having *romances, love affairs,* and *liaisons* and *amours* (both French), which later graduated into *affairs.* In 1985, we were—depending, of course, on the topic of conversation—*involved,* or having an *involvement* or a *relationship,* or *seeing someone.*

Euphemism is also prominent in the areas of poverty and disability. We speak of the *underprivileged, disadvantaged,* and *culturally deprived* rather than insulting people by calling them *poor.* Countries are no longer socially and economically *backward* but are *developing* nations, which may be *underdeveloped* countries of the *Third World.* Animals, even intelligent ones, can be *dumb* (in that they do not use words), but human beings are *mute, speechless, nonverbal,* or *speech-impaired,* as *deaf* is often replaced by *hearing-impaired.* Similarly, *mentally* and *physically handicapped* have softened the indignity of *retarded* and *crippled.*

Taboo deformation is a related process whereby the unlucky or offensive term is disguised by mispronouncing it. In Judeo-Christian practice, it is forbidden to utter God's name except in certain prescribed circumstances. Even in spelling, the word customarily appears as *G__d.* This practice was so rigidly enforced by the Jews that we do not know for certain the vowels in the titular name for God because that name was deliberately mispronounced by using the vowels of a less sacrosanct name. Hence only the consonants *YHWH* survive, which we fill in with extraneous vowels: *Jehovah, Yahweh.* Similarly we distort the divine names and titles in English to give *gosh, gad, gee, gorry, golly,* and the British *cor.* It has been proposed that in Indo-European times the word for *bear* was unutterable because in the descendant languages the animal is often called by a euphemistic nickname—like *bear,* which translates as "the brown one" (compare *bruin*); where it is preserved, the original name has been so distorted that its descendants, though they are recognizably related, cannot be justified by applying the usual phonetic rules (see examples in the Introduction).

Circumlocutions ("to speak around"), although in full flourish along with euphemisms ("to speak well") but experiencing a far more precarious reputation, reached new heights—or, to many, sank to new depths—in the 1970s and 1980s. Defined objectively, circumlocution is a roundabout way of speaking, using superfluous words. On the down side, it has been referred to as the art of saying as little as possible with as many words as you can get in. It has gained for itself many harsh critics, who have referred to the growing tendency with such terms as psychobabble, mutter language, fodder language (no pun intended, I'm sure), handjive, semi-demi-quasi-pseudo speech, and echt-gibberish. One critic said that we were "being buried alive in an avalanche of jargon." A British reporter for *Punch* magazine, covering a computer convention in London, wrote "there was not a word of English anywhere."

A few examples of circumlocutory jargon are: maximally impactful advertising (=good, successful advertising); conceptualizing new thrusts (=thinking up new ideas); depolarization experience (=shock); microcluster of structured role expectations; resurgency in consumer outlay (=a buying spree); terminal behavioral objectives for continuous progression modules in early childhood education; instructional module (=a classroom); personal transportation module (=a car); preplanning (=planning); intergroup recognition function (=a handshake); lexico-grammatical sentence components (=words); at this temporal dimension spot (=now); stimulative approach opportunity (=foreplay, itself a quasi-euphemism for amorous play before sex); vocalize performance concerns (=talk about [something]); ingestion situation (=eating); data base (=records); oral incorporation (=a baby sucking a nipple); vertical transportation (=an elevator); retinal experience (=seeing things).

Also to be included are such words as *conclusionary, evidentiary, trialability, credentialing, semesterization, reconceptualization* (= thinking of something in a different way), *recontour* (=to lose weight), *momentaneous* (=covering a single moment), *armamentarium* (=a group, as of skills), *dysfunctional* (=unhelpful), *economization* (=economy), *prototypical* (= typical)—plus four for you to work on: *bourgeoizification, plebiscitarianism, mobilizeability,* and *classifactory.*

Circumlocution seems a mild term for some of these: *escalated interpersonal altercations* (=murder and assault); *relocate* (=kill, cremate); *liberate* (=to steal or loot); *manipulative methods* (=bribery). Should we call these determinative deceptualizations?

A lot of speech of this sort turns up in various branches of government writing, and in treatises, articles, proposals, and workshop and conference papers in the social sciences, linguistics, education, and other fields.

ASSIGNMENT

I. Learn the following **noun-forming suffixes** and their meanings:

-ance, -ancy; -ence, -ency, "quality of ___ing," "state of ___ing"

	VIGIL-	to watch	+ *-ance*	vigilance
	HESIT-	to stick fast	+ *-ancy*	hesitancy
in- +	FLU-	to flow	+ *-ence*	influence
	FLU-	to flow	+ *-ency*	fluency

This suffix is actually a combination of *-ant* or *-ent,* "-ing," (see Lesson X) and *-y,* "quality of," "state of" (see Lesson XV). Thus *vigilance* is literally "state of being watchful," and *hesitancy* is "state of sticking fast."

-or (in British usage often *-our*), "state of," "result of"

ARD-	to burn	+ *-or*	ardor
FUR-	to rage	+ *-or*	furor
ERR-	to wander	+ *-or*	error

-ary (-arium), "place for"

LIBR-	book	+ *-ary*	library
GRAN-	grain	+ *-ary*	granary
AQU-	water	+ *-arium*	aquarium

This suffix is actually a substantive form of *-ary,* "pertaining to," etc. (see Lesson IX).

-ory (-orium), "place for"

DORMIT-	to sleep	+ *-ory*	dormitory
LAVAT-	to wash	+ *-ory*	lavatory
AUDIT-	to hear	+ *-orium*	auditorium

This suffix is actually a substantive form of *-ory,* "serving for" (see Lesson XIII).

II. Learn the following bases and their meanings:

AG-, (IG-), ACT-	to do, drive	agent, agile, inactive, transact
CLAM-, [CLAIM-]	to cry out	exclamation, proclamation, declaim, proclaim

Note that English used the Latin CLAM- for its nouns and adjectives, and the French CLAIM- for its verbs. The English noun *claim* derives from the verb.

| COG- | to think, reflect, consider | cogent, cogitation |

This base derives from the prefix *co-* + the above base AG-.

DIC-, DICT-	to say	diction, contradiction, edict
GER-, GEST-	to carry, produce	exaggerate, congestion, digest
MIT(T)-, MIS(S)-	to send, let go	admit, transmitter, missile, transmission
SCI-	to know	science, conscientious
SON-	sound	supersonic, resonance, sonata
VAL-, [VAIL-]	to be strong, be worthy	value, equivalent, valid, avail, prevail

III. Analyze the following italicized words and define them as they are used in the sentence or phrase.

1. . . . like a growth of fungus or any unwholesome *excrescence* produced there in neglect and impurity.—Dickens

2. He was determined one could survive—nay, be completely healthy—on *predigested* protein liquid, apples, and bee pollen.

3. An *endurance* of my shortcomings is the price which my admirers are willing to pay for the satisfaction of my acquaintance. —Lord Sudeley

4. . . . each based on a market basket of currencies and *commodities.*—Alvin Toffler

5. The *fervor* of these radical groups was for a time kindled . . . by the success of the Bolshevik revolution.—*Harper's Magazine*

6. . . . the Italian genius as it expressed itself in society, scholarship, fine art and literature, at its most brilliant period of *renascence.*—John Addington Symonds

7. The voting papers, and all the elements of the calculation, would be placed in public *repositories,* accessible to all whom they concerned.—John Stuart Mill

8. A *conscience* cannot prevent sin. It only prevents you from enjoying it.—A.R. Magee

9. The words, spoken *sonorously,* with an even intonation, were heard all over the ship.—Joseph Conrad

10. He was with the battalion about two weeks when Jefferson reported to the little *dispensary* on sick call.—*Harper's Magazine*

11. This singular accident, by a strange *confluence* of emotions in him, was felt as the sharpest sting of all.—Thomas Hardy

12. The little bell giving *clamorous* notice of a visitor's approach. . . .—Dickens

13. . . .the people of one English colony, and of nearly half the United States, have been *interdicted* by law from making any use whatever of fermented drinks.—John Stuart Mill

14. Anyone knows the sharp *dissonance* resulting from two consecutive half-tones struck simultaneously on the piano. —*Atlantic Monthly*

15. Old men. . .harangued the warriors as they passed, exhorting them to *valorous* deeds.—Washington Irving

16. In Washington, U.S. officials kept up their steady pressure on Egypt to curb its *intransigence*. . . .—*Time*

17. In all the thousands of words of *malediction* which have been called down upon his head, very few have made him angry. —*Harper's Magazine*

18. Von Humboldt's story, preposterous as it sounds, has a faint claim to *credence.*—*Atlantic Monthly*

19. All his verse is written with amazing technical skill and a great richness of sound, with complex rhythms, intricate patterns of alliteration and *assonance.*—*The Reader's Companion to World Literature*

20. As the music came fresher on their ears, they danced to its *cadence,* extemporizing new steps.—Hawthorne

LESSON XIX

FOLK ETYMOLOGY

Another interesting process encountered in word study is folk etymology or, as it is sometimes called, popular etymology. This, however, affects the form of words more often than it does their meaning. Folk etymology is the attempt to make unfamiliar words resemble better-known words to which they are erroneously thought to be related, and it arises from ignorance of the true derivations of these words.

Thus, *female* is actually derived from the Latin *femella*, the diminutive of *femina*, "woman," but the English word owes its spelling to the fact that people felt it must somehow be derived from the word *male*, although there is no linguistic relationship between the two words. The *primrose* botanically has nothing to do with roses; it was originally spelled *primula* and meant "little flower of the prime or spring of the year," but popular usage gradually transformed the spelling of this foreign-sounding word to make it resemble something more familiar. Folk etymology has also caused the Spanish *cucaracha* to appear as *cockroach* in order to make it sound less strange. *Aecern* was altered to *acorn;* the nuts that grow on oak trees were apparently associated in the popular mind with *corn* because they can be ground into meal in the same way. Sometimes *hiccup* is spelled *hiccough*. The word arose simply as an imitation of the sound made when hiccuping, and so the first spelling is more natural; but people who do not understand this have tried to indicate some supposed resemblance to *cough*.

If a person has ever been tempted to spell or pronounce *sacrilegious* as if it were connected with *religious*, he has been influenced by the same tendency which gave rise to the previous examples of folk etymology; *sacrilegious* actually comes from the Latin *sacer*, "sacred," and *legere*, "to gather" (in the sense of "steal").

ASSIGNMENT

I. Learn the following **noun-forming suffixes** and their meanings:

-ure, "act of," "result of"

FRACT-	to break	+ *-ure*	fracture
PUNCT-	to prick	+ *-ure*	puncture
RUPT-	to break	+ *-ure*	rupture

- (u)lence, - (o)lence, "state or quality of being full of"

VI-	force	+ *-(o)lence*	violence
FRAUD-	deceit	+ *-(u)lence*	fraudulence

This suffix is a combination of *-(u)lent, -(o)lent,* "full of" (see Lesson IX) and *-y*, "state of," "quality of" (see Lesson XV).

-or, "one who does," "that which does"*

		ACT-	to do	+ *-or*	actor
ad-	+	GRESS-	to go	+ *-or*	aggressor
		TRACT-	to drag	+ *-or*	tractor
		MOT-	to move	+ *-or*	motor

-and(um), -(i)end (um), "that which must be ___-ed"

AG-   to do   + *-endum*   "that which must be
                                                    done" agendum

MEMOR- to remember + *-andum* "that which must be
                                                    remembered"
                                                    memorandum

The plural form of this suffix is *-anda, -(i)enda.*

II. Learn the following bases and their meanings:

ERR-	to wander	error, erratic
JAC-, JECT-	to throw	ejaculate, inject, projectile, reject
NOMEN-, NOMIN-	name, noun	nomenclature, nominate, pronominal
SCRIB-, SCRIPT-	to write	describe, inscribe, scribble, conscription, subscription
ST(A)-, STIT-, SIST-	to stand	stance, circumstance, station, insist
VOLV-, VOLUT-	to roll	revolve, involve, evolution, revolution

III. Analyze the following italicized words and define them as they are used in the sentence or phrase.

1. In states with *referendum* processes, very seldom do foolish proposals win.—*Wall Street Journal*

2. The woman herself was a *conjectural* creature who had little to do with the outlines presented to Sherton eyes; a shape in the gloom, whose true quality could only be approximated by putting together a movement now and a glance then. —Thomas Hardy

---

*The feminine form of this suffix, which occurs mainly in legal terminology, is *-rix:* testatrix, feminine of *testator; executrix,* feminine of *executor.* Dictionaries generally list this suffix as *-trix.* A more useful suffix of agency is derived from the French, *-ess,* as in *heiress, seamstress,* etc.

3. Do not let us add to our difficulties by any lack of clarity of thinking or any *restive* wavering in resolve.—Sir Winston Churchill

4. Wherever the sphere of action of human beings is artificially *circumscribed*, their sentiments are narrowed and dwarfed in the same proportion.—John Stuart Mill

5. So long as mankind shall continue to lavish more praise upon its destroyers than upon its *benefactors*, war shall remain the chief pursuit of ambitious minds.—Edward Gibbon

6. This is perhaps the fullest history of those early days *extant*. —Thoreau

7. To this I was securely bound by a long strap. . . . It passed in many *convolutions* about my limbs and body.—Edgar Allan Poe

8. . . . the right of Chieftainship attached to the blood of *primogeniture*, and, therefore, was incapable of being transferred. —James Boswell

9. Robert E. Lee's *stature* as a gentleman of honor, integrity, and intelligence won him the presidency of the fledgling Washington College in Virginia after the war.

10. An office in the household, with merely *nominal* duties, had been assigned to her as a pretext for the payment of a small pension.—Hawthorne

11. He dreamed that Minerva, whom he worshipped even to a *superstitious* excess, was withdrawing from her sanctuary. —Hugh J. Shonfield

12. No humane being, past the thoughtless age of boyhood, will wantonly murder any creature which holds its life by the same *tenure* that he does.—Thoreau

13. . . . a phonemic analysis of the phonic data is an essential *prerequisite*.—Hans Kurath

14. To *err* is human; to ask forgiveness is embarrassing and a nuisance.—Bill Mark

15. We know through what strange loopholes the human mind contrives to escape, when it wishes to avoid a disagreeable *inference* from an admitted proposition.—Macaulay

16. During my summer vacation out West, I took home a *terrarium* of miniature cactus plants from Arizona.—J.B. Walker

17. There is one thing that always struck me wherever I went: clothes make the man. Naked people have little or no *influence* in society.—Mark Twain

18. The need for union arises not from any inherent virtues of the large state but from the *exigencies* of survival.—*Harper's Magazine*

19. ...the handful of priests and war leaders enjoyed comparatively few *perquisites.*—Michael C. Meyer

20. Egg white takes on *consistency* if you whip it until it stands in peaks.

IV. With the aid of a dictionary determine the derivation of the following words whose forms have been influenced by folk etymology.

1. belfry (not connected with *bell*)
2. crayfish (not connected with *fish*)
3. curtail (not connected with *tail*)
4. cutlass (not connected with *cut*)
5. hangnail (not connected with *hang*)
6. headlong (not connected with *long*)
7. penthouse (not connected with *house*)
8. shamefaced (not connected with *face*)
9. sovereign (not connected with *reign*)
10. surround (not connected with *round*)

LESSON XX

CLIPPED WORDS

Another way in which the form of some words has been affected is by shortening or clipping. *Canter,* for instance, is short for *Canterbury* and originally referred to the kind of pace which was popular with pilgrims riding to the shrine of St. Thomas at Canterbury. Clipped words are usually the result of popular speech and are often labeled in dictionaries as *slang* or *informal,* but they are especially common in the language of college students, as may be seen from the many examples like *math, prof, exam,* and *psych.* Nevertheless, despite the fact that such shortening has been frowned upon by many purists, including Jonathan Swift, the author of *Gulliver's Travels,* who deplored in particular the use of *mob* (short for *mobile vulgus,* "the movable or fickle common people"), some of our most common words represent clipped forms which have become standard English. Thus *cute* was originally *acute, drawing room* was originally *withdrawing room,* and *brandy* was *brandywine* (that is, "burnt or distilled wine"). *Chum* is apparently a shortened form of *chamber fellow,* while *rum* is from *rumbullion.*

Some of these can move around to different parts of speech: you can get *psyched* (or *out,* or *up*), *mob* the ticket office, have an attack of the *cutes,* and *chum* around with the wrong people.

Originally (and perhaps still, to some extent) as an effort to save space, much of our abbreviated language has for many years come from the press, a purpose which gradually shifted over the years toward an effort to be a leader (or at least to keep up) with 'modern' language. Therefore, many clips are quickly picked up by national magazines, the popular press, disk jockeys, TV sitcoms, and the like, thus gaining for these clips a certain respectability and a possible ticket to a place in tomorrow's dictionary. Clips generally fall into three classes:

Regular clips: *quake* (=earthquake), *copter, comp* (=complimentary, as tickets), *comp time* (=compensatory time), *amp* (=ampere, amplifier), *limo* (=limousine), *semi* (=semitrailer), *jock* (=jockey; jockstrap; an athlete), *ex* (=ex-spouse; ex-lover), *juvie* or *juvey* (=juvenile), *lab, blitz* (=blitzkrieg).

Clip-blends (in which two words are blended but only one is clipped): *agribusiness* (=agriculture), *bookmobile* (=automobile), *motorcade* (=cavalcade), *helipad* (=helicopter), *agitrock* (=agitation + rock [music]), *docudrama* (=documentary).

Clips that are suffixed: *civies,* or *civvies* (=civilian clothes), *fresher* (=a freshman), *comfy* (=comfortable), *vibes* (=vibraharp; vibration[s]), *grotty* (=grotesque), *commie* and *Commie.*

Blends are further discussed in Lesson XXI. Meanwhile, on hot days keep your *marge* in the *fridge.*

ASSIGNMENT

I. Learn the following **verb-forming suffix** and its meaning:

-esce, "to begin," "to become"

con-	+ VAL-	to be strong	+ *-esce*		convalesce
ob-	+ SOL-	to be accustomed	+ *-esce*	+ *-ent*	obsolescent
af-	+ FLOR-	to flower	+ *-esce*		affloresce

II. Learn the following bases and their meanings:

CAPIT, (CIPIT-)	head	capital, decapitate, precipitate
GNO-, NO-, NOT-	to know	recognize, ignore, noble, note
LOC-	place	local, dislocate
PUT-	to prune, reckon, think	amputate, compute, impute
RADIC-	root	radical, eradicate
ROG-	to ask	arrogant, derogatory
SPIR-	to breathe	spirit, conspire, inspiration

III. Analyze the following italicized words and define them as they are used in the sentence or phrase.

1. He said it was no *derogation* from a man's dignity to confess I was a devilish good fellow.—Dickens

2. Over it hung the *attenuated* skeleton of a chrome-yellow moon, which had only a few days to last.—Thomas Hardy

3. St. John Bosco...was an outstanding figure in the *efflorescence* of heroic sanctity in north Italy in the nineteenth century.—Donald Attwater

4. Even if the thing were *indisputably* miraculous, it would not follow that the miracle had occurred because of your prayers. —C.S. Lewis

5. ...viral *respiratory* infections.—*Time*

6. This was indeed a time of grave uncertainty and *circumstances* called for an agonizing reappraisal.—Hugh J. Schonfield

7. The blackness of the water was streaked with trails of light which *undulated* gently on slight ripples.—Joseph Conrad

8. Labor, naturally, claims that this bill nullifies its most precious *prerogative*, the right to strike....—*Harper's Magazine*

9. It proved far less easy to *eradicate* evil passions than to repeal evil laws.—Macaulay

10. The look carried the *imputation* that she 'picked up' acquaintances.—Henry James

11. The lower-class person's actions oscillate between conformity to values and to *countervailing* circumstances.— Frederick Elkin, *Child and Society*

12. The critic is quick to shred the artist who blindly and persistently labors under the *aberrant* assumption that bigness equals monumentality.

13. ...a green spotlight fixed immovably in the wall. Its ghastly *luminescence* flooded, from end to end, the steel bunk that was my bed.—*Harper's Magazine*

14. A thick crayon of white chalk lay on my desk for the convenience of *elucidating* any grammatical or verbal obscurity which might occur in my lesson.—Charlotte Brontë

15. ...classical Darwinian selection at the level of the individual is adequate to explain the majority of *putatively* "group-selected" attributes of populations and species.—Eric R. Pianka

16. ...an *ignominious* peace.

17. In *consonance* with our emphasis on responsibility, we advocate dispensing with psychiatric labels.—William Glasser

18. ...produces a music of technical *excogitation* in which the listener finds neither pleasure nor reflection of anything of concern to him.—Henry Pleasants, *The Agony of Modern Music*

19. You must all confess that I was not *ignoble* of descent. —William Shakespeare

20. Amanda is flinty, not flighty...a bustling den mother, not a *senescent* teenager.—*Time*

IV. With the aid of a dictionary give the unshortened form from which each of the following clipped words has come.

Example: disco—discotèque

1. bus
2. cab
3. cad
4. narc
5. gin (both the drink and the machine)
6. pep
7. (stage) prop
8. van (both "forefront" and "covered vehicle")
9. varsity
10. wayward
11. wig

V. Give as many examples as you can of clipped words arising from campus life; e.g., *prof, exam,* etc.

LESSON XXI

BLENDS

A blended word, or blend, is produced by combining two words so that only a part of each remains. The meaning is also a blend of the two component words. For example, *brunch* (breakfast + lunch) is a combination of breakfast and lunch and also it occurs midway between breakfast time and lunch time. Other blends are *smog* (smoke + fog), *radiclib* (radical + liberal), *slurb* (slum + suburb) and its extension *slurbia, Comsymp* (Communist sympathizer), *harmolodic* (harmonic + melodic), *comsat* (communications + satellite), *simulcast* (simultaneous + broadcast), *quaver* (quake + waver), *jargonaut* (jargon + argonaut = a person who uses jargon excessively), *druther* (would + rather) and its plural *druthers,* a noun meaning "preference," as in "If I had my druthers, I'd go bowling."

Blending—or, in some cases, clip-blending, as we have called it in Lesson XX—reached a new plateau in the 1970s and 1980s, when it became increasingly popular to snip off the latter part of a word, usually from one to three syllables, and to this new "combining form" attach whatever suited one's purposes. (For a discussion of combining forms see Greek Lesson XII.) Some of these words are coined for an occasion, as a political event—such as *Watergate,* which provided the combining form *-gate* (=scandal), which later produced *Koreagate, oilgate, computergate,* and others. Some of these combining forms come out of an activity, such as *-thon* (=any unusually long and uninterrupted activity) from *marathon,* from Marathon, Greece, from which a messenger ran to Athens to announce a victory over the Persians in 490 B.C. The word in time spawned *begathons, danceathons, telethons, walkathons, bikeathons, swimathons, workathons, phoneathons, talkathons,* and others.* The modern *decathlon* has blended into *athlete* to give us *decathletes.* The exercise vogue of the 1970s and 1980s has not only given new meanings to the words *spa* and *jog* (itself a blend, from *jot* "to jog," + the obsolete English word *shog* "to shake"), but has produced *-(er)cize* (=to exercise using [a specified activity]), allowing us to *dancercize, jazzercize, sexercize,* and

---

*Some of these examples are taken from *The Second Barnhart Dictionary of New English,* Barnhart/Harper & Row, 1980.

aerobicize—in our *duplexes, fourplexes, sixplexes,* or maybe in a *condotel* or on a *boatel. Aquacizers* also teach *aquacizing* in your local pool.

It seems, however, that many of these false combining forms are concocted out of the fever of fashion, such as *-oholic* or *-aholic* (= a person addicted to or obsessed with [a specified thing or activity]), generating *workaholic, pen-, word-, sex-, drug-, exer-, charge-, gas-* (in reference to the so-called gas guzzlers), *vida-* and *tela-* and *tube-* (i.e., TV), and "Curseaholics Anonymous has kicked off a nationwide campaign to make public profanity a felony offense" (*Playboy*). According to a headline in the *Dallas Times Herald,* a "'Shopaholic' wife kills bank account, credit." In addition, there is *sexploitation, blaxploitation,* and *gaysploitation* from *exploitation, exclave* from *enclave, binant* from *quadrant, groceteria* from *cafeteria, guesstimate* from *estimate, house-* and *dog-* and *plant-sit* from *babysit, rockabilly* from *hillbilly, stagflation* from *inflation, countrypolitan* from *cosmopolitan,* and the *breath analyzer* begot the *breathalizer* begot the *intoxilizer* (or *intoxalizer*).

However, none of this is anything new. Thoreau, for example, back in the 1840s, coined *able-souled* (from *able-bodied*), *blue angels* (from *blue devils*), *brain rot* (from *potato rot*), *now-a-nights* (from *now-a-days,* or *nowadays* as we currently spell it), and many others.

After the fun has worn off, many blends disappear from use. Still, many others have had long lives and remain in our common vocabulary, such as *smash* (smack + mash), *bash* (bat + mash), *flare* (flame + glare), and *glimmer* (gleam + shimmer), all of which date from between the fifteenth and eighteenth centuries. Other unsuspecting blends in our common vocabulary are *about* (*on* "on" + *be* "by" + *utan* "outside"), *among* (*on* "in" + *gemang* "crowd"), *answer* (*and* "in reply" + *swaru* "a swearing"), *also* (*eal* "all" + *swa* "so"; i.e., quite so), and *world* (*wer* "man" + *yldu* "age"; i.e., age of man).

There is also a phenomenon known as false blending. An example of this is *doofer* (also spelled *doofah, doovah, doover*), which is a "thingamabob" or a "thingumajig," that is, any gadget or other thing the name of which we do not know or have not cared to remember. It is from "do for," as in "that will do for now." Another example is *gofer,* "an employee who runs errands, in addition to any other regular duties," from "go for," as in "one who goes for coffee or snacks."

ASSIGNMENT

I. Learn the following **verb-forming suffix** and its meaning:

-(i)fy, -(e)fy, "to make"

PAC-	peace	+	*-(i)fy*	pacify
MAGN-	large	+	*-(i)fy*	magnify
LIQU-	to be liquid	+	*-(e)fy*	liquify

The following suffix, though it forms **adjectives**, is considered here because it is a form of the previous suffix. Both are related to the base FAC-, (FIC-), "to do," "to make" from Lesson XII.

-(i)fic, "making," "causing"

PAC-	peace	+	*-(i)fic*	pacific
TERR-	to frighten	+	*-(i)fic*	terrific

II. Learn the following bases and their meanings:

AL-, ALT-	to nourish, grow tall	alumnus, alimony, altitude
MEDI-	middle	median, medium, immediate
MIGR-	to move from one place to another	migratory, transmigrate, immigrant
MORT-	death	mortal, mortuary
PET-	to seek, assail	compete, petition, appetite
PUG(N)-	to fight; a fist	repugnant, impugn, pugilist

III. Analyze the following italicized words and define them as they are used in the sentence or phrase.

1. Some of the *migrants* had been working the east coast for thirty years, picking apples and tobacco in Virginia, peaches in Georgia, and oranges in Florida.

2. The reason that my works are accused of pessimism is low sales. Readers who wish to cheer me up have only to buy my books *prodigiously.**—Thomas Hardy

3. ...but what politician has a right to *deification* or posthumous respect?—*Harper's Magazine*

4. Will you be my *intermediary* in these negotiations? I am afraid to approach her.

**prod-* here is a variant of *pro-.*

5. "I arst you civil enough, didn't I?" said the old man straightening his shoulders *pugnaciously.*—George Orwell

6. Siegfried stalked about, occasionally bursting forth with a *petulant* scream.—James Herriot

7. Cessation in his love-making had *revivified* her love. —Thomas Hardy

8. We rejected the compulsory jurisdiction of the International Court of Justice, which means that we refused to obligate ourselves even to submit our legal disputes to impartial *adjudication.*—Harper's Magazine

9. Syracuse...had not only become *inexpugnable* but had assumed the aggressive.—Grote

10. The 1-9 season was powerful: it *dispirited* the team as well as the entire school, provoked twenty-eight fights, initiated nine lawsuits, and cost the coach his job.—William Mark

11. ...doors which were intended for (a) *ingress* and (b) *egress,* windows which were meant to give light.—John Addington Symonds

12. ...contracts in which...there may have been no direct fraud or deceit, sufficient to *invalidate* them in a court of law.—*The Federalist*

13. "I expect you're right, Stack," said Colonel Melchette, disguising his usual *repugnance.*—Agatha Christie

14. A reproductive system to *perpetuate* the species.... —*Review of Medical Physiology*

15. In 1890 his grandparents *emigrated* from France to go live in Quebec.

16. Upon this ground, which is evidently the true one, it will not be difficult to *obviate* the objections....—*The Federalist*

17. And therefore we are often *constrained* to stand alone against the strength of opinion.—Sir Thomas Browne

18. The plumber then proceeded to give me a fascinating *disquisition* on how a professional traces leaks.—*Atlantic Monthly*

19. ...a youth of restless and *impetuous* activity.—Francis Parkman

20. The distinguishing mental features of melancholia are a profoundly painful dejection, *abrogation* of interest in the outside world....—Sigmund Freud

IV. With the aid of a dictionary, list the words which have been combined to produce each of the following blends:

1. Amerind
2. dumfound
3. electrocute
4. agitprop
5. Gestapo
6. motel
7. quasar
8. moped
9. telecast
10. transistor

LESSON XXII

DOUBLETS

We have seen from the introduction that there were a number of different periods during which English borrowed from Latin and a number of different routes by way of which Latin words entered our language. In the Renaissance many words were borrowed directly from Latin by scholars and so more nearly preserve their original forms; but in earlier times Latin words entered English generally by way of Old French or occasionally Germanic, and often in such cases their forms became considerably altered. Thus, frequently the same Latin word has been borrowed with different spelling and often with different meaning during successive periods and so has supplied our vocabulary with two or more English words. Sometimes, also, such variations have appeared because a Latin word has entered English by way of different dialects of French. Such words that are different in spelling but are derived ultimately from the same parent word are called doublets. For example, the Latin word *dignitas* entered English through Old French as *dainty,* but was borrowed again as *dignity.* The process might be diagrammed as follows:

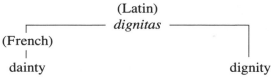

Sometimes doublets have completely different meanings, as in the previous example or in the case of the following:

cruise—cross (from Latin *crux,* "cross")

When a ship cruises, it "crosses" back and forth over its previous course.

chamber—camera (from Latin *camera* "room," as in *unicameral*)

An early device for taking photographs was called by its inventor *camera obscura* ("dark room"), and the first part of this name came to be applied to all such devices.

ray—radius (from Latin *radius,* "spoke of a wheel")

ennui—annoy (from Latin *in odio,* "in hatred"; cf. English *odious*)

Many times, however, the meanings of doublets vary only slightly, and thus it is possible to see how the tendency to borrow has greatly increased the richness and variety of the English language. The following doublets, for instance, are fairly close in meaning but yet are not exact synonyms.

fragile—frail	*regal—royal*
abbreviate—abridge	*compute—count*

Languages other than Latin have of course supplied doublets, as, for example, *shirt—skirt,* and *ward—guard,* which are of Germanic origin, and *cipher—zero,* from Arabic.

Sometimes a single parent word has given our language three or more different words, as in the following instances:

ratio—ration—reason

capital—cattle—chattel (from Latin *caput, capitis,* "head")

Cattle at one time formed a very important item of "capital" (literally, "chief property").

gentle—gentile—genteel—jaunty

There are linguistic reasons for doublets looking and sounding so differently. In the development of the French language from Latin, most of the vowel sounds and many of the consonantal ones underwent change. During this evolution, syllables were dropped out or added as well, so that the sound and also the spelling of the French word—for example, *dainty* (from French *deinté*)—was completely altered from its Latin parent *dignitas.* When this word was borrowed into English, it was made to conform to English sound and spelling, the end result being *dainty.* On the other hand, when the English borrowed a word from Latin, a great deal less molding had to take place, which is why the above *dignity* looks a lot more like the Latin *dignitas* than does *dainty.*

There are too many situations for them all to be explained here, but the following will explain a few:

Some doublets reflect merely a spelling difference, as with the French *co(i)* = Latin *qu-* (both pronounced /kw/)—as in *coy/quaint, antic/antique.*

Some changes are concerned with vowel modification—as in *cloak/clock, close/clause, poignant/pungent, pity/piety, aggrieve/aggravate* (here with the added verbal suffix *-at-* from Lesson II).

Some alterations are contractions—as with *sure,* a contraction of *secure,* also *naive/native, parcel/particle, ancestor/antecessor, count/compute.*

Some changes involve voicing—as in *stance* (with voiceless /s/) and *stanza* (with voiced /z/), *chart/card* (/t/ and /d/).

In French, a circumflexed vowel before *t* indicates the dropping of *s,* a procedure that was incorporated during the period of Old French. This gave rise to doublets in English since we borrowed the word first in its old form and again in its new form. Examples are *maître (d'hôtel)/master, hotel/hostel,* and *fête/feast* (together with *fiesta,* an English word on loan from Spanish).

ASSIGNMENT

I. Learn the following bases and their meanings:

GRAT-	pleasing, grateful	gratitude, gratuitous
MISC-, MIXT-	to mix	promiscuous, immiscible, admixture
MOV-, MOT-	to move	movement, remove, motion, remote
NEG-	to deny	negative, renegade
PURG-	to clean	purge, purgative
VULG-	common, ordinary	vulgar, vulgate

II. Analyze the following italicized words as they are used in the sentence or phrase.

1. ...the solemn pledge we had already signed agreeing not to *divulge* classified information we might acquire.—*Harper's Magazine*

2. Hitting hard at *pretentious* commencements, big time football ...Conant snorts that all such status seeking is utterly without "sound educational reason."—*Time*

3. *Miscegenation* may now be handled discreetly, but anything inciting hatred among peoples is taboo.—*Time*

4. A tortured and complicated character, full of *ambivalences* and utter contradictions....—*Harper's Magazine*

5. The extraordinary length and magnificence of this fish tale

(no pun intended) aroused considerable *incredulity* in the minds of all within earshot.—S.D. Kinsley

6. The man shook his fist and gnashed his teeth as he uttered these words *incoherently.*—Dickens

7. . . . Hoover endured not only the *emotional* torment of the Depression, but two decades of obloquy in which his name was equated with economic disaster and social injustice.—*Time*

8. On a large centre table a number of artistic objects were lying together in a *promiscuous* jumble.—W.H. Hudson

9. Every eye and every tongue affected to express their sense of the general happiness, and the veil of ceremony and *dissimulation* was drawn for a while over the darkest designs of revenge and murder.—Edward Gibbon

10. The idea of *Purgatory* has always seemed too facile to me. Can any sin or inadequacy be washed away simply by enduring a hellish sojourn?

11. Nor is it possible to plead, in *extenuation* of his guilt, that he was misled by inordinate zeal for the public good.—Macaulay

12. The *prevailing* view seemed to be that his opinion was not worth a pair of fetid dingo's kidneys.—Douglas Adams

13. When you used to sit on the shore of your pond on Sunday morning, listening to the church bells of Acton and Concord, you were aware of the excellent filter of the *intervening* atmosphere.—E.B. White

14. We all know what *specious* fallacies may be urged in defence of every act of injustice yet proposed for the imaginary benefit of the mass.—John Stuart Mill

15. Many of the translations, they complain, are *expurgated* Victorian versions. . . .—*Time*

16. Debate could be protracted interminably, and an active minority, by *dilatory* motions and filibustering, could create preposterous delays.—Allan Nevins

17. . . . air assault, which Hitler was led to believe would shatter our industries and reduce us to *impotence* and subjection. —Sir Winston Churchill

18. Our life has been a vain attempt at self-delight. But self-*abnegation* is the higher road. We should mortify the flesh. —Thomas Hardy

19. He was kind, cordial, open, even *convivial* and jocose, would sit at table many hours, and would bear his full share of festive conversation.—Macaulay

20. We have seen with what sagacious policy the French had labored to *ingratiate* themselves with the Indians.—Francis Parkman

III. With the aid of a dictionary give the doublet(s) of each of the following:

Example: feat—fact

On looking up *feat* you will find that it is derived from the Latin *factum,* "that which is done." The form *factum* should suggest the obvious derivative, which is the doublet *fact.* Some of the following may not be quite this easy, however.

1. overture	7. chase
2. ancestor	8. fashion
3. attitude	9. grace
4. hostel	10. comprise
5. slander	11. comply
6. balm	12. treasure

LESSON XXIII

LATINISMS IN SHAKESPEARE

One of the reasons why modern readers have difficulty appreciating older writers is that they encounter many obsolete words or words used in a sense different from that of today. College students find this type of difficulty most frequently perhaps in the works of Shakespeare. In *Henry V,* for instance, the line occurs, "By my troth, I will speak my conscience of the king." *Conscience* (SCI-, "to know") here does not mean, however, "knowledge of right and wrong," the modern meaning, but "inmost thoughts," "mind." In *Hamlet* Ophelia, who has become insane, is described as "a document in madness," *document* (DOC-, "to teach") here being "lesson" rather than "written proof."

These two examples are instances of words which have since become specialized, although used in a generalized sense in Shakespeare's time. Likewise Shakespeare sometimes employs words in a literal sense whereas the modern meaning is figurative, such as *extravagant* in the third quotation below. Often a knowledge of bases combined with careful attention to the context will enable a student to determine more precisely the meaning of a word as it occurs in one of Shakespeare's plays.

ASSIGNMENT

I. On the basis of your knowledge of bases, prefixes, and suffixes, give the meanings of the italicized words as they occur in the following quotations from Shakespeare.*

    1. The people love me, and the sea is mine;
       My powers are *crescent*. . . .   —Antony and Cleopatra

    2. . . .an excellent play, well *digested* in the scenes. . . .
                                           —*Hamlet*

    3.   . . .and at his warning,
      Whether in sea or fire, in earth or air,
      the *extravagant* and erring spirit hies
      To his confine. (VAG-, to wander)

                                           —*Hamlet*

    4.   . . .falling in the land,
      Have every pelting river made so proud,
      That they have overborne their *continents*.
                      —*A Midsummer Night's Dream*

    5. The Turk with a most mighty preparation makes for Cyprus.
       Othello, the *fortitude* of the place is best known to you.
                                        —*Othello*

    6. Whose white *investments* figure innocence. . . .
                                       —*Henry IV*

    7.   . . .and of the truth herein
      This present object made *probation*.
                                       —*Hamlet*

---

*Many of these examples have been taken from Edith F. Claflin, "The Latinisms in Shakespeare's Diction," *Classical Journal,* 16 (1920–21), pp. 346-59, and C.C. Hower, "Importance of a Knowledge of Latin for Understanding the Language of Shakespeare," *Classical Journal,* 46 (1950-51), pp. 221–7.

8. Abate the edge of traitors, gracious Lord,
   that would *reduce* these bloody days again.

   —Richard III

9. If you have hitherto conceal'd this sight,
   Let it be *tenable* in your silence still.

   —Hamlet

II. Give the meanings of the following italicized obsolete or archaic
    words as they are used in the passages below:

1. Let it stamp wrinkles in her brow of youth;
   With *cadent* tears fret channels in her cheeks.

   —King Lear

2. Then weigh what loss your honour may sustain,
   If with too *credent* ear you list his songs.

   —Hamlet

3. The presence of a king engenders love
   Amongst his subjects and his loyal friends,
   As it *disanimates* his enemies.

   —Henry VI

4. For ever should they be *expulsed* from France,
   And not have title of an earldom here.

   —Henry VI

5. What *propugnation* is in one man's valour,
   To stand the push and enmity of those
   This quarrel would excite?

   —Troilus and Cressida

6. . . . stubbornly he did *repugn* the truth.

   —Henry VI

7.   Now, the next day
   Was our sea-fight; and what to this was *sequent*
   Thou know'st already.

   —Hamlet

8. Thou perjured, and thou *simular* man of virtue . . . .

   —King Lear

9. As knots, by the conflux of meeting sap,
   Infect the sound pine and divert his grain
   Tortive and errant from his course of growth.

   —Troilus and Cressida

III. Learn the following bases and their meanings:

   CORD-   heart   cordial, accord, record

FLECT-, FLEX-	to bend	deflection, reflection, flexible, reflex
MAN(U)-	hand	manicure, manipulate, manual, manuscript
PORT-	to carry	portable, deport, report
STRU-, STRUCT-	to build	instrument, structure, instruct
TERMIN-	boundary, end	terminal, determine
VINC-, VICT-	to conquer	convince, evince, victor, convict

IV. Analyze the following italicized words and define them as they are used in the sentence or phrase:

1. They made a mad attempt to follow us in the fractured canoe, but finding it useless, again vented their rage in a series of hideous *vociferations.* —Edgar Allan Poe

2. They exclaimed that they were betrayed, and that the truce had been only an *artifice* to secure their inactivity until the arrival of the expected succours. —William Hickling Prescott

3. . . . laying his finger on his lip, drew his companions back again, with the greatest caution and *circumspection.* —Dickens

4. His stern features expressed *inflexible* resolution; his brows were puckered, and his lips compressed, with deep and settled purpose. —Dickens

5. . . . rightly *construed* this as an acquiescence in his proposition. —Dickens

6. The claims of the rival nations were in fact so *discordant* that any attempt to reconcile them must needs produce a fresh quarrel. —Francis Parkman

7. Men, seeing the nature of this man like that of the brute, think that he has never possessed the *innate* faculty of reason. —Thoreau

8. . . . would cling with an *invincible* tenacity of grip to any purpose which he might espouse. —Francis Parkman

9. Form and material are among the major *determinants* of house design. —Brian Fagan

10. The cold beer he drew from the keg was certainly *effervescent,* an adjective that could scarcely be applied, however, to his present drunken stupor.

11. Plays and poems, hunting and dancing, were *proscribed* by the austere discipline of his saintly family. —Macaulay

12. The resolution was, of course, carried with loud *acclamations,* every man holding up both hands in favour of it. —Dickens

13. Let us examine the point of the story. . . . We will introduce it by an *apposite* anecdote.—Charles Lamb

14. . . .his face expressive of pain and care, —not *transitory,* but settled pain, of long and forcedly patient endurance. —Hawthorne

15. . . .the vista of that noble street, stretching into the *interminable* distance between two rows of lofty edifices. —Hawthorne

16. *Dictionary*: a malevolent literary device for cramping the growth of a language and making it hard and inelastic.—Ambrose Bierce, *The Devil's Dictionary*

17. As it proved, science has achieved the possibility of that *emancipation* from want. . . .—*Harper's Magazine*

18. . . .had sunk into a chair, with an expression of the most *abject* and hopeless misery that the human mind can imagine portrayed in every lineament of his expressive face. —Dickens

19. . . .hearty *extroverts* with the ever-ready smile, the big hello, the manly handshake, the sure-fire memory for first names. —*Harper's Magazine*

20. The Emancipation Proclamation together with the 13th amendment to the Constitution guaranteed the *manumission* of all slaves in the United States.

LESSON XXIV

METATHESIS

One of the events in the history of language that remains shrouded in mystery is a phenomenon called metathesis, which is a transposition of two letters or sounds in a word. Sometimes the new form completely replaced the old form, such as the word *bird*, which mysteriously crept into Middle English alongside the original Old English *bridd*, eventually in Modern English to supplant it. Likewise, the modern *frost* displaced the original Old English *forst; gaers* became *grass; naefre* became *never;* and *beorht* changed to *bright.*

Sometimes both forms lived together, such as the Latin root *cla-* "to cry out, to call" (connected with the base CLAM- in Lesson XVIII), which is in the word *nomenclature,* and the form *cal-,* which survives in *intercalate;* also the two bases CERT- and CRET- "to separate." The Latin base CRE- had *cer-* as its older form. The base TURB- "to disturb" (Lesson IV) came into Old French as *trub-* and *troub-,* which slipped into English as *trouble.* So *gul-* (Latin "throat") and *glut-* (Latin "to gulp down") have supplied the English words *gullet* and *glutton.* Latin for "three" is *tres*; but "third" is *tertius*— both cognate with our *three* and *third.* *Thrill* is a metathesized form of *thirl* (=to pierce), which came from Old English *thurh,* which also turned into our present *through.* And *thorough,* also from *thurh,* got caught in the middle, with a vowel on either side of the *r.*

Some words changed in their spelling but the pronunciation did not change. *Where* used to be *hwar,* but we still pronounce the word with a little puff of air (the *h*) before we pronounce *w*—as with many *wh-* words that were once *hw-: whither* from *hwider, while* from *hwil, white* from *hwit, when* from *hwanne,* and so on.

Some words have metathesized pronunciations (which do not appear in dictionaries but which are on our lips nevertheless) but their spellings have remained unchanged. Some speakers consistently use a *pretty apron* in the kitchen, while others will always put on a "purdy apern.'"

Even entire words are known to have swapped places. The Old English *horshwael* got metathesized twice: the *hw* changed to *wh,* giving *whale,* and the original "horse whale" changed to "whale horse," ending up in English as *walrus.*

ASSIGNMENT

I. Many other writers besides Shakespeare have of course used familiar words with meanings not found today. On the basis of your knowledge of bases, prefixes, and suffixes, give the **uncommon meanings** of the italicized words as they occur in the following passages, most of which have been taken from the *Oxford English Dictionary.*

1. In order to lighten the crown still further, they *aggravated* responsibility on ministers of state.   —Burke (1790)

2. The moste *comfortable* Sacrament of the body and bloud of Christe. . . .   —Ordre of Communion (1547 − 8)

3. There is no *convenience* between Christ and Belial.
   —Sampson (1554)

4. The *conversion* of Jupiter about his own axis. . . . (1655 – 6)

5. At length *convinced* with the heavinesse of sleep. . . he turned him to the wall. —Munday (1633)

6. The insatiable Appetites of a *decimating* Clergy. . . .
   —Penn (1670)

7. Venice was a Colonie *deducted* and drawne from thence.
   —Holland (1600)

8. . . .to be exiled and *dejected* from those high mansions.
   —Mede (1638)

9. The drapery. . . that *depends* from his shoulders. . . .
   —Hogarth (1753)

10. An *excursion* of land shooting out directly. . . .
    —Browne (1682)

11. An accessory before the *fact*. . . .

12. All these afflictions. . . they knowingly did *object* themselves to. —Barrow (1677)

13. God. . . had *pretended* a remedie in that behalfe which was . . .Manna. —Carew (1594)

14. Love is more *prevalent* in obtaining what you desire than fear. —King (1711)

15. The fortunate soil assisted, and even *prevented,* the hand of cultivation. —Gibbon (1776)

16. An insect with the extremity of its abdomen *produced* into a sharp point. . . . —Darwin (1877)

17. . . .and have *punctuated* unto me so many remarkeable things and novelties. . . . —Tirwhyte (1634)

18. Morley, made at first bishop of Worcester, and soon after . . .*translated* to Winchester. . . . —Burnet (1683)

II. Learn the following bases and their meanings:

Base	Meaning	Examples
AUD-	to hear	audience, audit, auditorium
CARN-	flesh	carnage, incarnation
NUNCI-, [NOUNC-]	to announce	annunciation, denunciation, denounce, pronounce
PRESS-	to press	pressure, compression
PROPRI-	one's own; fitting	proprietary, appropriate
SAT(IS)-	enough	satiate, satisfy

III. Analyze the following italicized words and define them as they are used in the sentence or phrase.

1. He found the country was pouring forth its legions from every quarter, and perceived that there was no safety but in *precipitate* flight.—Washington Irving

2. ...Russia's two great *expatriates*—one of whom had not set foot in his homeland for half a century, the other for better than 35 years.—*Time*

3. All honour to those who can abnegate for themselves the personal enjoyment of life, when by such *renunciation* they contribute worthily to increase the amount of happiness in the world.—John Stuart Mill

4. Under cover of the rustle of the tracings, he murmured...in a low voice *inaudible* to the other two.—Thomas Hardy

5. A *prescient* analyst of Far East development in the 1930's, Close predicted Japanese war aims and the rise of Red China. —*Time*

6. Under the ruins were human skeletons and a great mass of pottery, clay figurines and other *artifacts.*—*Time*

7. ...drew up an address to Dr. Johnson on the occasion, *replete* with wit and humour, but which it was feared the Doctor might think treated the subject with too much levity.—James Boswell

8. I do this with no desire to make *invidious* comparisons or rouse purposeless rivalries with our greatest ally, the United States.—Sir Winston Churchill

9. It seemed worth putting down among the noblest sentiments *enunciated* by the best of men.—Dickens

10. Thou lovest; but ne'er knew love's sad *satiety.*—Shelley

11. I would not, at twenty years, be a preaching missionary of abstemiousness and sobriety; and I should let other people do as they would, without formally and *sententiously* rebuking them for it.—Lord Chesterfield

12. "No, dearie, better stay home and snuggle up with TV tonight. I mean, listen, the guy's got *carnal* appetites you wouldn't believe."—Brian Levin

13. He *comported* himself with great dignity.—Joseph Conrad

14. The *oppression* of a majority is destestable and odious; the oppression of a minority is only by one degree less detestable and odious.—William Gladstone

15. The great landed properties were *expropriated* by the state a generation ago and parcelled out among the indigent peasantry.—*Atlantic Monthly*
16. Never was there a sweeter-tempered, a better-mannered member of that often *contentious* and not infrequently acrimonious body.—Samuel Hopkins Adams
17. Increasingly *repressive* legislation—certain to limit and restrict our civil liberties—would certainly result.... —*Harper's Magazine*
18. ...watching the monotony of everyday occurrences with a kind of *inconsequential* interest and earnestness.—Hawthorne
19. ...that morbid condition of the *auditory* nerve which rendered all music intolerable to the sufferer.—Edgar Allan Poe
20. With his captivating flattery and seductive magnetism, I felt the devil *incarnate* was standing before me.—F. O'Sullivan

LESSON XXV

LATIN WORDS AND PHRASES IN ENGLISH

Some words have entered English from Latin without becoming completely anglicized; thus they still retain their Latin endings and consequently have a foreign, un-English appearance. In some cases the plurals of such words are formed in the Latin fashion; in other cases the regular English plural -*s* or -*es* is used; while in still other cases both English and Latin plural forms are to be found. One can be certain only by consulting a dictionary.

There are a number of different Latin plural endings for nouns, too many in fact to attempt to classify fully here. For our purposes, it is enough to learn the most frequently occurring Latin singular endings,

-*us*,-*a*, and -*um*, with their corresponding plurals, -*i* (usually), -*ae*, and -*a*. Thus:

alumnus—alumni
alumna—alumnae
medium—media

Also might be mentioned words ending in -*ix* and -*ex*, with plurals in -*ices*. Thus:

appendix—appendices
vortex—vortices

Besides having carried on wholesale borrowing of individual words from the Latin language, English has adopted many Latin phrases in their original form. Some of these are so familiar that we scarcely think of them any longer as belonging to a foreign tongue, *post mortem* (literally, "after death"), for instance, and *vice versa* (literally, "the alternation or order being turned about"). Others are less familiar but are not infrequently found in literary and legal language.

Perhaps the biggest problem in connection with Latin phrases in English is pronunciation (and this holds true as well for Latin words like those listed in the preceding lesson). Dictionaries often give an anglicized pronunciation for such phrases and words, but many people who have studied Latin prefer to use the system of pronunciation taught in most schools in this country, where Latin is pronounced as nearly as possible in the manner of the ancient Romans. Thus, although some dictionaries give the pronunciation of *per diem* as "per DYE-em," one is probably more likely to hear it as "per DEE-em." Likewise, the pronunciation of *antennae* (the plural of *antenna*) is given in dictionaries as "antenn-EE," but many, including some zoologists, say "antenn-EYE." We are not justified in insisting that one system is correct and the other incorrect, or even that one system is better than the other. (As a matter of fact, there is still a third system of Latin pronunciation, which in this country is used principally in the Roman Catholic Church.) We can only observe the way these phrases are pronounced by educated users with whom we are acquainted and, when in doubt, rely upon the dictionary.

Loan words are further discussed, and more broadly, in Lesson VII of Part Two, the Greek section.

ASSIGNMENT

I. The following italicized words contain bases which have already been studied. Define each word as it is used in the sentence or phrase, and give the base and its meaning.

1. The committee was unprepared for the proposal since it had not been listed in the *agenda.*

2. It will be all the easier for us to conduct ourselves as belligerents in a high spirit of right and fairness because we act without *animus,* not in enmity towards a people. . . . —Woodrow Wilson

3. . . .a *congeries* of brilliant passages in support of an untenable thesis.—*Harper's Magazine*

4. The *consensus* is that the trial will not be concluded before May at the earliest.—*Atlantic Monthly*

5. The following errors have not been listed in the *corrigenda* of the book.

6. Early councils were primarily concerned with combating heresy and defining the truths that form the *credo* of most believing Christians.—*Time*

7. This effort of the Germans to secure daylight mastery of the air over England is, of course, the *crux* of the whole war. —Sir Winston Churchill

8. Men still quoted with approval Jefferson's *dictum* that government is best when governing least.—*Atlantic Monthly*

9. An indescribable and complicated smell, made up of damp earth below, of the taint of dried fish and of the *effluvia* of rotting vegetable matter, pervaded the place.—Joseph Conrad

10. They are so natural that they seem to be the *extempore* conversations of two people of wit, rather than letters.—Lord Chesterfield

11. It is inconsistent to pay the one, and accept the service of the other *gratis.*—Thomas Paine

12. As an *interim* measure, before the full scientific treatment can be given to this procedure....—Sir Winston Churchill

13. Cortés established a control over his band of bold and reckless adventurers, such as a pedantic martinet, scrupulous in enforcing the *minutiae* of military etiquette, could never have obtained.—William Hickling Prescott

14. A report-drafting committee gathers memoranda from the economists and co-ordinates the stuff into a kind of *omnibus* draft embodying the suggestions.—*Harper's Magazine*

15. A written *prospectus* of this issue of stock will be sent upon request.

II. Give the plural or plurals of each of the following singular forms:

1. apex	8. focus
2. apparatus	9. formula
3. arena	10. genus
4. cactus	11. index
5. campus	12. memorandum
6. crux	13. species
7. curriculum	14. stadium

III. Unlike the case with English phrases in a dictionary, where *keep tabs on* will be under *tab* (see Idiomatic Uses in Lesson I), foreign expressions are always under the first word, regardless of its part of speech. Also, as there is no *a, an,* or *the* in Latin, these are always supplied by the translator, who also has to supply the preposition *of,* which in Latin is added to a noun stem the same way we can add *'s* to *dog* and get *dog's*—where the *dog's fur* means the *fur of the dog.* An example of this *of* is in number 16 below, in which *operand-* means *operating* and *-i* means *of*; or in number 27, in which *qu-* means *who/whom* and *-orum* means *of* plural. Other Latin prepositions are often right there, as *pro,* meaning *for,* in number 26 (which is where the prefix *pro-* came from), or *ex,* meaning *from,* in number 11. However, many times the preposition is built onto the noun, as with *of.* In number 32, the *-o* on *quo* means *in*; and in number 15, the *-o* on both *ipso* and *facto* means *by.*

In the example phrases or sentences, you will notice that some of the Latin phrases are italicized (which means the author considers them as foreign words) and some are not (which means the author considers them to be English). The issue as to whether or not these expressions when used in English are, in fact, Latin or English has been up for grabs for many years: some dictionaries consider all of them Latin, some dictionaries consider all of them English, and yes, some dictionaries consider some of them English and some of them Latin. But do not be confused by what dictionary editors think. As a general rule, many academic books and learned journals frequently italicize these Latin expressions indiscriminately where newspapers and newsstand magazines do not. Whichever you choose, you won't be wrong, except that numbers 5, 22, 25, 27, 28, and 32 are generally not italicized.

You will notice that some of these expressions in translation fit nicely into English word order, as in number 13 ("the officer was 'by the very fact' a gentleman"); but most do not. Whereas in number 8, "the Allies give de jure recognition" is perfectly acceptable, we could never say "the Allies gave by right recognition."

The following Latin phrases in English are listed together with the literal meaning of the Latin. Using your dictionary, define them as they are used in the accompanying phrase or sentence.

1. ad hoc (with regard to this)

...responsibility for the study and its findings fell on an "*ad hoc* citizens committee of 22."—*Time*

2. ad hominem (to the [individual] person)

The argument here alleged is only *ad hominem.*—Hartley

3. ad nauseam (to nausea)

My friend of the pit repeated it *ad nauseam* during the performance.—Thackeray

4. ad valorem (according to value)

. . .the British Board of Trade announced the application of a 75 per cent ad valorem tax against foreign film-earnings in the United Kingdom.—*Harper's Magazine*

5. alma mater (bounteous mother)

My dear old alma mater. . . .

6. alter ego (another I)

The Governor sits in on many of these discussions and is usually represented by his alter ego. . .when he cannot attend.—*Harper's Magazine*

7. de facto (from the fact)

A growing problem in every big Northern city, *de facto* segregation results from slum housing, racial ghettos and rigid school zoning laws.—*Time*

8. de jure (by right, according to law)

It was not until late in 1940 that the Allies gave *de jure* recognition to the Czechoslovak government-in-exile. —*Harper's Magazine*

9. et cetera (and other things)

It is concluded between the two *et ceteras* that a cessation of arms. . .should be agreed on.—John Cotgrave

10. ex cathedra (from the chair)

He advanced with a very doctorial air, placed himself behind a chair, on which he leaned as on a desk or pulpit, and then delivered, ex cathedra, a mock solemn charge. —Washington Irving

11. ex officio (from the office)

At the top, of course, are the officers of the Corps of Engineers, who are ex officio members of the Rivers and Harbors Congress.—*Harper's Magazine*

12. ex post facto (from what is done afterwards)

Ex post facto laws are prohibited by our constitution and are rightfully considered contrary to good morals and natural law.—*Atlantic Monthly*

13. habeas corpus (you must have the body)

The great and efficacious writ, in all manner of illegal confinement, is that of *habeas corpus.* —Blackstone

14. in toto (in the whole)

For example, a supersonic beam may be reflected almost *in toto* by a brick wall, but only partially by a privet hedge. —*Atlantic Monthly*

15. ipso facto (by the very fact)

As the Army expanded, everyone managed to have some innocent fun with the idea that the officer was *ipso facto* a gentleman. —*Harper's Magazine*

16. modus operandi (manner of operating)

But for the present the committee has decided to seek with the New York publishers a voluntary *modus operandi* under which both courts and newspapers would endeavor to protect the rights of defendants. —*Harper's Magazine*

17. modus vivendi (way of living)

This government at last even considered offering the Japanese a "modus vivendi" calling for a three months' truce. . . . —*Harper's Magazine*

18. ne plus ultra (no more beyond)

All those works of scholarship, which seemed to our ancestors the *ne plus ultra* of refinement, are now relegated to the lumberroom of erudition that has been superseded. —John Addington Symonds

19. non sequitur (it does not follow)

. . . evade the law by patching together a rat's nest of innuendo, *non sequitur* and irrelevancy. —*Time*

20. per capita (by heads)

New England still produces some lumber, but well below the national average per capita. . . . —*Harper's Magazine*

21. per diem (by the day)

. . . generous per diem allowances for employees trapped by high hotel expenses. —*Harper's Magazine*

22. per se (by himself or itself)

No man was either great or good per se, but as compared with others not so good or great. —James Boswell

23. persona non grata (a person not acceptable)

The embassy official was declared *persona non grata* by the Cuban government.

24. prima facie (on the first appearance)

If anyone does an act hurtful to others, there is a prima facie case for punishing him, by law, or where legal penalties are not applicable, by general disapprobation.—John Stuart Mill

25. (a) quasi (as if)

In the American Dream there is no room for quasi success.

(b) quasi- (a combining form, from above)

In ancient times astrology was quasi-scientific but is now considered to be a pseudoscience.

26. quid pro quo (something for something)

An...apothecary that understands not his bile but gives *quid pro quo.*—Calfhill

27. quorum (of whom)

There being a *quorum* present, I call the meeting to order.

28. quota (of what number)

Will the business community meet its quota in the coming United Way campaign?

29. reductio ad absurdum (reduction to an absurdity)

In this unlucky chapter the argument of the book confutes itself by a *reductio ad absurdum.*—Arnold Toynbee

30. sic (thus)

John writes in his letter, "I like Massachusets [*sic*] but its [*sic*] too cold in the winter."

31. sine qua non (without which not)

...an enlightened electorate is a *sine qua non* for success in our kind of government.—*Harper's Magazine*

32. status quo (the situation in which)

The status quo was to be maintained in Luxemburg during negotiations respecting that duchy.—*The Edinburgh Review*

INDEX OF WORDS APPEARING IN CONTEXT (LATIN)

The Roman numerals appearing after the word indicate the lesson in which the word is to be found.

expropriated xxiv
expulsed xxiii
expunged iv
expurgated xxii
exquisite xvii
extant xix
extempore xxiv
extenuation xxii
extravagant xxiii
extroverts xxiii

F

fact xxiv
factitious xii
fallacious xi
fallible xi
Fates xi
feasible xii
fervor xviii
fidelity xv
firmament xvi
flagrant x
florid xii
forte ii
fortitude xiv, xxiii

G

generate ix
generic ix
genitally xi
grandeur ii
gratis xxv
gregarious ix

H

habeas corpus xxv

I

ignoble xx
ignominious xx
immutable xi
impartiality ii
imperturbable iv

imperviousness iv
impetuous xxi
implement v
impotence xxii
imprecations iv
improbity xvi
impulsive xiii
imputation xx
inadvertently iv
inanimate vii
inaudible xxiv
incantations vii
incarnate xxiv
incessant iv
incisive xv
incoherently xxii
incompatible xvii
inconsequential xxiv
incontrovertible xi
incorporeal viii
incorrigible xvii
incredulity xxii
incredulous xii
increment xvi
incumbent x
incursions vi
indigenous xi
indisputably xx
induces iv
ineffable xi
inequity xiv
inexorably xiv
inexpugnable xxi
infer ix
inference xix
infinitesimal ii
infinitude ii
infirmity xiv
inflame ix
inflexible xxiii
influence xix
infrangible xvii
ingratiate xxii

ingress xxi
inherent x
iniquitous vii
injudiciously viii
injustice iv
innate xxiii
inordinate x
insensate iv
insubordinate x
insuperable v
intangible xi
intercession iv
interdicted xviii
interim xxv
interlineations iv
interlocutor vi
interlocutress iv
intermediary xxi
interminable xxiii
intervening xxii
interventionist vii
in toto xxv
intractable xi
intransigence xviii
introspectiveness xiii
invalidate xxi
investiture ii
investments xxiii
invidious xxiv
invincible xxiii
invoke ix
ipso facto xxv
irrevocable v

J

jugular xvii

L

lineaments ii
lucidity xiv
luminary ix
luminescence xx
luminous ix

PREFIXES (LATIN)

The Roman numerals in parentheses following the meanings indicate the lesson in which each prefix is to be found.

ab-, a-, abs-, away, from (III)
ad-, ac-, etc., to, toward (III)
ambi-, both, around (III)
ante-, before, in front of (III)
circum-, around (III)
con-, com-, co-, etc., with, together, very (III)
contra-, contro-, counter-, against (III)
de-, down, off, thoroughly (III)
dis-, di-, dif-, apart, in different directions, not (III)
en-, em-, in, into, against (IV)
ex-, e-, ef-, out, from, completely (IV)
extra-, extro-, outside, beyond (IV)
in-, im-, etc., in, into, against; not (IV)
infra-, below, beneath (IV)

inter-, between, among (IV)
intra-, intro-, within (IV)
non-, not (IV)
ob-, etc., toward, against, completely (IV)
per-, through, wrongly, completely (IV)
post-, after, behind (V)
pre-, before, in front of (V)
pro-, forward, in front of, for (V)
re-, red-, back, again (V)
retro-, backward, behind (V)
se-, sed-, aside, away (V)
sub-, sus-, suc-, etc., under, up from under, secretly (V)
super-, above, over (V)
trans-, tran-, tra-, across, through (V)
ultra-, beyond, exceedingly (V)

SUFFIXES (LATIN)

The Roman numerals in parentheses following the meanings indicate the lesson in which each suffix is to be found.

-able, able to be, etc. (XI)
-acious, tending to, etc. (XI)
-acity, quality of being inclined to (XV)
-acy, quality of being or having (XIV)
-ain, pertaining to, etc. (VIII)
-al (-ial, -eal), pertaining to, etc. (VIII)
-an (-ian), pertaining to, etc. (VIII)

-ance, -ancy, quality of ___ing, etc. (XVIII)
-and(um), -(i)end(um), that which must be ___-ed (XIX)
-ane, pertaining to, etc. (VIII)
-ant, present participle ending -ing (X)
-ar, pertaining to, etc. (VIII)
-ary, pertaining to, etc. (IX)
-ary (-arium), place for (XVIII)
-at(e), verbal suffix (II)

-*ate*, possessing, etc. (X)
-*ate*, office of, etc. (XV)
-*cle* (-*icle*), little (XVII)
-*cule* (-*icule*), little (XVII)
-*el*, little (XVII)
-*ence*, -*ency*, quality of ___ing, etc. (XVIII)
-*ent* (-*ient*), present participle ending -ing (X)
-*esce*, to begin, etc. (XX)
-*et*, -*ette*, little (XVII, footnote)
-(*i*)*fic*, making, etc. (XXI)
-(*i*)*fy*, -(*e*)*fy*, to make (XXI)
-*ible*, able to be, etc. (XI)
-*ic*, pertaining to, etc. (IX)
-*id*, tending to, etc. (XII)
-*il*, little (XVII)
-*il*, pertaining to, etc. (IX)
-*ile*, pertaining to, etc. (IX)
-*ile*, able to be, etc. (XI)
-*ine*, pertaining to, etc. (X)
-*ion*, act of, etc. (XVI)
-*it*(*e*), possessing, etc. (X)
-*it*(*e*), verbal suffix (II)
-*itude*, quality of, etc. (XIV)
-*itious*, tending to, etc. (XII)

-*ity* (-*ety*, -*ty*), quality of, etc. (XIV)
-*ive*, tending to, etc. (XIII)
-*le*, little (XVII)
-(*u*)*lence*, -(*o*)*lence*, state or quality of, etc. (XIV)
-(*u*)*lent*, (*o*)*lent*, full of, etc. (IX)
-*men*, result of, etc. (XVI)
-*ment*, result of, etc. (XVI)
-(*i*)*mony*, quality of (XV)
-*ole*, little (XVII)
-*or*, one who does, etc. (XIX)
-*or* (-*our*), state of, etc. (XVIII)
-*ory*, tending to, etc. (XIII)
-*ory* (-*orium*), place for (XVIII)
-*ose* (-*iose*), full of (VIII)
-*ous* (-*ious*, -eous), full of, etc. (VIII)
-*rix*, she who does (XIX)
-*tic*, pertaining to, etc. (IX)
-*ule*, little (XVII)
-*ulous*, tending to, etc. (XII)
-*uous*, tending to, etc. (XIII)
-*ure*, act of, etc. (XIX)
-*y*, quality of, etc. (XV)

BASES (LATIN)

The Roman numerals in parentheses following the meanings indicate the lesson in which each base is to be found.

A

AB-, to have, hold as customary (IV)
AC(U)-, ACR-, ACET-, sharp, bitter (XII)
ACT-, to do, drive (XVIII)
AG-, to do, drive (XVIII)
AL-, ALT-, to nourish, grow tall (XXI)
ALIEN-, of another (II)

AM-, to love (XIV)
ANIM-, mind, feeling, life (VII)
ANN(U)-, year (VII)
AQU(A)-, water (VIII)
ART-, art, skill (II)
AUD-, to hear (XXIV)

B

BENE-, well; good (VII)

BI-, BIN-, two; twice (VI)
BON-, well; good (VII)

C

CAD-, to fall, befall (XII)
CANT-, to sing (VII)
CAP-, CAPT-, to take, seize
  (XII)
CAPIT-, head (XX)
CARN-, flesh (XXIV)
CAS-, to fall, befall (XII)
CED-, to go, yield (III)
CEIV-, to take, seize (XII)
CENT-, hundred (VI)
CENT-, to sing (VII)
CEPT-, to take, seize (XII)
CERN-, CERT-, to separate,
  distinguish (XIII)
CESS-, to go, yield (III)
CHANT-, to sing (VII)
CID-, to fall, befall (XII)
CID-, to kill, cut (XV)
CIP-, to take, seize (XII)
CIPIT-, head (XX)
CIS-, to kill, cut (XV)
CLAIM-, to cry out (XVIII)
CLAM-, to cry out (XVIII)
CLOS-, to shut (V)
CLUD-, CLUS-, to shut (V)
COG-, to think, reflect,
  consider (XVIII)
CORD-, heart (XXIII)
COR(S)-, to run, go (V)
CORPOR-, CORP(US)-, body
  (VIII)
COURS-, to run, go (V)
CRE-, to grow (XVI)
CRED-, to believe, trust (XI)
CRESC-, CRET-, to grow
  (XVI)
CRET-, to separate, distinguish
  (XIII)
CRUC-, cross (IV)

CUB-, to lie down (X)
CUMB-, to lie down (X)
CUR-, cure, care (VII)
CUR(R)-, CURS-, to run, go
  (V)

D

DE-, god (XIV)
DECI(M)-, tenth (VI)
DIC-, DICT-, to say (XVIII)
DIV-, god (XIV)
DOC-, DOCT-, to teach (XI)
DOM(IN)-, house, master (IX)
DU-, two (VI)
DUC-, DUCT-, to lead (III)
DUR-, hard; to last (XIII)

E

ENNI-, year (VII)
EQU-, equal, even (VII)
ERR-, to wander (XIX)

F

FA(B)-, to speak (XI)
FAC-, FACT-, to do, make (XII)
FAIL-, to deceive (XI)
FALL-, FALS-, to deceive (XI)
FAM-, FAT-, to speak (XI)
FAULT-, to deceive (XI)
FEAS-, FEAT-, FECT-, to do,
  make (XII)
FEDER-, treaty, league (X)
FER-, to bear, carry (VII)
FERV-, to boil, bubble (XVII)
FESS-, to speak (XI)
FIC-, to do, make (XII)
FID-, faith (X)
FIDEL-, faithful (X)
FIN-, end, limit (II)
FIRM-, firm, strong (II)
FLAG(R)-, FLAM(M)-, to burn;
  flame (IX)
FLAT-, to blow (IX)
FLECT-, FLEX-, to bend
  (XXIII)

FLOR-, flower (XII)

FLU-, FLUX-, FLUV-, FLUOR(O)-, to flow (XII)

FOLI-, FOIL-, leaf (XII)

FORT-, strong (II)

FOUND-, to pour, melt (XIII)

FRANG-, FRING-, FRACT-, to break (XVII)

FUND-, FUS-, to pour, melt (XIII)

G

GEN-, to give birth to, produce (IX)

GEN-, GENER-, race, kind, origin (IX)

GER-, GEST-, to carry, produce (XVIII)

GNO-, to know (XX)

GRAD-, to step, go (V)

GRAN-, grain (XVII)

GRAND-, great (II)

GRAT-, pleasing, grateful (XXII)

GRAV-, heavy (II)

GREG-, flock, herd (IV)

GRESS-, to step, go (V)

GRIEV-, heavy (II)

H

HAB-, to have, hold as customary (IV)

HER-, HES-, to stick (X)

HIB-, to have, hold as customary (IV)

I

I-, to go (XVI)

IG-, to do, drive (XVIII)

IQU-, equal, even (VII)

IT-, to go (XVI)

J

JAC-, JECT-, to throw (XIX)

JOIN-, JOINT-, a yoke; to join (XVI)

JOURN-, day (XIV)

JUDIC-, judgment (III)

JUG-, JUNCT-, a yoke; to join (XVI)

JUR-, JUST-, right, law; to take an oath, form an opinion (III)

L

LAT-, to bear, carry (VII)

LATER-, side (IX)

LECT-, to choose, pick out, read (XVI)

LEG-, to choose, pick out, read (XVI)

LEV-, light (in weight); to lift (III)

LIG-, to choose, pick out, read (XVI)

LIGN-, line (II)

LINE-, line (II)

LOC-, place (XX)

LOCUT-, to speak (III)

LOQU-, to speak (III)

LUC-, to shine; light (IX)

LUD-, to play, mock (III)

LUMIN-, to shine; light (IX)

LUS-, to play, mock (III)

M

MAGN-, great (VII)

MAL(E)-, bad (VII)

MAN(U), hand (XXIII)

MATR-, MATERN-, mother (XV)

MEDI-, middle (XXI)

MIGR-, to move from one place to another (XXI)

MILL-, thousand (VI)

MINOR-, MINUS-, MINUT-, small, smaller (XVII)

MISC-, to mix (XXII)

MIS(S)-, to send, let go (XVIII)
MIT(T)-, to send, let go (XVIII)
MIXT-, to mix (XXII)
MOD-, measure (XI)
MON-, to warn, advise (XVI)
MORT-, death (XXI)
MOT-, to move (XXII)
MOV-, to move (XXII)
MULT-, many (VII)
MUT-, to change (XI)

N

NASC-, NAT-, to be born (XIII)
NEC-, to harm, kill (XII)
NEG-, to deny (XXII)
NIC-, to harm, kill (XII)
NIHIL-, nothing (II)
NO-, to know (XX)
NOC-, to harm, kill (XII)
NOMEN-, NOMIN-, name, noun (XIX)
NOT-, to know (XX)
NOUNC-, to announce (XXIV)
NOV-, new (XII)
NOX-, to harm, kill (XII)
NUL(L)-, nothing (II)
NUNCI-, to announce (XXIV)

O

OCT-, eight (VI)
OCTAV-, eighth (VI)
OMN-, all (VIII)
OPTIM-, best (VII)
OR-, to speak formally, plead (XIV)
ORD(IN)-, to put in order, arrange (X)
OUND-, wave (V)

P

PAR-, to ready, bring forth, provide (IX)
PART-, part (II)

PASS-, to endure, suffer (XVII)
PATI-, to endure, suffer (XVII)
PATR-, PATERN-, father (XV)
PATRI-, fatherland, country (XV)
PATRON-, protector (XV)
PED-, foot (IV)
PEL(L)-, to drive, push (XIII)
PEND-, PENS-, to hang, weigh, pay (V)
PET-, to seek, assail (XXI)
PLE-, PLET-, PLEN-, to fill; full (V)
PLEX-, PLIC-, PLY-, to fold, tangle, interweave (VII)
PON-, to place, put (XIII)
PORT-, to carry (XXIII)
POSE-, POSIT-, to place, put (XIII)
POSS-, POT-, to be able, have power (X)
POUND-, to place, put (XIII)
PREC-, to request, beg; prayer (III)
PRESS-, to press (XXIV)
PRIM-, first (VI)
PROB-, good; to test (XIV)
PROPRI-, one's own, fitting (XXIV)
PROV-, good; to test (XIV)
PUG(N)-, to fight; fist (XXI)
PULS-, to drive, push (XIII)
PUNCT-, to prick; point (IV)
PUNG-, to prick; point (IV)
PURG-, to clean (XXII)
PUT-, to prune, reckon, think (XX)

Q

QUADR(U)-, four (VI)
QUART-, fourth (VI)
QUEST-, to ask, seek (XVII)

QUINT-, fifth (VI)
QUIR-, QUISIT-, to ask, seek
(XVII)

R

RADIC-, root (XX)
RAP-, RAPT-, to seize (XIV)
RECT-, REG-, right, straight; to
rule, straighten, stiffen (VIII)
REPT-, to seize (XIV)
RIG-, right, straight; to rule,
straighten, stiffen (VIII)
ROG-, to ask (XX)

S

SACR-, sacred (IV)
SAL-, SALT-, to leap (X)
SANCT-, holy (IV)
SAT(IS)-, enough (XXIV)
SCI-, to know (XIII)
SCRIB-, SCRIPT-, to write
(XIX)
SEC-, to cut (XVII)
SECR-, sacred (IV)
SECT-, to cut (XVII)
SECUT-, to follow (XV)
SED-, to sit, settle (X)
SEG-, to cut (XVII)
SEMI-, half, partly (VI)
SEN-, old (IX)
SENS-, to feel, think (IV)
SENT-, to feel, think (IV)
SEPT(EM)-, seven (VI)
SEQU-, to follow (XV)
SERV-, to serve, save (IX)
SESS-, to sit, settle (X)
SEXT-, six; sixth (VI)
SID-, to sit, settle (X)
SIL-, to leap (X)
SIMIL-, SIMUL-, like, similar
(VIII)
SIST-, to stand (XIX)
SOL-, alone (XV)

SOLUT-, to free, loosen (XVI)
SOLV-, to free, loosen (XVI)
SON-, sound (XVIII)
SPEC-, SPIC-, SPECT-, to
look (V)
SPIR-, to breathe (XX)
ST(A)-, STIT-, to stand (XIX)
STRAIN-, STRICT-,
STRING-, to draw tight (XIV)
STRU-, STRUCT-, to build
(XXIII)
SULT-, to leap (X)

T

TACT-, to touch (XI)
TAIN-, to hold (VIII)
TANG-, to touch (XI)
TEMPER-, TEMPOR-, time,
due season; to set bounds (VIII)
TEN-, to hold, (VIII)
TEND-, TENS-, to stretch,
strive (VIII)
TENT-, to hold (VIII)
TENT-, to stretch, strive (VIII)
TENU-, stretched, thin (VIII)
TERMIN-, boundary, end
(XXIII)
TERR-, land, earth (X)
TIN-, to hold (VIII)
TING-, to touch (XI)
TRI-, three (VI)
TRACT-, to drag, draw (XI)
TORT-, to twist (XIII)
TRUD-, TRUS-, to push, thrust
(III)
TURB-, to disturb (IV)

U

UN-, one (VI)
UND-, wave (V)

V

VAIL-, to be strong, be worthy
(XVIII)

VAL-, to be strong, bc worthy (XVIII)

VEN-, VENT-, VENU-, to come (III)

VER-, true (XIV)

VERB-, word, verb (II)

VERS-, to turn (IV)

VERT-, to turn (IV)

VEST-, garment (II)

VI(A)-, way, road (IV)

VID-, VIEW-, to see (V)

VINC-, VINCT-, to conquer (XXIII)

VIS-, to see (V)

VIV-, to live (XV)

VOC-, VOK-, voice; to call (V)

VOLUT-, to roll (XIX)

VOLV-, to roll (XIX)

VULG-, common, ordinary (XXII)

PART II

Word elements
from Greek

INTRODUCTION

In general, Greek has not exerted so continuous nor so extensive an influence upon English as Latin has. In many specialized areas of study, however, Greek has furnished the majority of technical terms and even more than Latin has become the language of science. Since we live in a scientific age, therefore, the study of the Greek elements in our language will be found as useful as the study of the Latin elements. Furthermore, compound words of Greek origin tend to be more self-explanatory than those of Latin, so that a knowledge of bases, prefixes, and suffixes is often even more helpful in the case of the former.

Words of Greek origin have generally entered English in one of three ways: (1) they have come indirectly by way of Latin; (2) they have been borrowed directly from Greek writers; (3) especially in the case of scientific terms, they have been formed in modern times by combining Greek elements in new ways.

I.   Until the Renaissance there was little direct contact between Greek and English; Greek was known to only a handful of scholars in Western Europe during the Middle Ages. But, as we have seen from the Introduction to Part I, there was considerable borrowing from Latin by English during the early periods, and many Greek words had become part of the Latin language.

The reason why Latin was greatly influenced by Greek is not difficult to see. When Rome was little more than a collection of shepherds' huts beside the Tiber, Greece possessed a great and flourishing civilization. Eventually, of course, Roman armies conquered Greece, but the conqueror was in turn taken captive by Greek culture. Greek poetry and drama provided the models for Roman literature; Greek statues adorned the homes of Roman statesmen; Roman students flocked to Athens to complete their education by studying Greek philosophy and oratory. It was only natural, then, that many Greek words should have been introduced into Latin.

Thus, on the various occasions when Latin words were being borrowed by English, words of Greek were entering as well. Some of the products, for instance, which Roman civilization introduced to the primitive Germanic tribes who later brought their language to the British Isles bore Greek names; e.g., *butter* (Greek, *boutyron*), *dish* (Greek, *diskos*), and *anchor* (Greek, *ankyra*). Christianity arose in an area where Greek served as the common language and, when the new religion reached Rome, it brought with it a number of Greek words.

These were in turn introduced into English when Roman missionaries converted the Angles and Saxons. Such Greek words as *alms, anthem,* and *deacon* were borrowed in this fashion by our language.

II.   The great majority of words from Greek, however, have been borrowed in a more direct fashion. With the Renaissance came a revival of interest in classical antiquity. The study of Greek began to flourish again, and terms were borrowed from the works of the great Greek writers by men who were almost as familiar with the language of Plato and Aristotle as with their own and who regarded the ancient authors as the supreme thinkers and models of literary expression.

III.   Once a considerable number of Greek words were to be found in English, these began to be combined and recombined in ways never known to the Greeks, and among many of the sciences today this has become the accepted practice in forming words to designate new discoveries. Such modern medical terms as *antibiotic, leukemia, allergy, poliomyelitis,* and *electrocardiograph* were coined in this way from Greek elements, while in other biological sciences have appeared terms like *chromosome, protoplasm,* and *chlorophyll,* also formed in recent times from the Greek. In psychology the same process has given us *schizophrenia, psychiatry, kleptomania,* and *psychoneurosis.*

ASSIGNMENT

The words which came from Greek before the Renaissance were generally popular borrowings, that is, they were adopted by the common people, who knew no Greek, rather than by scholars. Furthermore, such words often entered English indirectly, not only by way of Latin, but sometimes by way of Old French, or even, in some cases, through Arabic. They therefore usually show considerable divergence in form from the Greek original. Sometimes the same Greek word was later reborrowed with a different meaning and in a form more closely resembling the Greek.

I.   The following words have come from Greek. With the aid of a dictionary give the Greek word from which each is derived and the meaning of the Greek word; also give another English derivative more closely resembling the original Greek form. (In most cases this will be a doublet.)

Examples: 1. dish—(Gk diskos, quoit, discus)—disk   (or discus)
            2. treasure—(Gk thesauros, a treasure)—thesaurus

1. bishop
2. blame
3. chair
4. desk
5. devil

6. glamour
7. palsy
8. parole
9. priest
10. story

II. With the aid of a dictionary trace the route of each of the following words from Greek to Modern English:

1. alms
2. box
3. chimney
4. church

5. elixir
6. pew
7. prow (of a ship)

III. The following common English words are also derived from Greek. In the case of each give the Greek original and its meaning.

1. almond
2. cherry
3. date (fruit)
4. fancy
5. frantic
6. guitar

7. lantern
8. licorice
9. place
10. surgeon, surgery
11. truck (vehicle)

LESSON I

WORDS FROM GREEK MYTHOLOGY

Many words in our language have been derived from proper names, the names of people, cities, etc. One obvious purpose in the formation of such words is to designate scientific or technical processes and inventions. For example, the verb *pasteurize* is derived from the name of the celebrated scientist who discovered the process, Louis Pasteur. A grimmer example of this type is seen in the French instrument of execution, the guillotine, which is called by the name of the man who proposed its use during the Reign of Terror. (He was not himself executed by this device, as is often supposed.) The origins of many terms, however, are more obscure although they are just as interesting; for example, the word *derrick,* which now has a quite commonplace meaning, comes from the surname of a well-known seventeenth-century hangman of Tyburn Prison in London.

Frequently a product is named from the place where it was first produced. This is particularly true with types of cloth and clothing. Thus, *calico* was originally imported from Calicut, a city in India; *muslin,* from Mosul, a city in what is now Iraq. *Jean,* a cloth used in blue jeans, was first made in Genoa, and *denim* is short for *serge de Nîmes,* "serge of Nîmes," a city in Southern France. Also, this practice of naming products after places seems almost invariable in the case of European wines, *port,* for instance, coming from Oporto, in Portugal, and *sherry,* from Xeres (Jerez), a Spanish town near Cádiz.

In other cases, the name of an individual famous in history, literature, or legend has become proverbial for some particular characteristic. Thus, we speak of a traitor as a *Judas;* and an uncultured, unenlightened person is a *Philistine.* Both of these examples are, of course, taken from the Bible, which has given us many other terms including *babel, Nimrod, doubting Thomas,* and *good Samaritan.* Along with the Bible, Greek culture has also greatly enriched the vocabulary of our language in this fashion. The mythology of the Greeks especially has impressed itself upon European literature and art, as is shown by the following passage from Shakespeare, where Hamlet describes his dead father:

> See what a grace was seated on this brow;
> Hyperion's curls, the front of Jove himself,
> An eye like Mars to threaten and command;
> A station like the herald Mercury
> New-lighted on a heaven-kissing hill.

The legends of Greece, with their gods and heroes, have consequently provided English with more words derived from proper names than perhaps any other single source, and many of these words have extremely interesting backgrounds.

The following are some of the words which Greek mythology has contributed to English together with examples of their use and brief descriptions of their origins. You will find that a knowledge of the background of such words will make them more vivid and will often give them added significance. Note that some of these words are still capitalized, while others have been used as common nouns to such an extent that they are generally written with a small initial letter.

1. *Achilles' heel,* "a single vulnerable spot"

The ability of consuming nations to reduce their consumption voluntarily proved to be the *Achilles' heel* in the OPEC plan to raise oil prices and keep them high.

Achilles was the greatest of the Greek heroes who took part in the Trojan War, and in this war he was killed. His mother, a goddess, was aware that her son was fated to die in battle, and she did everything in her power to protect him. When he was a baby, she dipped him in the River Styx (see *Stygian* below), the waters of which rendered his body invulnerable. But she held Achilles by his heel, which the water consequently did not touch. During the siege of Troy he received a fatal wound from an arrow that struck this one unprotected part.

2. *Adonis,* "an extremely handsome young man"

The casting director's office was full of *Adonises* waiting for screen tests.

Adonis was a very beautiful youth, so beautiful in fact that the goddess Aphrodite (the Romans called her Venus) fell in love with him. When Adonis was killed while hunting a wild boar, Aphrodite was inconsolable and obtained from Zeus, king of the gods, the promise that her beloved might leave the Underworld to spend part of each year with her.

3. *aegis,* "sponsorship or protection"

Rome remained inviolable beneath the *aegis* of her ancient prestige. —John Addington Symonds

In Greek mythology the aegis was a piece of armor or shield worn by Zeus and later by the goddess Athena. It was not only an awesome defense but filled with horror those against whom it was shaken.

4. *amazon,* "a powerful, masculine woman"

Detractors of the women's liberation movement seem to proclaim the stereotype that its advocates are unfeminine *amazons.*

The Amazons were a legendary race of female warriors who supposedly lived in the region of the Black Sea and often fought the Greeks. In the Trojan War they were allies of Troy, and their queen was slain by Achilles. The great Amazon River in South America received its name from the fact that early Spanish explorers, during battles with the Indians along its banks, observed women fighting beside the men.

5. *atlas,* "a collection of maps"

Atlas, one of the Titans (see *titanic* below), was condemned to support the world on his shoulders. Apparently because early books of maps so frequently pictured Atlas performing this task, they came to bear his name. In anatomical terminology *atlas* refers also to the first vertebra of the neck, which supports the skull as the giant supposedly did the world.

6. *Cassandra,* "a person who warns of coming evil but whose prophecies are disregarded"

I have, as you know, long foretold the now approaching catastrophe; but I was *Cassandra.*—Lord Chesterfield

Cassandra was a Trojan princess with whom the god Apollo fell in love. To win her favors, he bestowed on her the gift of prophecy, but when she resisted his advances, instead of taking back his gift, he decreed a far worse punishment, that no one should believe her warnings. Thus Cassandra was condemned to the frustration of prophesying in vain the fall of Troy, while her hearers not only failed to heed her but regarded her dire predictions as the ravings of an insane person.

7. *chimera,* "a foolish or idle fancy"

All those alarms which have been sounded...must be ascribed to the *chimerical* fears of the authors of them.—*The Federalist*

The Chimera was a fire-breathing monster with the head of a lion, the body of a goat, and the tail of a dragon. It was so fantastic a hybrid that it became the symbol of vain imaginings.

8. *Elysium,* "place or state of blissful happiness"

Again you say, you much fear that that *Elysium* of which you have dreamed so much is never to be realized.—Abraham Lincoln

In Greek mythology the Elysian Fields, or Elysium, was the abode after death of those who had led good lives; it was a region of ideal happiness, to some extent the equivalent of the Christian heaven.

9. *Gorgon,* "a snaky-haired creature so ugly as to petrify an onlooker"

When he plays Dirty Harry Callahan, Clint Eastwood acts with his pulsating blood vessels. Two veins run down his high forehead like stray hairs on a *Gorgon.*—*Time*

The Gorgons were three sister monsters with wings of gold, bronze hands, and with purple tongues protruding from their mouths between swine-tusk teeth; serpents writhing on their head replaced their hair. A glimpse of them would turn a man to stone. Perseus managed to kill Medusa, the mortal Gorgon, with the aid of a magic sword and a polished shield which he used for guiding the mortal blow.

10. *halcyon,* "calm; peaceful"

During those *halcyon* years before the invasion of Charles VIII, it seemed as though the peace of Italy might last unbroken.—Symonds

The expression *halcyon days,* meaning a period of calm and tranquility, takes its origin from the ancient belief that the kingfisher, called *halcyon* by the Greeks, hatched its young in a nest floating on the sea. During its nesting period the bird supposedly calmed the weather by means of a magic charm so that the waves were quiet and it could brood undisturbed.

According to myth, the kingfisher, whose Greek name was also spelled *alcyon,* had once been a woman, Alcyone, wife of Ceyx, the king of Thessaly. Alcyone had mourned so piteously for her husband who was drowned in the ocean that the gods changed both into sea birds so that they might be reunited.

11. *herculean,* "very powerful"

He was short in stature...but his limbs were of *Herculean* mold. —Edgar Allan Poe

Hercules, son of Zeus and a mortal mother, was of course the strongest of all the heroes of Greek fable. In particular, he was renowned for a series of mighty deeds, the "labors of Hercules," imposed upon him by the goddess Hera, who hoped that he would be killed in the performance of them.

12. *hydra,* "a persistent evil, one difficult to eradicate"

Thirteen independent courts of final jurisdiction over the same causes ...is a *hydra* in government from which nothing but contradiction and confusion can proceed.—*The Federalist*

One of the labors of Hercules was to slay the Hydra, a poisonous water serpent with nine heads whose very breath was fatal. The difficulty of this task was increased by the fact that, when one of the heads was cut off, two more grew in its place; but Hercules solved the problem by having an assistant sear the neck with a hot iron after each head had been severed.

13. *labyrinth,* "a complicated arrangement of passageways or roads; a maze"

We rattled with great rapidity through such a *labyrinth* of streets, that I soon lost all idea where we were.—Dickens

The original labyrinth was a huge structure full of intricate passageways, which was built at the order of King Minos of Crete as a place of confinement for the Minotaur, a monster half bull and half man. Those whom the King wished to destroy were placed in the labyrinth, from which they were unable to find an exit, and where they wandered until they were discovered and eaten by the Minotaur or died of starvation.

14. *mentor,* "a wise counselor"

Had she been brought up by any sterner *mentor* than that fond father...she might perhaps have saved herself from this great fault.
—Anthony Trollope

Mentor, a word usually found nowadays in the sports section of newspapers where it refers to a football coach, comes from the name of the faithful adviser to whom Odysseus entrusted the education of his son when he sailed away to fight at Troy.

15. *Midas,* "a very rich man"

You could feel just as certain that he was opulent as if he had exhibited his bank account, or as if you had seen him touching the twigs of the Pyncheon Elm, and *Midas*-like, transmuting them to gold.
—Hawthorne

Midas was a legendary king of Asia Minor, whose desire for riches was apparently exceeded only by his lack of intelligence. Once he had performed a service for one of the gods and in return was granted the fulfillment of a wish. Without thinking, Midas asked to be given the power of turning into gold whatever he touched. To his dismay, however, he discovered that not only the roses in his garden and the tables in his palace were changed to gold, but also the food and drink which he tried in vain to swallow. So he was the richest and hungriest king in all the world until the god had pity on him and told him to rid himself of this fatal gift by bathing in the River Pactolus, whose sands were ever after rich in gold.

16. *narcissism,* "abnormal attachment to one's own appearance and personality"

Psychologists set forth that anyone who becomes an actor in the first place must be a *narcissist,* yearning for ever-new romantic mirrors to provide adoration.—*Time*

Narcissus was a beautiful youth whom the nymph Echo loved. When he did not return her affection, Echo pined away from grief until nothing was left of her but her voice. Aphrodite, however, punished Narcissus for his cruel neglect. One day, as he leaned down to drink from a clear pool, he spied his own reflection in the water and at once fell in love with it. Unable to tear himself away, he was consumed by his longing for this figure which he saw in the pool and finally was changed into the flower which bears his name.

17. *nemesis,* "retribution; one who inflicts retribution"

The fantastic valuation which we put upon youthful beauty in women, for example, brings its *nemesis* in bedizened crones.—*Atlantic Monthly*

Nemesis was a goddess, the personification of righteous anger. She hated every transgression of the proper order of things and inflicted punishment on the wicked for their sins.

18. *odyssey,* "a long series of wanderings"

He made his way on foot from Cairo to South Africa, and on his return to America he described his *odyssey* in a long article.

Homer's epic poem, the *Odyssey,* tells of the wanderings of the Greek hero Odysseus in attempting to return to his home and family at the conclusion of the Trojan War. After being driven by adverse winds and by the anger of the gods over the wide reaches of the Mediterranean, and after encountering many strange adventures and misfortunes, Odysseus finally reached his native land ten years after he had set sail from Troy.

19. *Oedipus* (complex), "an abnormal attachment to one's parent of the opposite sex with corresponding hostility to the other"

Also, Freud's unusual family setting, with a young mother, but a father old enough to be his grandfather, led to overemphasis on *Oedipal* feelings.—*Time*

Like the story of Narcissus, the myth of Oedipus has suggested to modern psychologists the name for a mental state. Oedipus, the subject of a famous tragedy by Sophocles, learned of a prophecy that he would one day kill his father and marry his mother. He did all in his power to avoid this dreadful fate, only to discover, after he had risen to greatness, that despite his efforts the prophecy had come true, whereupon he blinded himself and went into exile.

20. *Olympian,* "exalted; majestic"

He, the ruler of that minute world, seldom descended from the *Olympian* heights.—Joseph Conrad

The most familiar of the Greek gods are those who dwelt on Mt. Olympus: Zeus, or Jupiter, to give him his Roman name, Hera or Juno, Aphrodite or Venus, and the rest. Though there are many stories about their scandalous behavior, *Olympian* today refers to the calm, imposing, majestic natures of these divine beings in their better moments, as they are represented, for instance, in classical Greek sculpture.

21. *paean,* "a song of thanksgiving or praise"

The press received the news of Gordon's mission with a *paean* of approbation.—Lord Elton

Paean came to be a name of the god Apollo, one of whose attributes was the power of healing. Many hymns of thanksgiving for recovery from illness and for averting evil were addressed to him under this title, and eventually *paean* was used to designate any hymn of thanksgiving or praise.

22. *procrustean,* also *Procrustean,* "forcing rigid conformity"

He was disposed to place all their separate and individual charters on a *Procrustean* bed, and shape them all into uniformity simply by reducing the whole to a nullity.—John Lothrop Motley

Procrustes was a legendary highwayman who possessed a grim sense of humor. He forced his victims to lie in an iron bed. Those who were too short he stretched; the limbs of those who were too long he lopped off with his sword, so that one way or the other all who fell into his hands were killed by being made to fit exactly his famous bed.

23. *protean,* "extremely changeable"

Man, being a *Protean* animal, swiftly shares and changes with his company and surroundings.—Robert Louis Stevenson

Proteus, the herdsman of the sea in Greek mythology, was able to change his shape at will. In the *Odyssey* an incident is described where one of the Greek heroes attempted to capture him. Trying to escape, Proteus turned himself first into a lion, then a snake, finally into running water and even into a tree.

24. *siren,* "an alluring but dangerous woman; seductive"

The *siren* cries of nothing down, easy credit and pay later have made the installment plan an essential part of the U.S. economy.—*Time*

The Sirens were nymphs, part woman and part bird, who sat on an island surrounded by the bones of sailors whom they had lured to destruction by the magic of their singing. Odysseus in his wanderings sailed past this island but stuffed the ears of his crewmen with wax so that they were immune to the charms of the Sirens' song. Leaving his own ears unplugged, however, he had himself bound to the ship's mast so that he could hear and yet not be enticed to his death.

25. *stentorian,* "very loud"

In another second or two the nightcap was thrust out of the chaise-window, and a *stentorian* voice bellowed to the driver to stop.
—Dickens

Stentor, who was the herald of the Greek army at Troy, was reputed to have a voice as loud as the voices of fifty ordinary men.

26. *Stygian,* also *stygian,* "dark, gloomy"

His debauched and reprobate life cast a *Stygian* gloom over the evening of his father's days.—Samuel Johnson

The Styx, as we saw in connection with Achilles, was a river of the Underworld; across it the souls of the dead were ferried by the grim old boatman Charon. To the ancients the Underworld was generally a place of darkness and gloom.

27. *tantalize,* "tease"

There lives no man who at some period has not been tormented, for example, by an earnest desire to *tantalize* a listener by circumlocution. —Edgar Allan Poe

Tantalus was admitted to the friendship of the gods, but then tried to deceive them. As punishment they decreed that he should stand eternally in a pool of water in Hades over which hung fruit-laden boughs. Whenever he leaned down for a drink, however, the water receded, and whenever he tried to pick the fruit, the branches were blown out of his reach. Thus Tantalus stood, suffering forever the pangs of hunger and thirst which were made all the keener by the nearness of food and drink.

28. *titanic,* "of enormous size and power"

General Smith does not expect that Stalin's death will precipitate a *titanic* struggle such as followed Lenin's.—*Atlantic Monthly*

The Titans were a race of primeval giants, the children of Earth and heaven, who ruled the universe before the Olympian gods with whom they fought long and bitterly. Finally the Titans were overthrown by the thunderbolts of Zeus in a war that lasted for ten years and almost destroyed the world.

Not included here are the innumerable botanical and zoological names drawn from classical mythology. Some of these names have little or no connection with their source, but others were bestowed because the organism thus designated has some characteristic of the person after whom it was named. Thus *Hydra* also refers to a genus of fresh-water polyps, so called by Linnaeus because cutting apart the bodies of these animals only serves to increase their numbers.

To cite a few more examples, Atropos was one of the Three Fates, the grim sisters who were thought of by the Greeks as spinning out the destiny of each man's life in the form of a thread and who cut it at the appointed time. Her name has provided the scientific designation for the deadly nightshade, *Atropa belladonna,* the source of the highly poisonous alkaloid atropine. Lachesis, another of the Fates, has given her name to the bushmaster, *Lachesis mutus,* the deadliest snake in the Western Hemisphere.

The Polyphemus moth (*Telea polyphemus*) was named for the grotesque giant Polyphemus, who had a single huge eye in the middle of his forehead. (He tried to eat Odysseus and was blinded by the hero.) The scientific use of the name is an allusion to the fact that the moth has a large eye-shaped marking on its wings.

ASSIGNMENT

I. Indicate the pronunciation of the following:

    1. The **ae** of *aegis* is pronounced like (1) the **i** in *bite* (2) the **a** in *gate* (3) the **e** in *equal* (4) the **e** in *tent.*

    2. The **g** of *aegis* is pronounced like the **g** in (1) *get* (2) *gem* (3) *tongue.*

    3. The **ch** of *chimera* is pronounced like (1) the **c** in *certain* (2) the **c** in *can* (3) the **sh** in *shell* (4) the **ch** in *chair.*

    4. The **i** of *chimera* is pronounced like the **i** in (1) *bite* (2) *sanity* (3) *tin.*

    5. The **c** of *halcyon* is pronounced like (1) the **c** in *certain* (2) the **c** in *can* (3) the **sh** in *shell* (4) the **ch** in *chair.*

    6. The **a** of *labyrinth* is pronounced like the **a** in (1) *gate* (2) *father* (3) *about* (4) *land.*

    7. The **y** of *labyrinth* is pronounced like the **i** in (1) *bite* (2) *sanity* (3) *tin.*

    8. The **i** of *Midas* is pronounced like the **i** in (1) *bite* (2) *sanity* (3) *tin.*

    9. The **oe** of *Oedipus* is pronounced like the **e** in (1) *equal* (2) *agent* (3) *tent.*

    10. The **u** of *Oedipus* is pronounced like the **u** in (1) *sue* (2) *put* (3) *cube* (4) *up.*

    11. The **ae** of *paean* is pronounced like (1) the **i** in *bite* (2) the **a** in *gate* (3) the **e** in *equal* (4) the **e** in *tent.*

    12. The **e** of *siren* is pronounced like the **e** in (1) *equal* (2) *agent* (3) *tent.*

    13. The **y** of *Stygian* is pronounced like the **i** in (1) *bite* (2) *sanity* (3) *tin.*

II. Circle the syllable on which the primary accent falls in each of the following:

    1. aeolian   5. narcissism

    2. chimera   6. nemesis

    3. herculean   7. Procrustean

    4. labyrinth   8. stentorian

LESSON II

WORDS FROM GREEK HISTORY AND PHILOSOPHY

At a time when a thorough acquaintance with classical culture was the mark of an educated man, a number of words from the names of persons, or places, or institutions connected with Greek history and philosophy entered our language. In fact, by tracing the origins of many of these words, one can see reflected some of the great events of Greek life and thought. Thus, the long race known as a *marathon* received its designation from the Plain of Marathon, the site of a historic victory by the Athenians over the Persian invaders, because the messenger who reported the good news to Athens ran so swiftly. The modern race of approximately 26 miles represents the distance between Athens and Marathon. *Solon,* a term generally seen nowadays in newspapers with reference to a senator, was originally the name of a statesman who was commissioned to reform the laws of Athens and whose wise measures marked perhaps the beginning of Western democracy.

The following are some of the words which Greek culture and history have contributed to English, together with examples of their use and brief descriptions of their origins.

1. *academy,* "a school or learned society"

The financially successful painters were the *academicians* who perpetuated the mannerisms of the past.—*Harper's Magazine*

Near Athens was a grove of olive trees sacred to the hero Academus. In this grove the philosopher Plato and his successors taught, and this school of philosophy was consequently known as the *Academy.* Because of the school's vast influence upon European thought, the name passed into the language to designate various types of educational institutions or learned groups.

2. *Arcadian,* "simple, peaceful, rustic"

We had in this region, twenty years ago, among our educated men, a sort of *Arcadian* fanaticism, a passionate desire to go upon the land and unite farming to intellectual pursuits.—Emerson

The region of Greece known in classical times as Arcadia is quite mountainous. It was therefore rather inaccessible and so was well known for its peaceful, rustic way of life.

3. *Croesus,* "a very rich man"

You are aware that my father—once reckoned a *Croesus* of wealth—became bankrupt a short time previous to his death.—Charlotte Brontë

Croesus, like Midas, was a very wealthy king of Asia Minor. Croesus, however, was a historical figure, while Midas was legendary. In an age of barter, Croesus' kingdom had been one of the first nations to mint coins of precious metal; it had, so to speak, invented money. (This was actually before Croesus' time, however.) Also, Croesus sent magnificent offerings to the temples of Greece, and these likewise impressed the Greeks with his wealth and luxury. Later his kingdom was conquered by the Persians, and his life was consequently regarded as furnishing the supreme example of a disastrous change of fortune.

4. *cynic,* "one who sarcastically doubts human motives"

To every remonstrance he listened with a *cynical* sneer, wondering within himself whether those who lectured him were such fools as they professed to be, or were only shamming.—Macaulay

A *Cynic* was originally a member of a Greek philosophical school noted for its exaggerated contempt of social conventions and institutions. The most famous of the Cynics, Diogenes, since he wished to show the uselessness of civilized customs, lived in a large earthenware tub; and to demonstrate his scorn for the rest of society, he went about in broad daylight with a lantern looking, as he said, for an honest man.

5. *Draconian,* "extremely severe"

Thanks to Macmillan's *Draconian* measures, Britain stood a good chance of staving off fiscal disaster.—*Time*

In the seventh century B.C. Draco was given special authority by the Athenians to codify and systemize their laws. In the resulting code certain minor offenses, such as stealing a cabbage, were made punishable by death, and the laws of Draco thus gained a reputation for severity that caused one Greek orator to describe them as having been written not in ink but in blood.

6. *epicure,* also *epicurean,* "a person of refined taste in matters of food and drink"

The price of artichoke hearts, the *epicure*'s staple, has risen out of sight.

Epicurus was the founder of a school of philosophy which held that the supreme goal of life should be pleasure. He carefully elaborated this doctrine, however, and taught that the most effective way to achieve pleasure is through the avoidance of pain. By living temperately and righteously, one might avoid the dissipation caused by immoral acts and the frustration of unfulfilled desires. The man who led a blameless life would find the greatest amount of pleasure in the long run. Unfortunately, many people, including some who claimed to be Epicurus's followers, failed to note his restriction of the idea of pleasure, and so his name has unfairly become associated with the doctrine of "eat, drink, and be merry," and in particular has reference to the delights of the table. The Greek word for pleasure gives us a blanket term for all such indulgent attitudes—*hedonism, hedonistic.*

7. to cut the *Gordian* knot, "to solve a difficult problem by direct and drastic means"

Never was such a tangled knottiness,
But this authority cuts the *Gordian* through.—Browning

According to legend, a king named Gordius once tied an extremely intricate knot, whereupon a prophecy arose that whoever untied it would rule Asia. Many tried and failed, and the knot remained on public display until Alexander the Great, on being shown it and finding himself unable to penetrate its intricacies, whipped out his sword and cut it, thus turning the prophecy to his advantage by showing that he would become ruler of Asia with the sword. The whole story is highly improbable but it has given our language an expressive phrase.

8. *laconic,* "brief, pithy, concise"

He seemed to be of a *laconic* disposition, and merely said, "How goes it?"—Dickens

Laconia was another name for Sparta. (Actually it was the district of Greece in which the city of Sparta was located.) The Spartan citizens were trained from childhood to be soldiers and little else; everything in their upbringing was aimed at making them perfectly disciplined warriors. They consequently acquired the reputation of being blunt and decisive men of few words. There is a story that an enemy, threatening war, sent the Spartans an ultimatum that if he invaded Laconia, he would raze Sparta to the ground, whereupon the Spartans sent back the reply, "If—."

9. *mausoleum,* "a large tomb"

He saw the house was occupied and animated—if animation might be talked about in a place which had hitherto answered to his idea of a magnificent *mausoleum.*—Henry James

When King Mausolus of Caria died, his wife was inconsolable. She built a magificent tomb in his honor called the Mausoleum, which was numbered among the Seven Wonders of the World.

10. *meander,* "to follow a winding course," "the Greek-key design"

Among their smooth trunks a clear brook *meandered* for a time in twining lacets before it made up its mind to take a leap into the hurrying river.—Joseph Conrad

The Meander, now called Menderes, is a river in Turkey which was proverbial in ancient times for its crooked, wandering course.

11. *ostracism,* "exclusion from society"

...the reason for the *ostracism:* the child has been infected from birth with herpes.—*Time*

Ancient Athens was one of the first democracies in the world and contributed many of its political ideals to later ages, but one rather peculiar Athenian institution may seem overly dramatic. To prevent an individual from demagoguery and to bar anyone from rising to dictatorship, Athens held, on occasion, a special election in which each voter inscribed on a broken piece of pottery (called *ostrakon* in Greek) the name of the man whom he considered most dangerous to the state. If 6000 ballots were cast, the person who received the greatest number of votes was sent into exile for ten years. Upon his return his family, property, and good name were resumable.

12. *philippic,* "a bitter denunciation"

Savonarola added withering *philippics* on the tyranny of Lorenzo the Magnificent.—*Time*

Philip of Macedon, the father of Alexander the Great, was determined to gain control of all Greece, but he carefully concealed his designs, playing the jealous and naive Greek city-states one against the other. The Athenian statesman Demosthenes, however, clearly realized Philip's intentions and, denouncing him in a series of bitter orations, sought to arouse the other Greek states against the common danger. From the subject of their attack, these orations were nicknamed the *Philippics.* Subsequently the term has come to refer to any bitter verbal attack.

13. a *Pyrrhic* victory, "a victory won at too great a cost"

His victory in securing the nomination could only be described as *Pyrrhic,* for the bad feeling caused by the struggle cost him the election.

Pyrrhus, King of Epirus and second cousin of Alexander the Great, was a skillful military commander; when he was exiled from his native land, he became a soldier of fortune. On one occasion he accepted the invitation of the Greeks in southern Italy to lead their armies against the Romans. The Roman generals were no match for Pyrrhus, who won several battles against them. But the Roman infantrymen showed great courage; they refused to retreat, and they died where they stood, inflicting such heavy losses on Pyrrhus's troops that after the Battle of Asculum Pyrrhus is reported to have said as he surveyed the gaps in the ranks of his armies, "One more such victory and we are undone."

14. *solecism,* "a substandard usage of language, a social blunder"

Ladies highly born, highly bred, and naturally quick witted, were unable to write a line in their mother tongue without *solecisms* and faults of spelling.—Macaulay

The Greeks sent many colonists to other lands in the Mediterranean, to southern Italy, the Black Sea region, and the coast of Asia Minor. At one such colony, Soli, the last outpost of Greek civilization, the inhabitants had developed such a barbarous dialect that the name of the town became proverbial for grammatical mistakes. By extension, *solecism* has come to mean "social error" as well as "incorrectness of speech."

15. *sophistry, sophism,* "clever but deceptive argumentation meant to mislead"

But he had one of those happily constituted intellects which, across labyrinths of *sophistry,* and through masses of immaterial facts, go straight to the true point.—Macaulay

Beyond elementary training in the reading and reciting of traditional texts, most Greek communities had no system for educating the young. To fill this need for the wealthy classes, a group of itinerant teachers traveled about giving instruction in grammar, rhetoric, logic, and, in some places, public speaking. Their elevated skills (*sophia* in Greek) gave them their name, sophists. In some communities speech to persuade the mob was more politically effective than analysis of the issues, and some sophists taught such politically motivated oratory as their stock-in-trade. The conservative opponents of higher education fastened upon this abuse to blacken the name sophist for all time. The chief spokesman for this attack on *sophistry* was the philosopher Plato, whose eloquence was owed, ironically, at least in part to the sophistic tradition.

16. *Spartan,* "rigorous, austere, disciplined"

They were in no sense elaborate or pretentious, but designed on simple, functional lines, not for luxurious but for rather *Spartan* living.—*Harper's Magazine*

The Spartans were famed as the bravest and hardiest warriors of Greece. Everything about their training from earliest childhood was designed to make them able to endure the rigors of military service and to instill in them a single-minded devotion to their country. At the age of seven, boys were taken from their mothers and sent to train in barracks, where they were made to do without any of the usual comforts. They were forced to wear thin clothing and go barefoot in winter, to sleep without covering, and to forage for their food. So that the citizens of Sparta would have nothing to distract them from their dedication to the state, they were forbidden to own private property, and their family life was rigidly restricted. All this resulted in an admirable simplicity and incorruptability; hence *Spartan* is usually a complimentary term.

17. *stoic,* "impassive"

He looked around him in agony, and was surprised, even in that moment, to see the *stoical* indifference of his fellow-prisoners.—Sir Walter Scott

One of the teachings of Stoicism, a Greek philosophical school, was that the universe is governed by a divine providence, and so whatever happens is for the best. Consequently, loss, pain, and death are evil only through the lens of an undisciplined attitude. In reality such events provide the opportunity for us to surmount our fallible natures and earn true inner peace by aligning ourselves with providence. *Stoic* endurance became legendary.

18. *sword of Damocles,* "a constantly threatening danger"

The nuclear arsenal is a sword of Damocles not only for those nations which persist in arming themselves with these weapons, but for the world at large which is threatened not by instant annihilation but by lingering death from radioactive fallout and nuclear winter.

Damocles, seeing the power and magnificence of Dionysius, tyrant or dictator of Syracuse, constantly referred to him as the happiest of men; whereupon Dionysius determined to show this deluded member of his court what a tyrant's life is really like. He invited Damocles to a delicious dinner; when in the midst of his enjoyment Damocles looked up, however, he saw a sword suspended over his head by a single thread, illustrating the ever-present danger in which a dictator lives.

19. *sybarite,* "one devoted to luxury and pleasure"

He led the life of a *sybarite* in the famous palace and gardens of Azahara, surrounding himself with all that could excite the imagination and delight the senses.—Washington Irving

Sybaris was a Greek colony in southern Italy famed for its wealth and luxurious living. It was destroyed by a less wealthy, but also less self-indulgent, neighbor.

The names of people and places in other ages have also greatly enriched the English vocabulary. For instance, the eighteenth-century Earl of Sandwich was so addicted to gambling that, according to report, he could not bring himself to leave the gaming table long enough for meals, but had food brought to him. In order to eat and at the same time hold his cards, he resorted to the practice of putting meat between two slices of bread and thus gave his name to the article of food which is so common today.

ASSIGNMENT

I. The following are some additional examples of words derived from proper names. With the aid of a dictionary identify the persons or places whose names they represent, and determine their meanings.

1. bedlam

The neighborhood surrounding Tiger Stadium became a *bedlam* following Detroit's victory in the World Series.

2. boycott

They are being ostracized, their shops...are completely *boycotted,* their children without a school.—*Time*

3. dunce

Great new theories share the fate of great old theories: they seem to be the work of *dunces.*

4. Frankenstein

Its advocates have not yet succeeded in stripping nuclear power of its *Frankensteinian* mask.

5. jeremiad

Dr. Caldecott's *jeremiad* against nuclear arms must be preached among all the nations.

6. maudlin

He burst into tears of *maudlin* pity for himself.—Dickens

7. quixotic

What wonder, then, if the Spaniard of that day, feeding his imagination with dreams of enchantment at home, and with its realities abroad, should have displayed a *Quixotic* enthusiasm!—William Hickling Prescott

8. simony

He did not scruple to become a broker in *simony* of a peculiarly discreditable kind, and to use a bishopric as a bait to tempt a divine to perjury.—Macaulay

9. tawdry

History is what happened, it is not what fits some scriptwriter's *tawdry* idea.—*Harper's Magazine*

10. utopia

It is often said that an ideal state—an *Utopia* where there is no folly, crime, or sorrow—has a singular fascination for the mind. —W.H. Hudson

II. Indicate the pronunciation of the following:

1. The **oe** of *Croesus* is pronounced like (1) the **oi** in *oil* (2) the **o** in *tone* (3) a combination of the **o** in *tone* and the **e** in *equal* (4) the **e** in *equal*.

2. The first **a** of *Draconian* is pronounced like the **a** in (1) *land* (2) *gate* (3) *father* (4) *about*.

3. The **o** of *Draconian* is pronounced like the **o** in (1) *pot* (2) *tone* (3) *wisdom*.

4. The **a** of *laconic* is pronounced like the **a** in (1) *land* (2) *about* (3) *gate* (4) *father*.

5. The **o** of *laconic* is pronounced like the **o** in (1) *pot* (2) *tone* (3) *wisdom*.

6. The **e** of *mausoleum* is pronounced like (1) the **e** in *tent* (2) the **i** in *tin* (3) the **a** in *gate* (4) the **e** in *equal*.

7. The **y** of *Pyrrhic* is pronounced like the **i** in (1) *bite* (2) *fir* (3) *tin*.

8. The **o** of *solecism* is pronounced like the **o** in (1) *pot* (2) *tone* (3) *wisdom*.

9. The **c** of *solecism* is pronounced like (1) the **c** in *can* (2) the **sh** in *shell* (3) the **c** in *certain*.

10. The **y** of *sybarite* is pronounced like the **i** in (1) *bite* (2) *sanity* (3) *tin*.

11. The **ei** of *Frankenstein* is pronounced like (1) the **i** in *tin* (2) the **i** in *bite* (3) the **e** in *equal* (4) the **e** in *tent*.

12. The **i** of *simony* is pronounced like the **i** in (1) *bite* (2) *sanity* (3) *tin*.

13. The **o** of *simony* is pronounced like the **o** in (1) *pot* (2) *tone* (3) *wisdom*.

III. Circle the syllable on which the primary accent falls in each of the following:

1. Damocles
2. Draconian
3. jeremiad
4. laconic
5. mausoleum
6. meander
7. philippic
8. quixotic
9. simony
10. solecism
11. sophistry
12. sybarite

LESSON III

GREEK BASES

Most of the English words derived from Greek are compounds formed from several different elements: prefixes, bases, and suffixes, which are used repeatedly in various combinations. In this lesson we shall consider Greek bases, that is, Greek words as they appear in English derivatives, without the characteristic Greek endings, *-os, -e, -on,* etc. (These bases are sometimes also called roots, stems, or combining forms. A combining form can also be a base + suffix. Combining forms are discussed and introduced at Lesson XII following.) As in the case of Latin bases, these will be printed in capital letters followed by a hyphen, e.g., CYCL-, PYR-, SPHER-. Later we shall see how, by the addition of various prefixes and suffixes, many English words have been formed from a single base. For example, from PSYCH-, "mind," "soul," have come:

PSYCH-IATR-y	PSYCH-osis
PSYCH-o-ana-LY-sis	PSYCH-o-SOMAT-ic
PSYCH-o-logy	PSYCH-o-tic
PSYCH-o-NEUR-osis	met-em-PSYCH-osis
PSYCH-o-PATH	

The meaning given for a base will in general represent its significance in the various compounds and combinations in which it appears in English. Language, however, is an extremely changeable and flexible instrument; consequently, in the course of the many centuries during which the process of forming new words has been going on, it is only to be expected that certain variations in the meanings of bases should have appeared. For example, from the base PYR- "fire," have been formed, among others, the following words:

pyromania	a psychopathic impulse to set fires
pyrometer	an instrument for measuring extreme temperatures
pyrogenic	produced by heat
pyrosis	a disorder of the stomach accompanied by a burning sensation
pyretic	pertaining to fever
pyre	a pile of combustible material on which a dead body is burned

In all of these words PYR- represents the basic idea of "fire," yet the concept of a literally blazing heap of fuel will not apply in many of these cases. One must therefore keep a flexible mind and be prepared for the different shades and nuances of meaning which are encountered everywhere in connection with language.

Sometimes Greek bases appear in English without the addition of any prefix or suffix.

I. Occasionally a base by itself forms an English word.

Greek Base		*English Derivative*
ORGAN-	instrument	organ
ANGEL-	messenger	angel
GRAPH-	to write	graph

II. In other cases a final silent *e* is added when the base appears in English. (This *e* is not a suffix and has no meaning.)

PYR- fire	pyre
CYCL- circle, wheel	cycle
SPHER- ball	sphere

Dictionaries, in describing the origin of an English word derived from Greek, will give the actual Greek word; e.g., *angel* is listed as coming from the Greek *angelos, organ* from the Greek *organon.* If one keeps in mind the English word, however, the base ANGEL- or ORGAN- can be readily seen. In this book we will be primarily concerned with Greek bases as they appear in English words.

Often, besides the addition of an ending, one will find a difference in spelling between the actual Greek word as it is transliterated in a dictionary and its English derivatives; e.g., *cycle* is listed as coming from the Greek *kyklos,* and *sphere* from *sphaira.* Such differences are due to the fact that originally Greek words entered English by way of Latin and thus acquired a Latinized spelling. Even though later borrowing from Greek has mostly been direct, the practice of Latinization has generally, but not always, been continued. These differences in spelling between the Greek and the English (or Latinized) form are summarized below. It will be useful to remember them, for one will thus be able to recognize more easily words which have been brought from Greek into English without first receiving a Latinized spelling, as, for example, *kaleidoscope.*

Greek	*English*
k (*kyklos, konos*)	c (*cycle, cone*)

(Occasionally the *k* is kept; for example, from the Greek word *kinein,* "to move," has come *kinetic* as well as *cinema,* also *leucocyte* but *leukemia.*)

ai (*sphaira, phainomenon*)	e (*sphere, phenomenon*)

(Sometimes this appears in English as *ae;* for example, from *aisthetikos* "perceptive," comes *aesthetics* as well as *anesthetic.* In British usage *ae* is more frequent than *e,* as, for example, in the British spellings *anaesthetic* and *haemorrhage* for the American spellings *anesthetic* and *hemorrhage.*)

ei (*eidolon, eikon*)	i (*idol, icon*)

(Occasionally the *ei* is kept as an alternate spelling; e.g., both *chirography* and *cheirography* are given by dictionaries, though the former is more usual.)

oi (*oikonomia, amoibe*)   e, oe (*economy, amoeba*)

(Note that dictionaries usually give *ameba* as a variant spelling. Also, in older books *economy* is sometimes spelled *oeconomy*.)

ou (*mousike, Ouranos*)   u (*music, Uranus*)

Greek words were of course originally written with different characters from those used for English, but since these words have been transliterated in dictionaries, the Greek alphabet has been omitted from consideration in this book. Note, however, that the names of the Greek letters have provided English with such words as *iota, delta, alpha, omega,* and *alphabet* itself, as well as having given such technical terms as *sigmoid* ("curved like the letter *s*"), *chiasma* ("a crossing, as in the Greek letter *chi*"), and *lambdacism* ("difficulty in pronouncing the letter *l*"). A listing of the Greek alphabet, along with the Russian and Hebrew, can be found in some dictionaries.

ASSIGNMENT

I. Learn the following bases and their meanings. Study each base so that you can recognize it in a long compound word.

BIBLI-	book
CANON-	rule
CRYPT-, CRYPH-	hidden, secret
CYCL-	circle, wheel
GLOSS-, GLOT(T)-	tongue, language
ICON-	image
MIM-	to imitate
OD-	song, poem
PYR-	fire
TOM-	to cut

II. The foregoing bases all appear as English words by themselves or with the addition of a final *e* (with a slight exception in the case of BIBLI-). Without using a dictionary, list as many additional words formed from them as you can. Then check these words in your dictionary to make sure that they actually contain the particular Greek base. For example, *odious* has nothing to do with OD-, "song poem," but is formed from the Latin base ODI-, "hatred."

III. List the base and its meaning in each of the following italicized words and define the word as it is used in the sentence or phrase.

Example: monody—OD- song, poem: a song in which one voice carries the melody.

1. He discovered that there were few *bibliographical* aids in the subject about which he was writing a term paper.

2. They determined to propose that, in the public services of the Church, lessons taken from the *canonical* books of Scripture should be substituted for the lessons taken from the *Apocrypha.*—Macaulay

3. ...a code unbreakable by any known *cryptographic* method. —*Time*

4. His *epiglottis* went berzerkers and he had to leave the room in a fit of coughing.—Brian Levin

5. ...despite his *encyclopedic* knowledge and amazing breadth and power of his intellect, he was using little more than half his brain.—*Time*

6. It is a significant fact, stated by *entomologists*...that "some insects, in their perfect state, though furnished with organs of feeding, make no use of them."—Thoreau

7. ...the Kremlin nonetheless kept up the momentum of its demolition of Stalin and, with that, of the *iconography* of the Communist way of life for the past 30 years.—*Time*

8. He used to amuse the company by his talent at story-telling and his powers of *mimicry,* giving capital imitations of... public characters of the day.—Washington Irving

9. *Parody* obviously demands that the original parodied should be well known to the reader....—*Time*

10. ...Singapore was in reality a defenseless, *polyglot* commercial town of Chinese, Japanese, Indians, Jews and British. —*Time*

IV. Define the following italicized words as they are used in the sentence or phrase. These represent various Greek words borrowed by English without prefixes or suffixes.

1. He did not at this time profess the *austere* devotion which, at a later period, gave his court the aspect of a monastery. —Macaulay

2. Or that the Everlasting has not fix'd
His *canon* 'gainst self-slaughter!—Shakespeare

3. Within the wall thus exposed by the displacing of the bones, we perceived a still interior *crypt* or recess, in depth about four feet.—Edgar Allan Poe

4. It has long...been a common saying, that if a good *despot* could be ensured, despotic monarchy would be the best form of government.—John Stuart Mill

5. ...an old lady buys, without even haggling, a few lilies to take to the sacred *icon* of the Most Holy Virgin in a neighborhood church.—*Atlantic Monthly*

6. Walden Pond was already...covered with *myriads* of ducks and geese.—Thoreau

7. But the *nomad* instinct, as I said, persists to drive us to fresh fields and pastures new.—Emerson

8. ...but the Iroquois had slept off the effect of their *orgies* and were again on the alert.—Francis Parkman

9. I pause with reverential awe when I contemplate the ponderous *tomes*, in different languages, with which they have endeavored to solve this question.—Washington Irving

10. I have spent many an hour, when I was younger, floating over its surface as the *zephyr* willed.—Thoreau

LESSON IV

COMBINATIONS OF BASES

Although, as we saw in the previous lesson, Greek bases are sometimes used by themselves, usually they occur in combination with other elements. Frequently two bases have been combined.

TELE-	far	+ PHON-	sound		telephone
PSYCH(o)-	mind	+ SOMAT-	body	+ *ic*	psychosomatic
THERM(o)-	heat	+ DYNAM-	power	+ *ics*	thermodynamics

Note that often an *o* is used as a connective between bases, usually when the second base begins with a consonant. Some dictionaries, in listing such Greek word elements (which they call "combining forms") as separate entries, include the *o*, giving PSYCHO-, THERMO-, etc. There are numerous instances, however, where this *o* does not appear, in *psychiatry, psychic,* and *thermal,* for example.

Sometimes Greek bases are combined with elements from other languages to form hybrids (see Part I, Lesson VII). Thus Latin and Greek have been combined in *dehydrate* (Latin, *de-*, "from," *-ate*, verbal suffix, and Greek, HYDR-, "water"), *automobile* (Greek, AUT(o)-, "self," and Latin, *mobilis*, "movable"), and *claustrophobia* (Latin, CLAUSTR-, "bar," "bolt," and Greek, PHOB-, "to be afraid").

PREFIXES

Often Greek bases appear in English with the addition of prefixes, that is, elements placed in front of the base which modify its meaning. Most of the prefixes were originally Greek prepositions or adverbs.

dia-	through, across	+ GRAM-	writing	diagram
epi-	upon	+ GRAM-		epigram
pro-	before	+ GRAM-		program

Most Greek prefixes end in a vowel which usually disappears before an initial vowel or *h* in a base.

parà-graph and *para-site*, but *par-ody*

cata-strophe and *cata-logue*, but *cat-holic*

hypo-dermic and *hypo-thesis*, but *hyp-hen*

A base may be preceded by more than one prefix.

a-, not + *sym-*, with + METR-, measure + *-ic* + *-al* asymmetrical
par-, beside + *en-*, in + THE-, to place + *-sis*   parenthesis

ASSIGNMENT

I. Learn the following **prefixes** and their meanings:

a- (**an-** before vowels or *h*),* not, without
   examples: abyss, anodyne, anarchy, anemic

amphi-, both, on both sides of, around
   examples: amphitheater, amphibious

ana- (**an-** before vowels or *h*),* up, back, again
   examples: analysis, anatomy, anode

---

*Therefore *an-* before a vowel or *h* will be ambiguous. You may need to consult a dictionary to determine which is the prefix in question.

anti- (*ant-* before vowels or *h*), against, opposite
    examples: antiseptic, antiaircraft, antarctic, antagonist

apo- (*ap-* before vowels or *h*), from, off
    examples: apology, apostle, aphelion

cata- (*cat-* before vowels or *h*), down, against, very. (In many
    English words it is difficult to see the force of this prefix.)
    examples: cataract, catastrophe, cathode, catholic

dia- (*di-* before vowels or *h*), through, across, between
    examples: diameter, diagnosis, diocese

II. Learn the following bases and their meanings:

Greek Base	Meanings	English Derivatives
ALG-	pain	neuralgia, nostalgia
BI-	life	biology, biography
CHRON-	time	chronic, chronicles
D(A)EMON-	spirit, evil spirit	demon
GE-	earth	geography, geology
LOG-	speech, word, pro- portion, reasoning	apology, epilogue, prologue

([LOGUE-] came into English through French.)

LY-	to loosen	analysis, paralysis
MNE-	to remember	amnesia
PAN(T)-	all, every	Pan-American, panorama, pantomime
POD-	foot	podium, tripod
THE-	god	theology, monotheism
TROPH-	to nourish, grow	atrophy

III. Define the following words in such a way that you indicate the
force of the prefix:

    Examples: 1. diagonal—at an angle <u>across</u>
              2. abyss—a pit <u>without</u> bottom

1. anonymous
2. antarctic
3. apostle
4. catastrophe
5. aseptic
6. antiseptic
7. amphitheater
8. anesthetic
9. diameter
10. amoral
11. catapult
12. anarchy

IV. List the base or bases and prefixes (if any), together with their meanings, in each of the following italicized words. Define each word as it is used in the sentence or phrase. In this and in similar exercises the bases contained in the words are ones assigned in the lesson or in previous lessons. If you cannot remember the meaning of a particular base, however, refer to the section at the end of Part II, where all bases are listed which students are expected to learn.

Example: apology—<u>apo</u>- off + LOG- speech: acknowledgement of improper conduct

1. I confess I was a little dubious at first whether it was not one of those *apocryphal* tales often passed off upon inquiring travellers like myself.—Washington Irving

2. The *analytical* power should not be confounded with simple ingenuity.—Edgar Allan Poe

3. Inactivity is the patients' worst enemy; their muscles *atrophy* and tendons shrink.—*Time*

4. If rightly made, a boat would be a sort of *amphibious* animal, a creature of two elements, related by one half its structure to some swift and shapely fish, and by the other to some strong-winged and graceful bird.—Thoreau

5. Neither scholar, *mnemonic* freak or gambler, Elfrida has hit the top in what is still the most demanding and sophisticated of all quiz shows.—*Time*

6. The whole Aztec *pantheon* partook more or less of the sanguinary spirit of the terrible war-god who presided over it. —William Hickling Prescott

7. Physically beautiful men — the glory of the race when it was young — are almost an *anachronism* now.—Thomas Hardy

8. ...her face enacting a vivid *pantomime* of the criticisms passing in her mind.—Thomas Hardy

9. There is no reasonable objection to examining an *atheist* in the evidences of Christianity, provided he is not required to profess a belief in them.—John Stuart Mill

10. The delegate of New Zealand, a country *antipodal* to Greece ....—*Atlantic Monthly*

11. ...it gives preliminary promise that a partial separation of the *analgesic* and addicting properties may have been achieved.—*Time*

12. There is an unmistakable *analogy* between these wicked weeds and the bad habits and sinful propensities which have overrun the moral world.—Hawthorne

13. The discovery of *antibiotics* greatly reduced the number of deaths from infection.

14. The depth of his knowledge of *anatomy* has no parallel among the artists of modern times.—Emerson

15. When I think of the benefactors of the race, whom we have *apotheosized* as messengers from heaven, bearers of divine gifts to man. . . .—Thoreau

16. His problem is therefore to find a way of becoming a *catalytic* agent for normalizing relations between the Soviets and the whole West.—Dorothy Thompson

17. . . . its scripts are full of insight and nicely caught *dialogue.* —*Time*

18. When night came, it brought with it a *pandemonium* of dancing and whooping, drumming and feasting.—Francis Parkman

19. A full *amnesty* for past offenses was granted to the citizens. —Macaulay

20. (a) When the Explorers' orbits were carrying them near the earth, they both reported reasonable numbers of cosmic rays . . . but as they climbed up towards their *apogees* the count became faster.—*Time*

(b) In the book as in history, John Adams emerges as the *apogee* of moral courage.—*Time*

LESSON V

HOMONYMS

Words which are the reverse of doublets (Latin Lesson XXII) are called homonyms (HOM- "same" + ONYM- "word" —both in Lesson VI following), that is, words similar in form or at least in pronunciation, but of different origin and meaning, as, for example, in *van,* "the forefront" and *van,* "a covered vehicle," or *gin,* "an alcoholic beverage," and *gin,* "a machine for removing the seeds from cotton." In the formation of homonyms there is nothing that can be described as a process; generally the similarity between the two words is due purely to chance. There are two types of homonyms: homographs (*-graph* "writing"—Lesson XIV) and homophones (PHON-"sound"—Lesson VIII).

Homographs are spelled the same but have a different origin and/or meaning. They may or may not be pronounced the same. Some examples are: *bass* (voice/fish), *buffet* (hit/sideboard), *close* (shut/near), *consort* (noun/verb), *entrance* (noun/verb), *forte* (one's strong point/a term in music), *contract* (noun/verb), *intimate* (verb/adjective), *invalid* (noun/adjective), *lead* (the metal/to show the way), *minute* (noun/adjective), *primer* (a first book/something that primes), *wound* (noun/past tense of wind), *wind* (noun/verb), *compact* (noun/adjective), *hide* (verb/noun).

Homophones are pronounced the same but have different meanings, origins, and spellings. Some examples are: *aisle, isle, I'll; barren, baron; base, bass; fisher, fissure; hoard, horde; mask, masque; mean, mien; peak, peek, pique; pole, poll; sac, sack; surf, serf; vain, vane, vein.*

Some situations are borderline. Some speakers do not feel that *there, their,* and *they're* are strictly homonyms; if *they're* is pronounced correctly, they say, it has more long *a* than the other two. Also, some words are homonyms when they stand alone, but when they are used in context they may not be. The letter *h* is often dropped in context when it is not stressed. For example, *him* and *hymn* sound alike, but to many speakers they do not in these two sentences: "Did you see him?" and "Let's sing hymn number 40." For *him* in that sentence, most of us are apt to say *'im.* Another situation is *he'll.* What would be your first guess as its homonym? Most of us would probably say *heel,* and most of us might be right once in a while, but if we open a sentence with it—as "He'll be here at five"—most of us might find that in fact we say *hill.* And if it is put elsewhere in a sentence—as "I don't know if he'll be here at five"—do not be surprised if what comes out is *ill.* Similarly, *he's* often becomes homophonic with *ease, hits* with *its / it's,* and *he'd* is often not homophonic with *heed.*

ASSIGNMENT

I. Learn the following **prefixes** and their meanings:

> *dys-,* bad, disordered, difficult
> examples: dysentery, dysfunction

ec-, (*ex-* before vowels or *h*), out, out of
    examples: eccentric, ecstasy, exodus

en- (*em-*, *el-*), in, into
    examples: energy, enthusiasm, emblem, emphasize, elliptical

endo-, *ento-* (*end-*, *ent-* before vowels or *h*), within
    examples: endocrine, endogamy, entophyte, endamoeba

epi- (*ep-* before vowels or *h*), upon, to, in addition to
    examples: epidemic, epidermis, epode

eu- (*ev-* before vowels), good, well
    examples: eugenics, euphony, evangelist

exo-, *ecto-*, outside, external
    examples: exogamy, exotic, ectoparasite

II. Learn the following bases and their meanings:

Greek Base	Meanings	English Derivatives
AGON-	struggle, contest	agony, protagonist
ANGEL-	messenger, message	angelic
CENTR-	center	concentric
DEM-	people	democracy, demagogue
GAM-	marriage	bigamy, polygamy
HEM(AT)-, HAEM(AT)-	blood	hemorrhage, hemoglobin, hematology, leukemia

(This base usually appears as EM- if preceded by a prefix or another base; e.g., *anemia*, *leukemia*.)

HEMER-	day	ephemeral, Decameron
OD-, HOD-	way, road	odometer, electrode, cathode
STOL-, STAL-, STLE-	to send, draw	epistolary, peristalsis, epistle
TAPH-	tomb	cenotaph, epitaph
THANAT-, THANAS-	death	thanatopsis

III. Define the following words in such a way that you indicate the force of the prefix.

1. exoskeleton
2. dysentery
3. embryo
4. dysfunction
5. enthusiasm
6. exotic
7. ectoparasite
8. epidermis
9. eugenics
10. endocrine

IV. List the base or bases and prefixes (if any), together with their meanings, in each of the following italicized words. Define each word as it is used in the sentence or phrase.

1. (a) Uttering a low querulous growl, the speaker, whose harsh countenance was the very *epitome* of selfishness....
   —Dickens

   (b) Such, in very brief *epitome,* are salient points in this lamentable and also memorable episode of which no doubt a much fuller account will be given by history.—Sir Winston Churchill

2. Precisely because the tyranny of opinion is such as to make *eccentricity* a reproach, it is desirable, in order to break through that tyranny, that people should be eccentric.—John Stuart Mill

3. Diseases which are *endemic* in Egypt include worms and other parasites, amoebic dysentery, malaria....—*Harper's Magazine*

4. Between it and ourselves is the Race—a place where *antagonistic* currents meet and form whirlpools—a spot which is rough in the smoothest weather, and terrific in a wind. —Thomas Hardy

5. The serious reader will be materially aided by an exceptionally complete index, a *glossary* of military terms and abbreviations, and a running commentary on world affairs. —*Atlantic Monthly*

6. Just as a man may not consent to *euthanasia* because religious law forbids him from doing away with himself....—*Time*

7. Nearly all the labourers...intended flight, and early in the morning there was a general *exodus* in the direction of the town.—Thomas Hardy

8. He had fallen a victim to that terrible *epidemic,* the smallpox, which was now sweeping over the land like fire over the prairies.—William Hickling Prescott

9. Finally, in 1918–19, it erupted in a global *pandemic,* one of the worst disease disasters in history, which claimed at least 15 million dead.—*Time*

10. The practice of *exogamy* among the northern tribes....

11. The *epitaph* composed by Lascaris for his own tomb in Santa Agata touchingly expresses the grief of an exile.—John Addington Symonds

12. A dull and *anemic* style. . . .

13. Last week, in the sixth *encyclical* of his reign, Pope John XXIII called on a Christianity surrounded by the forces of Communism and secularism to join together. . . . —*Time*

14. Muscular *dystrophy,* a progressive wasting of muscle power for which neither cause nor cure is known. . . . —*Time*

15. But what he seemed to be saying with the evanescent words of his music. . . was that life is *ephemeral* and let us make the most of it. —*Atlantic Monthly*

16. Something of the ancient prophetic and *apostolic* fire needs to be rekindled in the piety of peace of mind. . . . —*Atlantic Monthly*

17. I can imagine that at the end of ten years we might have a very pleasant correspondence. I shall have matured my *epistolary* style. —Henry James

18. . . .and there poured out such a *eulogy* upon her children's qualities as fond mothers know how to utter. —Thackeray

19. I owe to their spontaneous, genuine, genial compassion, as large a debt as to your *evangelical* charity. —Charlotte Brontë

20. The hero's old age was described in an *epilogue.*

V. With the aid of a dictionary determine the derivations of the following homonyms:

1.a. cashier (to dismiss with disgrace

1.b. cashier (one who has charge of money)

2.a. junk (a type of sailing vessel)

2.b. junk (useless material)

3.a. policy (course of action)

3.b. policy (insurance contract)

4.a. quarry (an object of pursuit)

4.b. quarry (excavation from which stone is obtained)

5.a. school (an educational institution)

5.b. school (a large number of fish)

6.a. tattoo (markings on the skin)

6.b. tattoo (a signal on a drum, or a bugle call)

REDUPLICATION AND ONOMATOPOEIA

Reduplication, in its grammatical meaning, is the process of repeating a syllable, or a part of it, at the beginning of a word. This is a standard and serious feature in some languages, such as Papago (Southwest Indian), where it is a common way to show plural in both nouns and verbs. For example, *ceoj* ("man" or "boy") is reduplicated in plural to *cecoj* (the singular here is often abbreviated), *cipkan* ("working" singular) to *cicpkan* ("working" plural), *gogs* ("dog") to *gogogs* ("dogs"). In Chinese, adverbs are made from adjectives by reduplication. In Greek, reduplication is also common as a method of tense formation. Note the Greek base GNO- (in the previous lesson), which is from the reduplicative verb *gignoskein;* and *leloipa* ("I have left") from *leipo* ("I leave"). Other examples are: *tsetse* fly (from Bantu, an African language), *Berber* (a member of an African Moslem tribe), the French *bonbon* (literally "good good"), the Latin *tetigi* (perfect tense of the Latin base TANG- "to touch"), the Latin *fefelli* (perfect tense of the Latin base FALL-, FALS-, "to deceive"), and *beriberi* (from Singhalese *beri* "weakness").

In English, however, reduplication does not have such grammatical purposes. Indeed, it has taken on an air of whimsy and has been stretched into so-called ricochet words and other humorous coinages. A few examples are *chitchat,* a *boo-boo* (from *boohoo*), *razzle-dazzle,* *heebie-jeebies* (which whelped *teevee-jeebies,* which is what you get when you watch too much TV), *hurly-burly, itsy-bitsy teeny weeny polka-dot bikini, hi-fi, sci-fi, fi-fi* (financial fiction), *jig-a-jig, go-go* (boys and girls, who make *goo-goo* eyes at you when they dance in those places where your *mama, dada,* and *nana* told you never to go; or maybe you would like to go on an *"exotic erotic booze cruise* for a *sneak week,"* as one travel agent advertises), *meter cheater, God squad, ground bound, gene machine* (a machine that assembles DNA segments automatically), *moldy-oldy, pooper-scooper, pot shot, quick fix, ragbag, tech talk,* and so on. Two synonyms or near-synonymous words connected by *and* constitute reduplicative expressions, such as *wild and wooly,* the trademark *Shake'n Bake, rock'n'roll, bag and baggage, hale and hearty,* and, as we all know, *time and tide* wait for no man (*tid* is an Old English word meaning "time").

Onomatopoeia (ONYM- "name," in the previous lesson, + *poi-* from a Greek verb meaning "to make") is the formation of a word by imitation of a sound made by, or in some other way associated with, its referent. Big guns go *boom;* bullets, cars, and people *whizz* by; shutters *thump* against the house; a batter *whacks* or *thwacks* a baseball; kids *splash* in a pool; your hamburger goes *plop* when you drop it; hot grease *sizzles* in a pan; and, of course, wimps *whimper.* Some onomatopoetic words describe the sounds of animals: flies *buzz;* cows go *moo;* bees *hum;* snakes *hiss;* sheep *baa;* monkeys (and people) *chatter;* cats *meow;* horses *whinny;* and dogs *yap, woof,* and *growl.* And, according to what dictionary you are looking at, owls may or may not *hoot* onomatopoetically; cymbals may or may not *clash;* and your soda pop may or may not *fizz.*

ASSIGNMENT

I. Learn the following **prefixes** and their meanings:

hyper-, over, excessive
examples: hypercritical, hypersonic, hypertension

hypo- (hyp- before vowels or *h),* below, less than normal
examples: hypodermic, hypothesis, hyphen

meta- (met- before vowels or *h),* after, changed
examples: metabolism, metamorphosis, method

para- (par- before vowels or *h),* beside, disordered
examples: paralysis, parasite, parenthesis, parody

peri-, around, near
examples: perimeter, periscope

pro-, before, in front of
examples: program, prologue

pros-, toward, in addition to
examples: proselyte, prosthetic

syn- (sym-, syl-, sy-, sys-), with, together
examples: syndicate, synonym, synthetic, sympathy,
symphony, syllable, systole, system

II. Learn the following bases and their meanings:

Base	*Meanings*	*English Derivatives*
BALL-, BOL-, BLE-	to throw, put	ballistics, symbol, emblem, problem

DERM(AT)-	skin	epidermis, pachyderm, dermatologist, dermatitis
DOX-, DOG-	opinion, teach-ing	heterodox, orthodox, dogma
GNO(S)-	to know	gnomic, diagnosis
HOM(E)-	same, similar, regular	homogenized, homosexual, homeopathy
MORPH-	form, shape	morphology, metamorphosis
ONYM-	name, word	anonymous, synonym
PHER-, PHOR-	to bear, go	periphery, semaphore, phosphorescent
TACT-, TAX-	to arrange, put in order	tactics, taxonomy, taxidermy

III. Define the following words in such a way that you indicate the force of the prefix:

1. hypersonic
2. parallel
3. syllable
4. hypertension
5. hypothyroidism
6. proscenium
7. periscope
8. sympathy
9. paranoia
10. perimeter
11. symphony
12. prosthetic

IV. List the base or bases and prefixes (if any), together with their meanings, in each of the following italicized words. Define each word as it is used in the sentence or phrase.

1. He knew...how America's illiterate and half-educted citizenry spoke, and mispronounced, foundered on *syntax,* floundered among clichés....—*Time*

2. The King's printing house...was—to use a coarse *metaphor* which then, for the first time, came into fashion—completely gutted.—Macaulay

3. A *hypodermic* injection....

4. ...the moral *anomaly* of punishing the accessory, when the principal is (and must be) allowed to go free.—John Stuart Mill

5. *Paradoxical* as the assertion may be, the conscious ability to do without happiness gives the best prospect of realising such happiness as is attainable.—John Stuart Mill

6. Moral insanity is often nothing more than the *hypertrophy* of some vulgar passion—lust, violence, cruelty, jealousy and the like.—John Addington Symonds

7. At the Roman Catholic University of Santa Clara, students formed a group to invite *agnostic,* anticlerical speakers to the campus.—*Time*

8. His optimism has no religious source but derives from youth, from the *euphoria* given by the joy of living under a bright sun and a clear, diaphanous sky.—*Atlantic Monthly*

9. ...eventually they die from a swift and general collapse of the body's *metabolic* processes.—*Time*

10. The hope that truth and wisdom would be found in the assemblies of the orthodox clergy induced the Emperor to convene, at Constantinople, a *synod* of one hundred and fifty bishops. —Edward Gibbon

11. The forests have departed, but the old customs of their shades remain. Many, however, linger only in *metamorphosed* or disguised form.—Thomas Hardy

12. Could you take all your *paraphernalia* out of the kitchen while I'm fixing lunch, please, so your stamps won't sneak over into our sandwiches and the marbles won't jump into the soup?—J.B. Walker

13. This victory, more complete than even the sanguine temper of Cortés had *prognosticated,* proved the superiority of the Spaniards.—William Hickling Prescott

14. At its highest point (apogee), the orbit rises to 1,700 miles above the earth, descending to about 200 miles (*perigee*). —*Time*

15. ...its numerous and spacious apartments, which Cortés, with enthusiastic *hyperbole,* does not hesitate to declare superior to anything of the kind in Spain.—William Hickling Prescott

16. The *antonym* of "attack" is "defend."

17. Progress has decreed their drainage, and we might well see the complete disappearance of the stilt and other island *endemics.*—Roger T. Peterson, *Field Guide to Western Birds*

18. ...it was anomalous that Russia, also on the *periphery* of modern Europe, should have been the theater of Marxist revolution.—*Time*

19. Two thirds of the people of America could not long be persuaded, upon the credit of artificial distinction and *syllogistic* subtleties, to submit their interests to the management and disposal of one third.—*The Federalist*

20. "Bore" and "boar" are *homonyms.*

V. By changing (or omitting) the prefix, form the antonym of each of the following:

Example: apogee—perigee

1. exoskeleton
2. sympathy
3. aphelion
4. proslavery
5. atheism

6. anabolism
7. ectoparasite
8. epilogue
9. hypertonic
10. euphoria

LESSON VII

LOAN WORDS

If you look up the phrase *loan word* in several dictionaries, you will find that there is some disagreement as to exactly what a loan word is. One dictionary will say that it is a "word borrowed from another language and at least partly naturalized," giving *hors d'ouevre* as an example. Another does not include the words "at least partly," and offers *khaki* and *intelligentsia* as examples. Still another includes "often with some modification of its form." A fourth says "in more or less modified form," giving *morale* as an example. Another dictionary uses *wine* and *blitz* as examples of loan words, stating that such words have been "borrowed or taken over."

It would probably be difficult for many people today to consider *wine* and *morale* as being loan words, any more than they would think of *several, disagreement, language, dictionary, naturalize, example, include, modification,* or *stating*—all used in the above paragraph—as loan words. These words today to us are English, although at one time they, too, were borrowed, and no doubt they were considered "foreign" to speakers of English who heard them for the first time. If we consider *loan word* in this sense, then more than eighty percent of the English language consists of loan words. Time, of course, and the compatibility of the sounds of the foreign language with the sounds of English, have a lot to do with this. Words like *modify, consist, elude,* and hundreds of other words from Latin had no problem at all slipping right into English because the sounds of the consonants and vowels match up very closely. (They slipped into Spanish—as *modificar, consistar, eludir*—just as easily.) Generally speaking, words that came in from Latin were therefore (and, of course, still are) relatively easy for English speakers to pronounce when first seen. Orthography is certainly a major consideration. Ask third graders to spell *modify, consist,* or *elude* and they will probably come pretty close. Ask them to spell *catastrophe, phonograph, rhythm, khaki,* or *hors d'ouevre,* and it will be a different story, as it would be if you asked them to pronounce the words given in the pronunciation exercise of Lesson I. They know in their hearts that the sound of 'f' looks like *f* on paper, and the trouble begins for many when you have to tell them that *ph* on paper also sounds like 'f.' How many of us started spelling *phone* as *fone* before we knew better?

Many such words from Greek, French, and other languages still have a slight foreignness to them that Latin imports do not. Consider *aikido, apartheid, autobahn, blini, ciao, détente, reggae,* and *aficionado.* Some of these words have been modified in spelling from the language of origin and some have not. Most of them are pronounced very closely to the way they are pronounced in the language of origin; and this is the second consideration: pronunciation. Words that come into English and that have sounds that are not in English, or that otherwise keep their foreign pronunciation, are not always quick to become naturalized, that is, become "English." Still, dictionaries disagree here, too. Some consider some of the above words to be foreign, while others consider some of the same words to be English. Some of the words receive only the foreign pronunciation in some dictionaries, some receive a sort of English equivalent, while some receive both pronunciations. The French *savoir faire* (spelled and generally pronounced just the way the French would have it) is labeled, in a spot check, "French" in three dictionaries and is considered English in three others, yet it has been used in English for more than 170 years.

Some words that we borrow never become completely Englished, and to many people these are the real loan words. Perhaps in a hundred years the words in the paragraph above will be so familiar to the English speaker that they will no longer be considered foreign, but even this possibility depends to a large extent upon usage. If there is a great increase in violence, perhaps aikido will be taught in schools and become standard fare. Perhaps some day we shall never again have to use the word apartheid. Blinis might become permanent fixtures in pancake houses. Almost anything could replace ciao (especially when the news gets around that it is a contraction that means "I am your slave"). Reggae may become passé. And we can all hope that we have détente around for a long time. On the other hand, words like *sauté, gemütlich, savoir faire,* and *hors d'oeuvre* may remain on the fence forever, to be considered for all eternity as half-breeds.

SUFFIXES

Along with bases and prefixes, suffixes have often been used in word formation. Suffixes are word elements attached to the end of a base which determine the part of speech of a word. Thus:

a-	+ THE-	god	+ *-ism* belief in		atheism
amphi-	+ BI-	life	+ *-ous* having the		amphibious
				character of	
ec-	+ CENTR-	center	+ *-ic*	pertaining to	eccentric

Atheism is a noun because *-ism* is a noun suffix. In the last two examples suffixes attached to noun bases have formed adjectives. Some adjectives can slip over and become nouns, such as *eccentric* (above) and *epidemic* (below.) We shall be dealing in the following lessons with three types of suffixes: adjective-forming, noun-forming, and verb-forming.

More than one suffix is sometimes found in a single word. For example:

CANON- rule + *-ic* pertaining to + *-al* pertaining to   canonical

a- + THE- god + *-ist* one who   + *-ic* pertaining to   atheistic
believes in

ASSIGNMENT

I. Learn the following **suffixes** and their meanings:

   -ic (*-ac* after the letter *i*), *-tic,* "pertaining to," "like"

	DESPOT-	absolute ruler + *-ic*	despotic
epi- +	DEM-	people + *-ic*	epidemic
	CARDI-	heart + *-ac*	cardiac
	STA-	to stand + *-tic*	static

   -ics, -tics, "art, science, or study of"

ETH-	custom	+ *-ics*	ethics
PHYS-	nature	+ *-ics*	physics
GENE-	to be produced	+ *-tics*	genetics

   (This was originally the plural form of the previous suffix and meant "things pertaining to," but words which exhibit this suffix are usually treated as singular; e.g., "Modern physics is a rapidly advancing science.")

   -oid, "like," "having the shape of"

ADEN-	gland	+ *-oid*	adenoid
SPHER-	ball	+ *-oid*	spheroid

II. Learn the following bases and their meanings:

Base	Meanings	Derivatives
AESTHE-, ESTHE-	to feel, perceive	aesthete, anesthetic
ANTHROP-	human being	anthropology, philanthropy
ARCHA(E)-, ARCHE-	ancient, primitive, beginning	archaeology, Archeozoic
AST(E)R-	star	astronomy, asterisk, disaster
GEN(E)-, GON-	to produce, originate	hydrogen, genesis, gene, theogeny
GER(ONT)-	old age, old people	geriatric, gerontocracy
HOL-	whole	holocaust
IATR-	physician, medicine	psychiatric, pediatric
PEP(T)-	to digest	peptic, pepsin
TECHN-	art, skill, craft	technical, polytechnic

III. List the prefixes, bases, and suffixes, together with their meanings, in the following italicized words. Define each word as it is used in the sentence or phrase.

Example: endemic— en- in, on + DEM- people + -ic pertaining to: peculiar to a certain district

1. Aristarchus of Samos anticipated Copernicus' heliocentric* universe, but Ptolemy perpetuated the *geocentric* views of Hipparchus.

2. ...a polemic against polytheism...as regards the *anthropomorphic* conception of deity prevalent in Greece.—John Addington Symonds

3. A scientific knowledge of *genetics* has greatly improved the breeding of cattle.

4. She murmurs *cryptic* remarks about life and love.—*Time*

5. "He's got money, time, and he's outrageous on the dance floor, but he's so...so *anthropoid*. No class. Know what I mean?"—Allan Magee

6. With a larger proportion of the American population approaching old age, *geriatrics* has come into prominence as an important branch of medicine.

*Measured, or as if seen, from the center of the sun, from *helio-* "sun."

7. Composer Poulenc abandoned...the brassy *pyrotechnics* which once made him the rage of the Left Bank.—*Time*

8. To say of an ancient literary composition that it has antiquarian interest often means that it has no distinct *aesthetic* interest for the reader of today.—Walter Pater

9. The *anthropocentric* goal of creation featured in Genesis 1 has often been used to justify human arrogance.

10. Most *asteroids* stay on the far side of Mars, but at least twelve are known whose eccentric orbits carry them near the earth. —*Time*

11. With all this, however, the Moslem empire in Spain was but a brilliant *exotic* that took no permanent root in the soil it embellished.—Washington Irving

12. *Dyspeptic* individuals bolted their food in wedges; feeding not themselves, but broods of nightmares, who were continually standing at livery within them.—Dickens

13. ...a magnificent panorama, only slightly spoiled by the odors bred by the *archaic* drainage system.—*Harper's Magazine*

14. The next thirty years were years of *chronic,* smothered war, disguised, but never quite at rest.—Francis Parkman

15. The hunter still kept his place and listened to the hounds. Still on they came, and now the near woods resounded through all their aisles with their *demoniac* cry.—Thoreau

16. The President headed west...on his congressional-election tour in such a cheerful, *eupeptic* and thoroughly nonpolitical mood.—*Time*

17. With these exceptions, I can read almost anything. I bless my stars for a taste so *catholic,* so unexcluding.—Charles Lamb

18. The techniques of supplanting defective DNA with restructured material will produce a *eugenic* effect without the chancy intermediary of sexual reproduction.

19. The physician decided on a regional *anesthetic* for his elderly patient.

20. Does reason constrain us to believe...in a *cyclic* movement of human history?—Arnold Toynbee

IV. Distinguish in meaning between the following pairs of words:

1. amnesia—anamnesis
2. anesthesia—paresthesia
3. anti-Christian—ante-Christian
4. antiseptic—aseptic
5. hypocritical—hypercritical
6. immoral—amoral
7. supersonic—hypersonic
8. symbolism—embolism
9. sympathy—empathy
10. synonym—homonym

V. With the aid of your dictionary, give the meaning of the following loan words and determine if your dictionary considers them to be "foreign" or "English." (It is possible that your dictionary may not record them all.) Before beginning this exercise, be sure that you understand the style of your dictionary with respect to the signaling of loan words.

1. angst
2. apparat
3. au jus
4. autostrada
5. baksheesh
6. enchilada
7. enfant terrible
8. gemütlich
9. machismo
10. samizdat
11. subito
12. table d'hôte

LESSON VIII

WORD ANALYSIS

Before doing the following assignment, read the section on word analysis in Lesson IX of Part I. One of the important points made there is that word analysis is not an infallible method of determining the meaning of words, with the three homonymous Latin bases PAR- cited as an example of how confusion can arise. And a few of the same traps are waiting for you in the analysis of Greek words.

If one had not analyzed *electrode, orthodontist,* and *melody,* it could be tempting to assume that OD- in the three words were the same base. However, in *electrode,* OD- means "way, road"; in *orthodontist,* OD- is part of the base ODONT- "tooth"; and in *melody,* OD- means "song, poem." Similarly, *aphasia* is from PHA- "to speak"; *phase* is from PHA- "to appear"; and *phagocyte* is from PHAG- "to eat." After you have studied these bases and learned these words, it is often a simple matter to analyze a word without a dictionary once you know its meaning. For example, when you learn that *threnody* is a "poem, speech, or song of lamentation for the dead," it is pretty safe to assume that OD- means "song, poem." It is, of course, the reverse process, that of defining after analyzing, that requires caution.

You may have already noticed that a few Greek and Latin bases are also identical in form, such as Latin BI- "two," and Greek BI- "life"; also Latin TACT- "to touch," and Greek TACT- "to arrange." Still, once you become accustomed to analyzing words like *pedal* and *pediatrics,* you will have no trouble remembering that one is from Latin PED- "foot," and the other is from Greek PED- "child."

ASSIGNMENT

I. The following **adjective-forming suffixes** treated in this lesson are actually of Latin origin (see Part I, Lesson VIII), but are frequently attached to Greek bases, so that it will be useful to study them again here.

-al, "pertaining to," "like," "belonging to," "having the character of"

	IDE-	idea	+ *-al*	ideal
dia- +	GON-	angle	+ *-al*	diagonal
	ETH-	custom + *-ic* + *-al*		ethical

-an (-ian), "pertaining to," "like," "one concerned with"

	BARBAR-	foreign	+ *-ian*	barbarian
u- +	TOP-	place	+ *-ian*	utopian
	THE(o)-	god	+ *-logy* + *-an*	theologian

-ous (-ious), "full of," "pertaining to," "like"

	BARBAR-	foreign	+ *-ous*	barbarous
amphi- +	BI-	life	+ *-ous*	amphibious
an- +	ONYM-	name	+ *-ous*	anonymous

II. Learn the following bases and their meanings:

CHROM(AT)-	color	chromosome, chromatic
CRI-	to judge, decide, separate	critic, crisis, endocrine
ETHN-	race, cultural group	ethnology, ethnography
LECT-	to speak, choose	dialect, analects
PHA(N)-	to show, appear	phantom, epiphany, phase, emphasis, fantasy
PHIL-	to love	philharmonic, philosophy
PHON-	sound, voice	phonetic, telephone
POLY-	many, much	polyglot, polygamy
TAUT-	the same	tautology, tautomerous
THERM-	heat	thermometer, thermodynamics

III. Analyze the following italicized words and define them as they are used in the sentence or phrase.

Example: anthropomorphic—ANTHROP(o)- human being + MORPH- form + -ic like: represented with human characteristics or form

1. The season was that period in the autumn when the foliage alone of an ordinary plantation is rich enough in hues to exhaust the *chromatic* combinations of an artist's palette. —Thomas Hardy

2. The orchestra played in a web of complicated *polyphony,* and the chorus sang in as many as twelve parts.—*Time*

3. Leaving things to the government, like leaving them to Providence, is *synonymous* with caring nothing about them. —John Stuart Mill

4. The ancient Hellenes were an *ethnic* mixture of prehistoric Mediterranean peoples and of northern invaders who, in successive waves, overran the country in the millenium before Christ.—*Atlantic Monthly*

5. Among other achievements, *bibliophile* Ransom has made the university one of the country's riches repositories of rare manuscripts.—*Time*

6. He mingled with his reverence for the Supreme, the *astral* worship which existed among the Toltecs.—William Hickling Prescott

7. "It was her father that I got acquainted with first. And through getting acquainted with him, you see,...I got acquainted with her," said Plornish *tautologically.*—Dickens

8. The *chromatic* scale is not used as much in music as the major and minor scales.*

9. It was a lovely May sunset, and the birch trees which grew on this margin of the vast Egdon wilderness had put on their new leaves, delicate as butterflies' wings, and *diaphanous* as amber.—Thomas Hardy

10. In order to equip our students to see through the legalized lying used by unscrupulous promoters, we need to reintroduce medieval *dialectics* into our school curriculum.

11. At the extremely low temperature of liquid helium, *thermal* motions almost stop.—*Time*

12. The most important and serious essay in this direction is a little book of great interest and almost *hypercritical* acumen published recently in Naples.—John Addington Symonds

---

*Several dictionaries have *chromatic scale* as a main entry.

13. The war is, perhaps, severest between the males of *polygamous* animals, and these seem oftenest provided with special weapons.—Darwin

14. To convey these directions, Laderman relies on musical notes together with music's *diacritical* markings; staccatos, rests, accents. . . .—*Time*

15. Master of an elegantly involuted style. . .James sometimes carried it to the point of "*euphonious* nothings."—*Time*

16. Besides our personal and familial prejudices, each of us is locked within the prison of our *ethnocentric* attitudes.

17. His account of that celebrated collection of books. . .cannot fail to impress all his readers with admiration of his *philological* attainments.—James Boswell

18. I never heard of a *philanthropic* meeting in which it was sincerely proposed to do any good to me, or the like of me. —Thoreau

19. What she wrote had never satisfied her; it was dull, labored, hampered, *amorphous,* as she knew.—*Harper's Magazine*

20. The main case that can be made against his music is that it is *eclectic.*—*Time*

IV. Separate the following into syllables:

1. amorphous	6. euphonious
2. astral	7. polygamous
3. diacritical	8. synonymous
4. diaphanous	9. tautological
5. eclectic	10. thermal

LESSON IX

PLACE NAMES

Up to now we have been concentrating on the analysis of words. There is more to vocabulary study, however, than simply breaking words down into their component parts. As we have seen from Lessons I and II, many terms which do not lend themselves to analysis of this sort or which are not derived from the classical languages at all have extremely interesting backgrounds, and in the next lessons we shall study some of these, for one of the purposes of this book is to develop an interest in words without which vocabulary study becomes mere meaningless drill.

Among the words whose origins and meanings many people find a fascinating study are place names. The names of cities and lakes and mountains and other locations are not usually just arbitrary choices selected at random; in the language of those who first applied it, a name often had a significance which may tell us something about the history of the place or at any rate may arouse our curiosity as to why the name was used.

The study of place names is difficult, however, for many are of great antiquity. New races which occupied the land, usually as the result of conquest, did not often change the names which they found there, but usually modified the pronunciation to resemble that of their own language. As a result, the earliest form of a place name may have little resemblance to later forms, and this causes difficulty in tracing its history. Thus *York* in the language of the ancient Britons was *Eburacon,* probably coming from the name of a man *Eburos.* When the Anglo-Saxon invaders displaced the Celts of Britain, this word became *Evuroc* and later *Eofor;* to it the suffix *wic,* meaning "dwelling place," was added. Under the influence of the invading Danes, the name *Eoforwic* acquired the pronunciation *Iorvik,* and eventually *York* was the result.

Since this book is primarily concerned with words derived from Greek and Latin, it might be well to start our consideration of place names with those which the early Greeks and Romans gave to settlements outside their homeland. Naples was originally a Greek colony, and its name is a contraction of *Neapolis,* literally "New City." (See NE- and POLIS- in the list of bases for this lesson.) Other places which were once settled by the Greeks and contain the Greek word for city, *polis,* are *Tripoli* (*Tripolis,* "Triple City"), *Gallipoli* (*kallos,* "beauty" and *polis*), and *Constantinople* ("Constantine's City"). Here also might be mentioned modern names like our own Annapolis (for Queen Anne), Indianapolis, and Arkopolis, which fortunately was discarded in favor of *Little Rock;* also the Russian Sevastopol (*sebastos,* "august").

The extent of the Roman Empire is likewise reflected by the names of some familiar cities. *Cologne* comes from *Colonia Agrippina,* an early Roman colony in Germany; the last part of *Lincoln,* the city in England, was also once *colonia,* i.e., "colony at Lindum." *Xeres,* or *Jerez,* in Spain, from which sherry takes its name, was originally *(Urbs) Caesaris,* "City of Caesar." The many English towns whose names end in -*chester* and -*caster,* such as *Winchester* and *Lancaster,* were once merely Roman military camps, the Latin word for which is *castra.*

In addition to the Romans, of course, each of the various other national groups which at one time or another invaded England (see Introduction to Part I) contributed its share of place names. A Celtic word for "river" is *avon,* and this is found today as the name of many English streams. The word *dun* in Celtic indicated a hill fortress, so names like *Dunstable, Dumbarton,* and *Dundee,* not to mention the French *Verdun,* belong to this early period. The Angles and the Saxons contributed, among others, the place names ending in *-ton, -ham, -bury, -burgh,* and the like, all conveying the idea of enclosure or protection. The towns settled by the Danish invaders a few centuries later are distinguished by such suffixes as *-thorp* and *-by,* originally "single farm" and later "village," e.g., *Derby* and *Rugby.**

In our country the place names which have perhaps the most universal appeal are those of the fifty states. These, like many other words in our language, reflect the varied national backgrounds of the early explorers and settlers. Twenty-six of the names of the states are from native Indian, eleven are of English origin, six are from Spanish, and three from French. Two (*Indiana* and *Washington*) might be described as genuine American, while Dutch has perhaps provided us with one name, and the designation of one of our newest states, Hawaii, come from a Polynesian language.†

Many of the states whose names have come from England were called after important persons. Virginia, for instance, was named by Sir Walter Raleigh for Elizabeth I, the Virgin Queen; Georgia, after King George II; Delaware, after Lord de la Ware, the first governor-general of Virginia; and the Carolinas, for King Charles I (*Carolus* being the Latin form of *Charles*).

Some of the most interesting names are those from Spanish. Florida, meaning "flowery," was discovered by Ponce de Leon shortly after Easter Sunday and was consequently named for that day, which in Spanish is called *Pascua Florida,* "Feast of the Flowers." The explorer meant also to indicate the fertility of this green land rich with the promise of spring flowers. *California* was originally the name of an imaginary land of gold and jewels, an island inhabited by Amazons, described in one of the Spanish romances of chivalry. The name was bestowed on this section of the New World (at first referring only to the peninsula of Lower California, which was thought to be an island) when one of Cortez's captains sent back a report from some

*Isaac Taylor, *Words and Places,* abridged and edited by Beatrice S. Snell, London, 1925.
†Based on Frederick Lawrence, "The Origin of American State Names," National Geographic, Aug. 1920, pp. 105–143.

Indians that such a very rich country was to be found to the northwest of Mexico. The name perhaps has no meaning at all and may simply have been coined by the writer of the popular romance in the same way as names of places in modern science-fiction stories.

Nevada in Spanish means "snowy," this name having been given to the state from the lofty Sierra Nevada range. *Colorado* (a cognate of English *colored*), meaning "red," was a term originally applied to the river because its waters contained so much reddish mud (cf. Red River and River Rouge); eventually the name was used for the state which is one of its sources. *Montana* means "mountainous."

French has given us *Vermont* (literally "Green Mountain"), *Louisiana* (after Louis XIV), and perhaps *Maine* (named for a province of France.) The only Dutch contribution is Rhode Island. Apparently the name was originally spelled "Roode Eyland," meaning in Dutch "reddish island" from the color in the soil of an island nearby; when the English disputed the Dutch holdings in the New World, they gave a similar but more English-sounding name to the region.

The names given by the Indians, which usually refer to some natural feature of the land, likewise have significance in their languages; thus, for example, *Connecticut* (originally spelled "Quinetucquet" and applied to the river) meant "long estuary"; *Arizona*, "little spring"; and *Minnesota*, "cloudy water," describing a river at flood stage.

Hundreds of thousands of less important place names in the United States are of course impossible to classify. But to give some idea of the manifold ways in which they have come to appear on the map, a few miscellaneous examples of more than usual interest have been included here.*

Baton Rouge

A group of Frenchmen exploring the Mississippi River came to a place called in the Choctaw language *Istrouma*, which means "red post," because such a marker was used to indicate the boundary between the lands of two tribes. The French simply translated this into their own tongue as Baton Rouge.

Sedalia

The founder of Sedalia, Missouri, had a daughter named Sarah, whom he called by the pet name of "Sed." He therefore decided to name the new town in her honor *Sedville*, until a friend persuaded him that -*ville* was not a very dignified suffix and that a more impressive sounding name would be *Sedalia*.

---

*Taken from George R. Stewart, *Names on the Land*, New York, 1945.

The Bronx

In the early days of New York, just north of Manhattan was a farm owned by a Danish settler named Jonas Bronck. The stream which flowed past his property was known as Bronck's river, and the region came to be called "the Broncks" (later "Bronx") just as people say "the Smiths" to mean "where the Smiths live."

Berkeley

When a name was being sought for what is now Berkeley, California, several prominent officials were one afternoon inspecting the site of the proposed city and could see in the distance the ships sailing out through the Golden Gate. One of their number happened to quote the line from Bishop Berkeley's writings, "Westward the course of empire takes its way," which seemed so appropriate that the name of its author was at once chosen for the new city.

ASSIGNMENT

I. Learn the following **noun-forming suffixes** and their meanings:

-ician, "specialist in," "practitioner of"

TECHN-	art, skill	+	-*ician*	technician
ELECTR-	electricity	+	-*ician*	electrician
TACT-	to arrange	+	-*ician*	tactician

(This suffix is actually a compound of -*ic,* or -*ics* from Lesson VII and -*ian* from Lesson VIII.)

-ism, "belief in," "practice of," "condition of"

	COMMUN-	common	+ -*ism*	Communism
	DESPOT-	absolute ruler	+ -*ism*	despotism
ant- +	AGON-	struggle	+ -*ism*	antagonism
	ALCOHOL		+ -*ism*	alcoholism

-ist, "one who believes in," "one engaged in"

	COMMUN-	common	+ -*ist*	Communist
ant- +	AGON-	struggle	+ -*ist*	antagonist

-ite, "one connected with," "inhabitant of" (also used to denote chemicals, minerals, etc.)

SYBAR-		+ -*ite*	sybarite
ISRAEL-		+ -*ite*	Israelite
DYNAM-	force	+ -*ite*	dynamite

If this is followed by an additional suffix, the *e* disappears.

SYBAR- + -*ite* + -*ic*   sybaritic

II. Learn the following bases and their meanings:

AGOG(UE)-	to lead	demagogic, synagogue
CH(E)IR-	hand	chiropractor
COSM-	universe, order	cosmic, cosmetic
HETER-	other, different	heterogeneous, heterosexual
NE-	new, new and different form of	neon, neoclassic, Neoplatonism
ODONT-	tooth	orthodontia, mastodon
OP(T)-	eye; to see	optic, autopsy
ORTH-	straight, correct	orthodox
P(A)ED-	child	pediatrician
PEDIA-	education	encyclopedia

(The two bases above are related.)

| POL(IS) | city, state | politician, policy, Annapolis |

III. Analyze the following italicized words and define them as they are used in the sentence or phrase.

1. Foot doctors began to be called *chiropodists* in the 18th century—just why is not certain.—*Time*

2. William, however, with *politic* clemency, abstained from shedding the blood even of the most culpable.—Macaulay

3. Frequently in the practice of *orthopaedic* surgery there is need for bone, either to pack an area from which diseased bone has been removed or to supply bone where bone has never grown.—*Harper's Magazine*

4. I cannot open my lips at home on the subject we have been discussing, and I am looked at coldly here, in my own village, on account of my *heterodox* opinions.—W.H. Hudson

5. The conditions after the war helped to encourage excursions into spiritual philosophy which brought *Gnosticism* into conjunction with both Judaism and Christianity.—Hugh J. Schonfield

6. He began to lecture his followers with the. . .air of a *pedagogue,* and sought out occasions to worry them with small discipline.—Henry Adams

7. The *polytheistic* system of the Indians, like that of the ancient Greeks, was of that accommodating kind which could admit within its elastic folds the deities of any other religion, without violence to itself.—William Hickling Prescott

8. A trek to the *orthodontist* every third Friday for an adjustment was not exactly my idea as to how to start a weekend.

9. Moreover, he is a polished gentleman—a citizen of the world—yes, a true *cosmopolite;* for he will speak like a native of each clime and country on the globe.—Hawthorne

10. She was referred by her dentist to a *periodontist* for a specialist's opinion of her particular problem.

11. He did not disdain the low arts of a *demagogue* to gain the favor of the populace.—William Hickling Prescott

12. It is not for nothing that Shakespeare was the greatest *neologist* who ever wrote in English.—*Harper's Magazine*

13. (a) Ikhnaton set aside the prevailing *pantheism* in which the God Amon and Amon's priests ruled over a motley array of other deities.—*Time*

    (b) His original attitude—a purely sensuous worship of nature—became steadily more spiritualized until it reached that of a wholly mystical *pantheistic* worship of the natural world.—*Atlantic Monthly*

14. . . . has set up widespread village nurse and sanitation programs, instructed village women in pregnancy and *pediatrics.* —*Time*

15. The expansionist strategy of the Nazis was generally dictated by considerations of *geopolitics.*

16. . . . the *synoptic* vision of an Augustine or St. Thomas Aquinas.—*Time*

17. The hunter took the animal which he had shot to a *taxidermist.*

18. The *ballistic* missile, then, runs out of fuel before apogee and is lobbed onto its target; therefore, it cannot be recalled. But the cruise missile is powered all the way.

19. *Orthodox* believers regarded his ideas as godless.

20. Last week the National Association of Chiropodists changed its name to American Podiatry Association, hoping that victims of corns, calluses and ingrown toenails would begin calling the nation's 8,000 foot doctors *"podiatrists."*—*Time*

IV. The following are common nouns formed from place names. List the place from which each has been derived and, in the case of cities and districts, give the location.

Example: <u>canter</u>—from <u>Canterbury</u>, England

1. bantam
2. bayonet
3. bungalow
4. bunk (nonsense)
5. currant
6. dollar
7. gypsy
8. magenta
9. milliner
10. peach
11. spaniel
12. spruce
13. tarantula
14. turquoise
15. tuxedo

LESSON X

EXPRESSIONS*

Not only individual words but also common phrases and expressions often have unusual histories, and many people find the explanation of their origins a most interesting study. Thus the expression "sold down the river" takes us back to the days of slavery in this country. In the nineteenth century the sugar and rice plantations of Louisiana were rapidly expanding, while agriculture in the upper South was declining. It therefore became a frequent and tragic practice to sell slaves from the plantations of Virginia and Kentucky, where they were used to less exhausting labor, to dealers "down river" in New Orleans. From here they were often shipped to the cane fields, where the climate was unwholesome and the work brutal.

The origin of the phrase "to look a gift horse in the mouth," meaning to be critical of something which one has been given, is not so apparent in modern times as it was in horse and buggy days, when the customary way of judging a horse's age was to examine its teeth. Thus it was impolite to show concern about the age of an animal which one had received as a present.

The sources of several expressions are to be found in absurd and long-forgotten beliefs about the habits of certain animals. "Crocodile tears" owes its origin to a notion, once actually believed, that the crocodile, after it had devoured its prey, shed tears over the fate of its victim. "Swan song," a last book or farewell speech, comes from the belief that the swan, which was unable to sing throughout its life, gave forth glorious melodies when it felt the approach of death. "To lick into shape" reflects the erroneous idea that, when a bear cub was first

*The examples in this lesson have been taken from Charles E. Funk, *A Hog on Ice and Other Curious Expressions*, New York, 1948.

born, it was merely a formless lump of flesh, and that only by the constant licking of its mother did it acquire its characteristic shape.

Another expression taken from animal lore is "show the white feather," that is, to play the coward. This actually comes from the so-called sport of cockfighting. At one time the belief was current that, if a gamecock had any white feathers in its tail, it was of an inferior breed and would immediately turn its back on an opponent and run.

Several curious phrases have undergone changes in form suggested by their meaning but actually reflecting a misunderstanding of their source (see Folk Etymology, Latin Lesson XIX); and so, while picturesque, they make literal sense only in terms of their actual origin. Thus the "favor" of "to curry favor" was once spelled *fauvel* or *favel* (meaning in French "chestnut horse"), and in a famous medieval French allegory such a horse appeared as a symbol of deceit (somewhat like Reynard the Fox). Perhaps as a result of this poem, then, "to curry Fauvel," meant to gain a person's friendship by cunning flattery; but, because of the meaning of the expression, and since "Fauvel" sounded unfamiliar, the word was eventually transformed into the more recognizable "favor." In the saying "to eat humble pie," *humble* was originally *umble* or *numble,* the numbles being an old term for the entrails of a deer or other animal, which were given to the servants, while the choicer parts were reserved for the nobles. "Forlorn hope" is simply the way in which the Dutch military expression *verloren hoop,* the equivalent of "lost battalion" (*verloren,* "lost," "abandoned"; *hoop,* "troop") sounded to English ears. The Dutch phrase referred to a small detachment of soldiers who undertook some especially dangerous mission. Since many such enterprises had little chance of success, the pronunciation of the words suggested in English "forlorn hope" and came to have the meaning of a desperate venture which will more than likely fail.

"Flash in the pan" likewise comes from military language. On the old flintlock musket there was a small pan containing gunpowder, which received the spark from the flint and was ignited. This in turn exploded the charge of powder in the barrel. Sometimes, however, although the powder in the pan was ignited, the main charge failed to fire, so that the only result of the long and laborious task of loading such a weapon was an ineffectual "flash in the pan."

Finally, a "red-letter day" was originally a holy day, one in honor of some saint or on which a church festival took place, so called from the custom of marking such days on the calendar in red. Now the expression means a day memorable because of some personal experience.

ASSIGNMENT

I. Learn the following **noun-forming suffixes** and their meanings:

-ast, -st, "one who does"

	GYMN-	naked	+	*-ast*	gymnast
en- +	THUS(i)- (THEOS-)	god	+	*-ast*	enthusiast
ana- +	LY-	to loosen	+	*-st*	analyst

-t, -te, "he who," "that which"

	POE-	to make	+	*-t*	poet
pro- +	PHE-	to speak	+	*-t*	prophet
	ATHLE-	to contend	+	*-te*	athlete
	PIRA-	to attempt	+	*-te*	pirate

-y, -ia, "quality of," "state of," "act of"

AGON-			struggle	+ *-y*	agony
PHIL-	to love + ANTHROP-	man		+ *-y*	philanthropy
an- + (H)EM-		blood		+ *-ia*	anemia

II. Learn the following bases and their meanings:

ALL-	other	allegory, parallel
CAC-	bad	cacogenics, cacophony
CAU(S)-	to burn	cauterize
CLA-	to break	iconoclast
DO-	to give	dose, antidote
DYN(AM)-	force, power	dynasty, dynamic, dynamo
ERG-, URG-	work	erg, energy, metallurgy
LAT(E)R-	to worship excessively, be fanatically devoted to	idolater, idolatry
PATH-	to feel, suffer; disease	sympathy, telepathy, pathology
PHY-	to grow	neophyte
PHYSI-	nature	physics, physiology

(The two bases above are related.)

STA-	to stand, stop	static
THE-	to place, put	thesis, theme, synthetic

III. Analyze the following italicized words and define them as they are used in the sentence or phrase.

1. . . . but the punishment of death is inflicted upon the *apostates* who have professed and deserted the law of Mahomet. —Edward Gibbon

2. The camera watches this grisly operation so closely that the moviegoer, with a little *empathy,* can feel the cold blade as it glides across the neck. —*Time*

3. The truths which are ultimately accepted as the first principles of a science are really the last results of *metaphysical* analysis. —John Stuart Mill

4. . . . noise, the grand *dynamism,* the audible expression of all that is exaltant, ruthless, and virile—noise which alone defends us from silly qualms, despairing scruples. —C.S. Lewis

5. I can think of no *epithet* but snaky to describe this man. —W.H. Hudson

6. Churchill was determined to avoid the *holocaust* of great casualties and long stalemate. —*Atlantic Monthly*

7. The skin eruption was due to an *allergy.*

8. In former times old women were sometimes accused of *demonolatry.*

9. (a) But the Henry Ford of the earlier Model T days was *an iconoclast* attacking in the name of morality and science the established order of J. P. Morgan. —*Harper's Magazine*

   (b) . . . cleared the way for Western experts to remove the plaster and paint which pious, *iconoclastic* Moslems had daubed over the great Christian mosaics. —*Time*

10. Nothing is more essential than that permanent, inveterate *antipathies* against particular nations and passionate attachments for others should be excluded. —George Washington

11. . . . the error commonly made by *neophyte* students of political science: that you can pass a law to stop almost everything, including sin. —*Harper's Magazine*

12. I cannot tolerate inhumane treatment of animals. My *thermostat* goes through the roof every time I see or hear of an animal being mistreated. —Brian Levin

13. In dark nights, when your thoughts had wandered to vast and *cosmogonal* themes in other spheres . . . —Thoreau

14. Her favorite strong blues and purples would have struck pain-fully on the refined colour-sense of an *aesthete.*—W.H. Hudson

15. Thirty years' observation of Roman society had sharpened her wit and given her an inexhaustible store of *anecdote.* —Henry James

16. Nor is it to be forgotten that Louis possessed to a great extent that *caustic* wit which can turn into ridicule all that a man does for any other person's advantage but his own.—Sir Walter Scott

17. These things are rank image-worship; and where *iconolatry* enters, the faith is dying.—*Harper's Magazine*

18. In the federal capital of Lagos...where gleaming buildings rise among the slums, the streets are a *cacophony* of honking autos and a torrent of heedless jaywalkers.—*Time*

19. Some stood aghast and bewildered at the fatal blow; others were sunk in the *apathy* of despair.—Francis Parkman

20. Nancy Hale descends from one of Boston's oldest *dynasties.*

LESSON XI

WORDS FROM RELIGION: CHRISTIAN SOURCES

Our vocabulary, as we have seen, has come from many different geographical sources: Greece, Rome, France, Arabia, India, etc. But there is another way of classifying the sources of numerous English words and expressions, and that is to consider them according to the various spheres of activity which have contributed them to our lang-uage. Thus, religion, farming, sport, seafaring, all have greatly en-riched our speech with their distinctive terminology which has passed into general usage; but often we are no longer aware of the origins of such words and so are not conscious of their one-time connection with a particular activity. *Adept* (Latin *adeptus,* "one who has arrived at"), for instance, was originally a term from alchemy and referred to a person who claimed to have "arrived at" the secret of transmuting base metals into gold. *Average* (French *avarie,* "damage to a ship or goods") is derived from the language of the sea, where it came to mean in maritime law the equitable division of such loss among the backers of the voyage, and through this step it acquired its current meaning. In tracing the histories of words contributed to our language in this fashion, we shall meet many examples which will illuminate the life and culture of the past and so serve as landmarks in the history of human progress.

In considering some of the areas from which words have become the common property of our speech, we might start with religion. The Bible has of course provided us with many such terms, and the sources of these are generally familiar to anyone acquainted with the Scriptures. Nevertheless, several are worth mentioning here if only because they are so common that their origin is often overlooked. *Scapegoat,* for instance, was originally *escape goat,* and referred in the Old Testament (see Lev. 16:10) to an animal over which the high priest of the Jews confessed the sins of the people; then the goat was allowed to "escape," and it wandered off into the wilderness symbolically carrying away upon itself all the wickedness of the Children of Israel.

The expression "the handwriting on the wall" comes from the Book of Daniel (5), where at the feast of King Belshazzar in Babylon the figure of a hand mysteriously appeared and wrote on the wall that Belshazzar had been weighed in the balance and found wanting, and that his rule was at an end. That very night Belshazzar was killed and his kingdom divided among the Medes and the Persians.

In New Testament times *talent* meant a weight of gold or silver and therefore referred to an amount of money. It acquired its modern meaning of "native ability" when Christ in a parable (Matt. 25:14 – 30) described three servants who had each been entrusted by their master with a certain number of talents of silver which he expected them to invest wisely. What Christ meant by the parable was that our inborn abilities, like the money given to the servants, is a trust from God to be used in His service, and from this passage *talent* acquired its figurative meaning.

To cite a less common example, *shibboleth,* a phrase or watchword which is the distinctive formula of a particular group, comes from the Book of Judges (12:6), where it was used as a test word to distinguish friend from foe, since the enemy could not pronounce the sound "sh."

Not so well known are the origins of certain words which have developed in the later ages of Christianity. Many have perhaps wondered what the connection was between "the Orient" and "Orientation," an introduction to college life offered to freshmen. Both words come from the Latin *oriri,* "to rise," and originally referred to the rising sun, that is, the east; when first used, the verb *orient* meant to place a church in the proper position, with its altar at the east end, to allow the congregation to face Jerusalem. Gradually the term became generalized to refer to the placing of anything in its proper position.

Dirge represents the first word of the Latin hymn for the burial of the dead, *Dirige, Domine, Dominus meus, in conspectu tuo viam meam,* "Direct, O Lord, my God, my way in thy sight." *Adieu* is from the French, meaning "to God" (cf. Spanish *adios*) and is roughly equivalent to the English *good-bye,* which is a contraction of "God be with ye." Originally *carnival* was specifically the festival of merrymaking just before Lent; it is derived from the Latin *carnem levare,* "to remove meat" (CARN-, "flesh," Part I, Lesson XXIV), from the religious practice of abstaining from meat during that period.

Bonfire, originally a *banefire* or *bonefire* (the Old English word for "bone" was *bān*), had an unfortunate smudge in its early history. During the reign of Henry VIII, saints were customarily burned in bone fires and afterwards "believers would fish the relics out of the embers." *Lewd* is from Old English *laewede,* meaning "unlettered," that is, referring to a lay person, or one outside the church family; hence, uneducated, ignorant and, later, base and vile, and eventually, lascivious, obscene—a good example of degeneration in meaning (discussed in Part I, Lesson XIV). A *miscreant,* now just a general rascal, was, at least in France where the word originated, a "non-believer," from Old French *mes-* wrongly + (ultimately) Latin CRED- to believe (Latin Lesson XI). *Holiday* is from Old English *haligdaeg* "holy day." *Halloween* means the eve of All Hallows (also called All Saints).[*]

The word *belfry* went in reverse. Originally a protective shed used by a besieging army, it passed on to mean the tower that protected a watchman, who needed little more than a bell to sound an alarm; by association, the word has come to mean a tower that holds a church bell.

ASSIGNMENT

I. Learn the following **noun-forming suffixes** and their meanings:

-ma, -m, -me, "result of," "thing that is the result of"

	DRA-	to do, to act	+ *-ma*	drama
pro- +	BLE-	to put	+ *-m*	problem
dia- +	DE-	to bind	+ *-m*	diadem
	THE-	to place	+ *-me*	theme

---

[*]Some of these examples are adapted in part from Wilfred Funk's *Word Origins and their Romantic Stories,* New York, 1950.

If this is followed by an additional suffix, it usually becomes
-*mat*-.

	DRA-	to do, to act	+ -*mat*- + -*ic*	dramatic
pro- +	BLE-	to put	+ -*mat*- + -*ic*	problematic
	THE-	to place	+ -*mat*- + -*ic*	thematic

-*sis*, -*se*, -*sy*, -*sia*, "act of," "state of," "result of"

ana-	+ LY-	to loosen	+ -*sis*	analysis
dia-	+ GNO-	to know	+ -*sis*	diagnosis
	DO-	to give	+ -*se*	dose
AUT(o)- self	+ OP-	to see	+ -*sy*	autopsy
a-	+ MNE-	to remember	+ -*sia*	amnesia

The adjectival form of this suffix sometimes appears as -*tic* and
sometimes as -*stic*.

ana-	+ LY-	to loosen	+ -*tic*	analytic
dia-	+ GNO-	to know	+ -*stic*	diagnostic

II. Learn the following bases and their meanings:

ANDR-	man, male	androgenic, philander
KINE-, CINE-	to move	kinetic, cinema
GEN(E)-	kind, race	genocide, genealogy
GYN(E)-, GYN(A)EC-	woman, female	gynarchy, gynecology
IDI-	one's own, peculiar	idiot, idiosyncrasy
LITH-, LITE-	stone	lithograph, phonolite
MIS-	hatred	misanthrope
PHE(M)-, PHA-	to speak	prophet, aphasia
SCHIZ-, SCHIS-	to split	schizophrenia, schism
STERE-	solid, three-dimensional	stereograph, stereopticon
TYP-	stamp, model	typographical, typical

III. Analyze the following italicized words and define them as they
are used in the sentence or phrase.

1. She haunted the San Francisco newspaper city room for six
months before penetrating the conventional *misogyny* of the
craft and persuading the weekly news review to hire her.
—*Time*

2. Older children respond to certain *kinesthetic* techniques. —*Psychology Today*

3. In the ruins of Hacilar, an ancient Anatolian town...Mellaart has discovered the remains of a culture so sophisticated as to shatter all previous notions about Late *Neolithic* man.—*Time*

4. It was a *heterogeneous* assemblage of people of all ranks and countries, who had arrived in all kinds of vehicles.—Washington Irving

5. I can account for the system of *polyandry*, as he calls it, in only one way; that it originated in necessity.—Southey

6. (a) There are those to whom this particular kind of biography is *anathema*, no matter who does it or how good it is.... —*Harper's Magazine*

    (b) A dire *anathema* was thundered against them and their posterity if they should dare to renew the same freedom of choice.—Edward Gibbon

7. ...it makes no difference to the *prognosis* whether treatment is given or not.—*Atlantic Monthly*

8. It involves what the experts call "vulnerability reduction"—a polite military *euphemism* to describe the relocation of populations, the decentralization of industry.—*Harper's Magazine*

9. Rowing himself right out of noon, up the long, bright air like an *apotheosis*, mounting into a drowsing infinity.... —William Faulkner

10. The *schism* which was then appearing in the nation, and which has been from that time almost constantly widening, had little in common with those schisms which had divided it during the reigns of the Tudors and the Stuarts.—Macaulay

11. The House of Commons, the *archetype* of all the representative assemblies which now meet, either in the old or in the new world....—Macaulay

12. The picture presents two hours and 25 minutes of continuously colossal spectacle in CinemaScope, Technicolor and *stereophonic* sound.—*Time*

13. The young man's reply marked him as a foreigner, not by any variation from the *idiom* and accent of good English, but because he spoke with more caution and accuracy, than if perfectly familiar with the language.—Hawthorne

14. Television is not just the latest and most miraculous of these media. It is a *synthesis* of them all.—*Harper's Magazine*

15. Without committing ourselves to the *dogmatism* of a theory, we are led to certain general conclusions.—John Addington Symonds

16. Even France, possessed of one of the most *homogeneous* communities in the world, is finding it a herculean task to draft a constitution which will satisfy conflicting class interests.—*Harper's Magazine*

17. Hence when experiments showed that light can travel in a vacuum, scientists evolved a *hypothetical* substance called "ether" which they decided must pervade all space and matter.—*Harper's Magazine*

18. ...useless ornamentation is the *antithesis* of beauty. —*Harper's Magazine*

19. The doctor's *misanthropic* mistrust of mankind (the bitterer because based on personal failure)....—Joseph Conrad

20. "...that *stereotype* of the Communist Russian which is too prevalent in American thinking."—*Time*

IV. The following words were originally associated with pagan or Christian religion but are not so today (with one exception). By using your dictionary, give for each word (a) its etymological definition showing the connection with religion, and (b) its current meanings.

1. bead
2. gossip
3. abominate
4. cretin
5. pittance
6. contemplate

LESSON XII

WORDS FROM RELIGION: NON-CHRISTIAN SOURCES

In continuing our discussion of words which have arisen in connection with religious beliefs and practices, we shall consider in this lesson some words coming from non-Christian sources. One important element in the religion of the ancient Greeks and Romans was the prediction of the future by means of omens, that is, by means of some unusual occurrence, such as a bolt of lightning, which could be regarded as a sign from heaven; and this practice has given us words like *ominous* and *abominate* (literally, "to regard as a bad omen"). Before any important course of action was decided upon at Rome, it was customary for certain priests called *augurs* to search for some omen which would indicate whether or not the gods looked with favor upon the enterprise; thus the word *inaugurate* meant (formerly) "to make a formal beginning by consulting the omens." One of the most usual ways of foretelling the future was to observe the flight of birds, and this practice was called in Latin *auspicium* (*avis,* "bird," and SPIC-, "to look"); so originally an *auspicious* occasion was one which had begun with some such good omen as the appearance of a flock of six white doves. *Monster,* as the root of the word indicates (MON-, "to warn," "to show"; cf. *demonstrate*), likewise owes its origin to this type of belief; an abnormally formed animal was regarded as a portent of evil.

Another religious belief of the Greeks and Romans is reflected in the word *enthusiasm,* literally, "state of having a god within" (Greek, *en-,* "in," and THE-, "god"), which indicates that a person in religious ecstasy was regarded as actually having been taken possession of by a divinity. But this is not a belief peculiar to the Greeks, as is shown by the original meaning of *giddy,* "god-possessed," which is of Germanic ancestry (apparently from **gud,* "god"). Likewise, when we speak of a statement as *oracular* in the sense of solemn and wise, we are recalling the oracles of the ancient world, the shrines at which were priests or priestesses who served as mediums through whom the gods foretold the future and who consequently spoke with the voices of the gods.

The religions of more distant lands have also contributed terms to the English language. Perhaps we should add that in some cases it is an erroneous idea of other beliefs which has been responsible for the appearance of such words in English. Westerners have not always understood the faiths of other peoples. Somehow Christians of the Middle Ages got the notion that Mohammedans worshiped a deity by the name of *Tervagant* or *Termagant,* which of course they do not. In the religious dramas of the times Termagant was represented as a violent, quarrelsome bully, naturally one of the villains of the piece. From this characterization the name came to mean a woman of violent temper. *Juggernaut* (a word that has been discussed in Lesson XI of Part I in relation to semantic change) is a distorted version of *Jagannath,* one of the avatars of the Hindu god Vishnu. At the festival in his honor a large image of this god is drawn through the streets in a wagon, and the erroneous belief arose among Europeans that his devotees in a frenzy of religious fervor threw themselves in front of the vehicle to be crushed by its wheels. Hence today *juggernaut* refers to an irresistible force which blindly runs over whatever gets in its way.

In one instance, unfortunately, the reputation of an Indian sect has been all too deserved. Until they were suppressed by the British, the *Thugs* (Hindi *thag,* "thief"), a secret religious group who worshiped Kali, the Hindu goddess of destruction, made it a practice to murder and rob in the service of the goddess. They usually selected as their victims wealthy travelers, whom they invariably killed, generally by strangulation, in honor of Kali; part of the proceeds from such activities were also devoted to the deity. The word *thug* has come into our language reminding us of their brutality.

The term *mufti* in reference to civilian clothes worn by soldiers apparently represents the Arab word for an expounder of Mohammedan religious law. This use of the word may have come from the resemblance between the costume of such a priestly official and the dressing gown and tasseled cap which so many British officers of the nineteenth century wore when off duty.

From the West African religions has come *fetish* (Portuguese *feitico,* "charm"), a term applied by the early explorers from Portugal to idols and amulets which the natives regarded as possessing magical powers because of an indwelling supernatural spirit. From Polynesia has come *taboo,* referring originally to religious prohibitions placed upon certain objects or words or actions, the violation of which would release evil magical forces, although the term today is often used simply to mean the restrictions enforced by social custom.

COMBINING FORMS

You have learned that a prefix changes the meaning of a base, and that a suffix makes or changes the part of speech (as well as sometimes changing the meaning). Further, not too many bases can stand alone as words; they need either a prefix, suffix, or another base to attach to. For example, with the Latin base SPIR- "to breathe," with prefixes we have *aspire, conspire, expire,* and so on; with a suffix, a *spirant;* with another base, a *spirograph* (an instrument that records respiratory movements). However, we cannot *spire* all by itself. (*Spire* meaning "steeple" is a homonym.) There are also many instances—hundreds, in fact—where a base is used so frequently with a particular suffix that the two connect and form a sort of package called a combining form, thus taking on the characteristics of the base (it contains meaning) as well as the suffix (it signals a particular part of speech and sometimes meaning). In other instances, only the base itself is considered a combining form. In some cases a base can swing both ways, that is, it can stand alone as a combining form and it can connect with suffixes to make combining forms. A good example is the base TROP-, which you will study in this lesson. Most dictionaries record all of the following with TROP-:

Combining Form	Words Formed
trop- (before vowels)	tropic, tropism
tropo- (before consonants)	tropology, troposphere
-trope	heliotrope
-tropism	heliotropism
-tropy	phototropy
-tropous	anatropous
-tropic	geotropic

The form *-tropism* is, of course, TROP- + *-ism; -tropous* is TROP- + *-ous;* and so on.

Since a combining form is the standard way of introducing bases in a dictionary, this lesson, and some of the others that follow, will consider the combining form so as to give you practice in recognizing and using them in words. Some forms, such as *-crat,* which came into French from Greek, thence into English, have never been anything but combining forms and are therefore usually not broken down into elements. Others, such as *-logy,* can be broken down (LOG- + *-y*) since the base can also form words on its own, in this case *dialogue* (or *dialog*), *catalog, analog,* and others. It should be pointed out here that the latest edition of AHD (1982) uses *-logy* as an example of a *combining form,* but under the main entry *-logy* labels it a *suffix.* But nowhere in its definition of *suffix* is such as *-logy* covered.

ASSIGNMENT

I. Learn the following **combining forms** and their meanings:

-logy, "science of," "systematic study of "

BI(o)-	life + *-logy*	biology
THE(o)-	god + *-logy*	theology
ASTR(o)-	star + *-logy*	astrology

-nomy, "science of," "system of laws governing"

ASTR(o)-	star	+ *-nomy*	astronomy
EC(o)-	house, community	+ *-nomy*	economy

AGR(o)- field + -*nomy* agronomy

When the two preceding suffixes are followed by additional elements, the final *y* is dropped.

BI(o)-   life + -*logy* + -*ist*   biologist
ASTR(o)- star + -*nomy* + -*ic* + -*al* astronomical

-*cracy*, "rule by," "type of government"

DEM(o)-   people + -*cracy* democracy
ARIST(o)- the best + -*cracy* aristocracy
BUREAU- office + -*cracy* bureaucracy

-*crat*, "one who advocates or practices rule by"

DEM(o)-   people + -*crat* democrat
ARIST(o)- the best + -*crat* aristocrat

II. Learn the following bases and their meanings:

AUT-	self	automobile, automatic
GASTR-	stomach	gastric, gastrointestinal
HELI-	sun	helium, heliocentric
IDE-	thought, idea	ideal, ideation
MANC-,	to devine by	bibliomancy, pyromancy,
MANT-	means of	mantic
MICR-	small, one millionth part of	microphone, microscope, microgram
NECR-	the dead, corpse, dead tissue	necrosis, necropolis
PAL(A)E-	old	paleontology, paleography
PSEUD-	false	pseudoscientific, pseudointellectual
PSYCH-	mind	psychology, psychosis
TROP-	to turn	tropic, phototropic

III. Analyze the following italicized words and define them as they are used in the sentence or phrase.

1. Christ was to be considered the Head of the State. This step at once gave a *theocratic* bias to the government which determined all the acts of the monk's administration.—John Addington Symonds

2. I again felt rather like an individual of but average *gastronomical* powers sitting down to a feast alone at a table spread with provisions for a hundred.—Charlotte Brontë

3. Suntan oils may cause inflammation at the very time they are protecting the skin against sunburn, warned *dermatologist* Wiley M. Sams of Miami.—*Time*

4. In jail and out, in Hollywood and during a self-imposed exile in Mexico, Dalton Trumbo wrote some 30 movies under assorted *pseudonyms.*—*Time*

5. She decided to specialize in obstetrics and *gynecology.*

6. R2D2 and C3PO are sexist robots; rather than clipping *android* to Droid, Lucas should have reduced anthropoid to Poid.

7. It is felt that possible damage to the child's emotional and social adjustment will be avoided by keeping him with children of his own *chronological* age.—*Atlantic Monthly*

8. Only fourteen miles to the west of Athens, Greek *archaeologists* found the great sanctuary of Demeter at Eleusis. . . . —*Atlantic Monthly*

9. This particular plant is *heliotropic.*

10. The doctors were so confident that. . .the diseased area showed no sign of malignancy that they did not bother to take a *biopsy* specimen.—*Time*

11. Publication of this novel was held up for two years in the Soviet Union because of its "*ideological* deviations."—*Time*

12. . . .and the islands, which so harmoniously unite earth and sea, farmer and fisherman, soldier and sailor. . .are, each individually, a *microcosm* of Greece, reflecting the whole course of its history.—*Atlantic Monthly*

13. Linnaeus's system of *taxonomy* has been elaborated and refined, but its basic framework remains intact.

14. A third guest was a hypochondriac, whose imagination wrought *necromancy* in its outward and inward world, and caused him to see monstrous faces in the household fires.—Hawthorne

15. In the hundred years since its christening, *psychiatry* has been much more successful in acquainting itself with the demons of the psyche than in casting them out.

16. The contentment of the Pygmies puzzled the *anthropologist,* and he searched for a reason for it.—*Time*

17. . . .*paleolithic* man, crouching in his cave a hundred thousand years ago.—*Atlantic Monthly*

18. ...the university protested that it was unable to compete for top teachers unless it had *autonomy* in hiring and firing. —*Time*

19. *Ethnologists,* classifying White men in accordance with their physical types, long heads and round heads, fair skins and dark skins, have sorted out three main White "races." —Arnold Toynbee

20. ...and the menace to that peace and freedom lies in the existence of *autocratic* governments backed by organized force which is controlled wholly by their will, not by the will of their people.—Woodrow Wilson

IV. Given names generally have a meaning in the language in which they have originated, although the etymology may have been lifted from another language. For example, *Leo, Leon,* and *Lionel* are given names that are used in English. *Leon* is the Greek for "lion"; when the Romans borrowed it, they altered the word to *Leo*; the French put their diminutive suffix *-el* (from the Latin *-il*—Latin Lesson XVII) onto the Greek and came up with *Lionel,* "young lion." *Michael* originated in Hebrew and means "Who is like God?" and in Anglo-Saxon *Edward* means "guardian of wealth" (from the Old English *weard,* meaning a "guardian or keeper," which also survives in the word *ward*).

With the aid of your dictionary give the literal meanings of the following given names, which are derived from Greek. (If your dictionary does not have given names, your library should be able to help.)

1. Alexander	6. George
2. Anastasia	7. Peter
3. Christopher	8. Philip
4. Dorothea	9. Sophia
5. Eugene	10. Theodore

V. The following words were originally not associated with religion but are so today. By using your dictionary, give for each word (a) its etymological definition, and (b) its modern meaning associated with religion.

1. pagan	5. pilgrim
2. providence	6. cathedral
3. psalm	7. paradise
4. Satan	

LESSON XIII

SEA TERMS

The sea has always played a large part in the lives of the English-speaking peoples, and this fact is reflected by the many words and expressions in our language which have become so much a part of our general everyday speech that we have forgotten their source. But a realization of their original application should serve to remind us of the romantic days before the invention of steam power when the oceans were sailed by iron men in wooden ships. Thus *aloof,* from the Dutch *loef,* "side toward the wind," was once used to describe a ship which kept well clear of the lee shore, toward which the wind might drive her, and it gradually passed into generalized use in the sense of remaining at a distance. "To be taken aback" referred to a vessel which had become unmanageable because its sails were pressed "backward" against the mast by a sudden shift of wind which struck their forward surface.

Rummage was originally the arrangement of cargo in a ship's hold, from Germanic *rum,* "room." The word acquired its present meaning of miscellaneous articles perhaps from the custom of holding "rummage sales," that is, sales of unclaimed articles at the docks; or perhaps the current meaning of the word was suggested by the confusion and clutter which seem to be present when goods are stowed in the hold. In the same way *junk* originally referred to pieces of old rope kept around a ship, from which were made mats and fenders and such.

Filibuster was a term at first applied to a privateer (by a series of changes in form ultimately from Dutch *vrijbuiter,* "freebooter"), in the seventeenth century little more than a pirate. Later it came to refer to one who made an unauthorized attack for personal gain against a country with which his own nation was at peace. Eventually, reflecting both the idea of irregular warfare and of piracy, the term was transferred to a member of a legislative body who obstructs passage of a bill by means of a long speech, and now it is used to designate the speech itself.

As a ship goes through the water, the wind striking against its side often causes a certain amount of lateral movement, and so in figuring a course some allowance must be made for this sideward motion, which is known as *leeway* (*lee,* the sheltered side, opposite to *windward*). This word has come into the language of landlubbers to mean margin for error.

227

Before the days of dry docks, it was the practice to tilt a vessel over on its side in order to make repairs on sections normally below the water line, and this was known as *careening* (Latin *carina,* "keel"). The term was also applied to a ship which a heavy sea caused to heel over, and eventually it came to refer to any moving object which lurches from side to side, as in the sentence, "The overloaded truck careened down the hill."

When we ask someone to lend us money to "tide us over" until payday, we are likewise using a nautical phrase, which originally meant to rely on a high tide to carry a ship over an obstruction. Some other common terms which were originally the exclusive property of sailors are *mainstay* (a cable supporting the mainmast), *make headway,* and *arrive* (literally, "to reach shore," from the Latin *ad,* "to," and *ripa,* "bank," "shore").

ASSIGNMENT

I. Learn the following **combining forms** and their meanings:

-archy, "rule by"

MON- one + *-archy* monarchy
MATRI- mother + *-archy* matriarchy

-arch, "one who rules"

MON- one + *-arch* monarch
MATRI- mother + *-arch* matriarch

Sometimes *arch(i)-* is placed in front of a base to mean "chief," "leading."

arch- + ANGEL messenger archangel
arch- + BISHOP overseer archbishop
archi- + TECT workman architect

-mania, "madness about," "passion for"

KLEPT(o)- thief + *-mania* kleptomania
DIPS(o)- thirst + *-mania* dipsomania

-maniac, "one having a madness or passion for"

KLEPT(o)- thief + *-maniac* kleptomaniac
DIPS(o)- thirst + *-maniac* dipsomaniac

-phobia, "abnormal fear or hatred of"

CLAUSTR(o)-	lock, bar	+ *-phobia*	claustrophobia
AGORA-	place of assembly, market place	+ *-phobia*	agoraphobia

-phobe, "one who fears or hates"

ANGL(o)-	English	+ *-phobe*	Anglophobe
FRANC(o)-	French	+ *-phobe*	Francophobe

II. Learn the following bases and their meanings:

ACR-	highest, the extremities	acrobat, acrostic
EGO- (Latin)	I	egotism, egoism
HIER-	sacred	hieroglyphic, hieratic
HYDR-	water	hydroelectric, hydraulic
MEGA(L)-	large; a million	megaphone, megacycle, megalomania
OLIG-	few	oligarchy
PATR-	father	patriot, patristic
PATRI-	family, clan	patriarch

(This base and the one above are related.)

SOPH-	wise	philosophy, sophomore
TELE-	afar, operating at a distance	telephone, telegraph
XEN-	stranger, foreigner	xenogamy
ZO-	animal	zoology

III. Analyze the following italicized words and define them as they are used in the sentence or phrase.

1. (a) Johnson's profound reverence for the *Hierarchy* made him expect from Bishops the highest degree of decorum. —James Boswell

   (b) Professional baseball is now organized into a *hierarchy* as rigid as Virginia Society. At the top, of course, are the two major leagues. . . . Below them stand the minor leagues, marshaled in carefully ordered ranks.—*Harper's Magazine*

2. I had always felt aversion to my uncourtly *patronymic* [Wilson].—Edgar Allan Poe

3. Greek scholars reserved for themselves the area of Athens and excavated the *Acropolis.—Atlantic Monthly*

4. ...lauding each other in terms that would make an *egomaniac* blush.—*Time*

5. He was introduced to *patristic* literature by finding at the bookseller's some volumes of the Fathers.—Thomas Hardy

6. Since several gasoline cans were found nearby, the fire obviously seemed the work of a *pyromaniac.*

7. ...that *telepathy* with which as children they seemed at times to anticipate one another's actions as two birds leave a limb at the same instant.—William Faulkner

8. ...climbed a 100-ft. tree, despite *acrophobia,* and with only one arm free.—*Time*

9. The assassination of the Prime Minister was followed by several months of *anarchy.*

10. ...blending the incoherence of delirium with fragments of *theosophy* which might have been imported from old Alexandrian sources or from dim regions of the East.—John Addington Symonds

11. We Americans have felt, this time, at least some of the same war-weariness, the same *xenophobia,* that caused our revulsion from foreign responsibilities last time.—*Harper's Magazine*

12. To explain the solar system, Alfven says, other scientists have used plain old *hydrodynamics* (the behavior of fluids, including gases).—*Time*

13. The high-risk driver's obvious faults are ill-concealed hostility lurking just below the surface, and an *egocentric* disregard for others' rights and feelings.—*Time*

14. The wings of bats are *homologous* to the front legs of mice.

15. The government of kings...gave place at long last, during a considerable lapse of time, to *oligarchies* of a few families. —John Stuart Mill

16. The local newspaper printed new versions of their earlier prewritten obituaries and brought their *necrology* up to date. —*Time*

17. He was a heavy man, with a *patriarchal* white beard, and of imposing stature.—Joseph Conrad

18. His particular egocentricity and *megalomania* made it seem that a composer who had not written for his ballet company was a composer whom he did not want.—*Atlantic Monthly*

19. In the adult it can cause *acromegaly* (a localized form of gigantism, with enlargement of the jaw and extremities). —*Time*

20. The development of reptiles began in the *Paleozoic* Era.

IV. By combining Greek elements which have been previously studied, form English words with the following meanings. Then look up these words in a dictionary to make sure that they are listed there.

Example: abnormal fear of death—<u>thanatophobia</u>.

1. hatred of marriage
2. rule by women
3. madness for books
4. having a love for animals
5. palmistry, i.e., art of divination by means of the hand
6. a scientist who studies water
7. condition of hating new things
8. having many forms
9. the study of the teeth
10. abnormal fear of pain

LESSON XIV

WORDS FROM SPORTS AND GAMES

The fact that many nautical terms have become a part of our general vocabulary indicates the large extent to which seafaring entered into the lives of our ancestors. But, if this is the case, what must we say about the emphasis which our forebears placed on sports and games? An even greater number of words and phrases from these activities have become generalized in meaning and have passed into our everyday language.

The word which perhaps best illustrates the pervasiveness of the influence of recreation upon our vocabulary is *check*, from the game of chess, the warning which one gives to an opponent that his king is in danger. (This word comes ultimately from the Persian *shāh*, "king," which is still the title for the ruler of Iran; *checkmate*, Persian *shāh māt,* means literally, "The king is dead or unable to escape.") So all of the various senses of *check* in modern English are metaphorical extensions of the original term, including *bank check* (the stubs act as a "check" or verification) and *checked,* "consisting of a pattern of small squares" (resembling a chessboard). *Exchequer,* a treasury, especially that of Great Britain, is likewise derived from the game of chess. In Norman England the accounts of public revenue were kept by placing counters on a table marked into squares like a chessboard.

Some words and expressions take us back to the sports of the Romans, "thumbs down," for instance, the supposed sign of the spectators at gladiatorial combats that the life of a beaten contestant should not be spared. Also *desultory,* "jumping from subject to subject, random," comes from the Latin *desultor,* an athlete who leaped from one horse to another while at full gallop.

In the Middle Ages the sport of falconry was popular, and though few people are interested in this today, it has left its mark on our vocabulary. *Haggard* originally referred to a hawk which had been captured at maturity and hence did not readily become used to captivity, keeping for a long time a wild, half-starved appearance. In the technical language of falconry a *lure* was a bunch of feathers used to recall a hawk which had been let fly, so the original meaning of *allure* was to "call back one's bird." *Reclaim* (Latin *re-,* "back," and *clamare,* "to cry out") also began as a technical term with the same meaning. Another popular medieval recreation is recalled by the expression "full tilt," which comes from tilting or jousting, the sport in which two horsemen galloped at one another, each trying to unseat his opponent with his lance.

Hunting, especially hunting with the hounds, has given our language many expressive terms and phrases. In the phrase "get wind of" *wind* refers of course to the air carrying the scent of the animal being chased. "At fault" originally meant having lost the trail, *fault* in hunting parlance referring to a dog's loss of scent. The expression became generalized to mean "perplexed and puzzled." Most people, however, are unaware of its origin, and it is normally used as the equivalent of "in fault," "guilty of error." The expression "at a loss" likewise first meant having lost the trail. "In full cry" referred to a pack of hunting dogs in pursuit of an animal; *cry* here describes the baying of the hounds.

Some methods of hunting unfamiliar to most of us, such as the use of beaters and nets, are recalled in the phrases "to beat around the bush" and "the toils of the law" (Old French *toile,* "net"). *Pitfall* originally denoted a concealed pit used as a trap for game.

In the case of various other sports, bowling has given us *bias* in its sense of "inclination," originally the oblique course which a ball follows, and *rub,* as in the expression "There's the rub," an obstacle which impedes a ball or turns it from its course. *Fluke* comes from billiards, where it meant a successful shot made by accident, while *bandy* is an old term from tennis and referred to a way of hitting the ball back and forth.

Less active and somewhat less respectable forms of recreation have also provided their share of additions to our general vocabulary. Even before the days of Julius Caesar and his traditional remark when crossing the Rubicon, "The die is cast," dicing had its devotees. *Hazard* meant originally a game of dice, the forerunner of craps (from Arabic *al-zahr,* "the die"). *Deuce,* though it is often used as a euphemism for devil, probably owes its origin to the exclamation of dismay from a gambler who has made the lowest possible throw, two. "Within an ace of" is also an expression derived from dicing, *ace* being originally a term for the single spot on a die, so the phrase means literally "within one point of."

Card games have of course provided many such terms. One of the most picturesque of these is the slang word *fourflusher,* "a person who makes a pretense." In poker a flush consists of five cards of the same suit, a relatively good hand, but a player with only four such cards may try to bluff his opponents into thinking he has a flush. "Pass the buck" also once was an expression used in poker; the *buck* was apparently a token which a player kept in front of him to remind him that it was his turn to deal next. If he did not care to deal, he "passed the buck" to the next player. The term *bunco,* "confidence game," reflects what happens all too often in gambling. It apparently comes from the Spanish *banco,* "bank," the name of an early card game. *Aboveboard* also suggests that cards are not always played fairly; the idea behind the term is that the players should keep their hands "above" the table so that they cannot substitute cards.

Finally, from cockfighting have come *crestfallen* and the slang *well-heeled* (referring originally to the custom of equipping the heels of the birds with sharp steel spurs); while "dark horse" has obviously been taken from racing and means specifically a horse whose background is little known, one about which we are "in the dark," in other words.

ASSIGNMENT

I. Learn the following **combining forms** and their meanings:

-meter, "measure," "instrument for measuring," "number of feet in poetry"

peri-   + -meter   perimeter

dia-   + -*meter* diameter
PENTA- five + -*meter* pentameter

-*metry*, "art or science of measuring"

GE(o)- earth   + -*metry*   geometry
TRI-   three + GON(o)- angle + -*metry*   trigonometry

-*graph*, "writing," "instrument for writing"

TELE-   far + -*graph*   telegraph
PHOT(o)- light + -*graph*   photograph

-*graphy*, "writing," "art or science of writing"

AUT(o)-   self + BI(o)- life + -*graphy*   autobiography
TELE-   far   + -*graphy*   telegraphy
PHOT(o)-   light   + -*graphy*   photography

-*gram*, "thing written"

TELE- far + -*gram*   telegram
dia-   + -*gram*   diagram

-*scope*, "instrument for viewing," "to view"

peri-   + -*scope*   periscope
MICR(o)- small + -*scope*   microscope
TELE-   far   + -*scope*   telescope

When this is followed by an additional suffix, the *e* is dropped.

TELE-   far   + -*scope*   + -*ic* telescopic
MICR(o)- small + -*scope*   + -*y*   microscopy

II. Learn the following bases and their meanings:

BAR-   weight, pressure   barometer, barograph
CAL(L)-,   beauty   calisthenics, kaleidoscope
   KAL(L)-
IS-   equal   isomerous, isosceles
MACR-   large, long   macron, macrocosm
ORA-   to see   panorama
PETR-   rock   petrify, petroleum
PHOT-   light   photograph, photosynthesis
TOP-   place   topic, utopia

III. Analyze the following italicized words and define them as they are used in the sentence or phrase.

1. But in her *topographical* ignorance as a late-comer to the place, she misreckoned the distance of her journey as not much more than half what it really was.—Thomas Hardy

2. . . . turning from the lonely *panorama* closed in by the distant Alps.—Dickens

3. The therapeutic application of radioactive *isotopes*** is a broad field for future research.—*Atlantic Monthly*

4. The compass, the *chronometer,* the sextant gradually changed navigation from an art to a science. . . . —*Time*

5. . . . not *symmetrically* arranged like houses in a town, but helter-skelter here and there, as if the builders of them had no plan about it.—*Harper's Magazine*

6. The *ideographic* nature of some Chinese symbols is obvious from their form while others remain difficult to understand even upon instruction.

7. In a nearby museum the battle is very realistically depicted in a *cyclorama.*

8. His eyes were examined for glasses by an *optometrist.*

9. After taking his degree in *petrography* he was employed by an oil company to explore new fields.

10. A *macroscopic* examination of this lesion fails to reveal its true nature.

11. How emancipated it sounds to dismiss in a moment's *epigram* an institution of nineteen hundred years!—*Harper's Magazine*

12. Within five months after his return from Nice, the deacon Athanasius was seated on the *archiepiscopal* throne of Egypt. —Edward Gibbon

13. The *telemetric* signals from Jupiter require some forty minutes to travel back to earth.

14. If she might speak of things worldly . . . she would hint to Mr. Warrington that his epistolary *orthography* was anything but correct.—Thackeray

15. We were warned by the sudden coldness of the weather, and the sinking of the mercury in the *barometer.* —Dickens

16. With the stilted gestures of *mimetic* tradition, he tells of his hopeless love for the leading lady of the troup.—*Time*

---

*To understand the etymology of this word, one must refer to the periodic table of the elements; isotopes, though they differ in weight, are numbered the same, and therefore occupy an *equal place* on the table.

17. The will was a *holograph,* for Mr. Utterson, though he took charge of it now that it was made, had refused to lend the least assistance in the making of it.—Robert Louis Stevenson

18. The difference in intensity of the two lights could be determined only by a very sensitive *photometer.*

19. For the Chinese art lover, the pleasure of viewing a painting includes enjoying the *calligraphy* of the written words as an art in itself.—*Time*

20. The daily weather maps published in many newspapers generally have the *isobars* marked on them.

IV. According to many psychologists we live in an age of anxiety. At any rate, one exhaustive medical dictionary includes a special list of over a hundred phobias, the names of most of which have been formed from Greek elements. In this list are to be found such neological absurdities as *siderodromophobia,* "morbid fear of railroad trains" (*sideros,* "iron," and *dromos,* "course," as in *airdrome* and *hippodrome*), and *triskaidekaphobia,* "morbid fear of the number thirteen." The following are the names of some obscure phobias which you are not likely to encounter again but which will give you practice in the recognition of Greek word elements. Match Column B with Column A.

1. scopophobia	(a)	fear of children
2. dysmorphophobia	(b)	fear of people
3. pedophobia	(c)	fear of rabies
4. ballistophobia	(d)	fear of insects
5. ergophobia	(e)	fear of animals' teeth
6. hydrophobophobia	(f)	fear of being seen
7. odontophobia	(g)	fear of certain places
8. topophobia	(h)	fear of missiles
9. anthropophobia	(i)	fear of deformity
10. entomophobia	(j)	fear of work

LESSON XV

MILITARY TERMS

In the previous lesson we studied words contributed to our general vocabulary by various types of recreation. In this lesson we shall consider a grimmer set of words, those which have been drawn from war. Thus, for instance, several terms in English which begin with the syllable *har-* (connected with an early Germanic word for "army" *heri*) originally had to do with military life. *Harbor* once meant "a shelter for the army." *Harbinger,* now by metaphorical extension "a forerunner," as in the stereotyped phrase "harbinger of spring," formerly designated an officer who went ahead of the army to arrange lodging for it, or an advance party sent to prepare a campground. *Harry,* a verb meaning "to raid and rob," first meant "to overrun with an army."

Some of our words recall the might of the Roman legions and the military organization which conquered the Mediterranean world. *Salary* is one such word. The ancients were well aware that salt is necessary for bodily health as well as convenient for seasoning food. Roman soldiers were consequently given an allowance for the purchase of salt, and this money was known as *salarium* (Latin *sal,* "salt," as in *saline, sal soda,* etc.), which has come into English as *salary.*

In exercise 5 of Lesson XII you learned about the word *pagan,* which owes its modern meaning to its use as a bit of military slang by the soldiers of Rome. Originally the word meant "peasant" (from Latin *pagus,* "village"), but the legionaries applied it in a somewhat contemptuous fashion to anyone who was not a soldier, and so it became the equivalent of "civilian." Later, the Christians, who felt a strong similarity between the sacrament of baptism and a Roman soldier's solemn oath of allegiance to his commander, and who thus regarded themselves as "soldiers of Christ," adopted the word *pagan* to refer to non-Christians.

The words *interval* (*inter-,* "between," + *vallum,* "palisade," "wall") and *subsidy* (*subsidium,* "reserve troops," from SED-, SID-, "to sit"; i.e., "those sitting and waiting") are likewise metaphors drawn from the technical language of Roman warfare. *Trophy* goes back to ancient Greece, where it was originally a monument consisting of pieces of armor taken from the defeated enemy which the victors set up on the field of battle as a token of their victory. The word is derived from the base TROP-, "to turn" (see Lesson XII) and signified a "turning back" or defeat of the enemy.

Warfare in the age when knighthood was in flower has added *pioneer* to our general vocabulary. The term originally meant "foot-soldier" (Latin *pedo, pedonis,* from *pes, pedis,* "foot"). At a time when cavalry formed the most important part of the army, *pioneers* were not considered of any great consequence. (*Peon* and *pawn* are derived from the same word as *pioneer.*). But they were useful since they went ahead and cleared obstacles from the way of the knight in armor mounted on his cumbersome charger. Gradually, therefore, *pioneer* lost its original lowly significance and came to have the more elevated meaning of one who goes in advance and blazes a trail. From the same period have come *squire* and *esquire* (ultimately from Latin *scutum,* "shield"), originally a young man who attended a knight and carried his shield.

The less romantic aspect of war in those days is reflected by the word *havoc,* which was formerly the signal given to an army to pillage a conquered town, as in the line from Shakespeare, "And Caesar's spirit...shall...cry 'Havoc,' and let slip the dogs of war." Also, not all warriors were knights fighting for the right; *free-lance* was used originally to refer to a mercenary soldier, one whose weapon and services were free to be sold to the highest bidder or who took part in battle for the sake of plunder.

To conclude with a few miscellaneous examples, *boulevard* is a French corruption of the Dutch *bolwerc,* "bulwark," in this instance, the fortification surrounding a city. As cities expanded, the original walls became useless and were torn down. On the site of the demolished ramparts were laid broad, tree-lined streets known from their location as *boulevards. Slogan* is from Gaelic where it designated the distinctive battle cry of each of the Irish or Scottish clans and was usually the name of the chief.

ASSIGNMENT

I. Learn the following **verb-forming suffix** and its meaning:

-ize, "to make," "to do something with," "to subject to," etc.

(This suffix has so many different senses that it is better in writing out the analysis of words to list it simply as "verbal suffix.")

ant- + AGON-	struggle	+ *-ize* antagonize
CRI-	to judge + *-tic*	+ *-ize* criticize
AMERICAN-		+ *-ize* Americanize
ANGL-	English + *-ic*	+ *-ize* anglicize

II. Learn the following bases and their meanings:

GON-	angle, angled figure	pentagon, trigonometry
LAB-, LEP-, LEM-	to take, seize	syllable, catalepsy, dilemma
MES-	middle	Mesopotamia, mesoderm
PHRA-	to speak	phrase, phraseology
STROPH-	to turn	strophe, catastrophe

III. Analyze the following italicized words and define them as they are used in the sentence or phrase.

1. The populace think that your rejection of popular standards is a rejection of all standard, and mere *antinomianism.* —Emerson

2. The instinctive act of human kind was to stand and listen, and learn how the trees on the right and the trees on the left wailed or chaunted to each other in the regular *antiphonies* of a cathedral choir.—Thomas Hardy

3. Nevertheless, the *cosmologists* are now giving us a logical, consistent pattern of the development of the universe. —*Atlantic Monthly*

4. In this *paraphrase,* I have, for the sake of brevity, modernised the language...while seeking to preserve the meaning. —John Addington Symonds

5. ...like an actor in a melodrama who *apostrophizes* the audience on the other side of the footlights.—Thomas Hardy

6. This specimen presents an *atypical* appearance.

7. By some process of *metathesis* he always pronounced "elevate" as "evelate."

8. The words came in a rush, broken by frequent *parenthetical* asides.—*Time*

9. It seems impossible for him to put pen to paper without inventing monstrous and ridiculous *periphrases.*—Symonds

10. ...turning his head, glanced at the coloured *lithograph* of Garibaldi in a black frame on the white wall.—Joseph Conrad

11. [He] had *metastases* throughout his liver and bile ducts from a primary malignancy of the pancreas.—*Time*

12. Stephen looked at the black form of the adjacent house, where it cut a dark *polygonal* notch out of the sky.—Hardy

13. The co-operation in nature is most plainly visable in true *symbiosis.* The crocodile bird picks the teeth of the crocodile and is spared the fatigue of foraging. The crocodile is possibly saved from caries and trench mouth.—*Harper's Magazine*

14. He appeared to have the convulsive strength of a man in an *epileptic* fit.—A. Conan Doyle

15. New Englanders...are skeptical about visions of the future involving drastic changes, either millennial or *catastrophic.* —*Harper's Magazine*

16. In old Colonel Pyncheon's funeral discourse, the clergy-
    man absolutely *canonized* his deceased parishioner, and...
    showed him seated, harp in hand, among the crowded chor-
    isters of the spiritual world.—Hawthorne
17. At the *autopsy,* the pathologists found no medical surprises.
18. The particles were *energized* by high voltage.
19. The *Mesozoic* life, animal and vegetable alike, was adapted to
    warm conditions and capable of little resistance to cold.
    —H.G. Wells
20. The dancers seemed unable to *synchronize* their leaps.

LESSON XVI

THE ARTS

Since at any given time the fine arts appeal to a relatively small
number of people, not many words from the language of painting,
sculpture, and architecture appear in English. Yet those that are to be
found reflect very interesting and unusual backgrounds. *Miniature,* for
instance, looks as if it were related to *minus* and *minimum* since it expresses the idea of smallness, and no doubt these words have influenced its current meaning. Historically, however, the word is derived
from *minium,* a red pigment used in the Middle Ages especially to
decorate the large initial letters in manuscripts, and to designate this
type of illumination the verb *miniare* was formed. Often in the space
around such letters a scene was painted, and, although various colors
were used, *miniare* came to refer to such painting as well. Then,
because manuscript illuminations are of necessity small, the word, or
rather its derivative *miniature,* lost its connection with a type of pigment and acquired its modern significance of "little."

The discovery in the Renaissance of some long-buried chambers
among Roman ruins contributed two words to our language, *grotesque*
and *antic.* The walls of these chambers were adorned with various fantastic pictures and, apparently from their location in a "grotto" or
vault, these paintings were called "grotesque." Eventually anything
fantastic or extravagant came to be called by this term, and it lost its
original significance of "characteristic of a grotto." Since these pictures had been made in an earlier age, they were also referred to in

Italian as *antico,* from Latin *antiquus,* "old," (which of course gives us *antique*). The Italian word, however, came into English as *antic,* with the meaning of posture or behavior as fantastic as that pictured in the "antique" style.

The origin of the word *maudlin,* "overly sentimental," might also be mentioned here. As we have seen, this comes from the name of St. Mary Magdalene, a woman of the Bible whom Christ redeemed from a sinful life. In early painting it became so customary to depict Mary Magdalene as deeply sorrowing in repentance for her past wickedness that her name has become proverbial for effusive sentimentality.

The language of sculpture has given us *colossal.* Originally *colossus* referred to a large statue like that at Rhodes where the gigantic bronze figure of a man stood across the entrance to the harbor. The Colosseum at Rome was so called from the fact that near it was a "colossal" statue of Nero. Eventually the word broadened in significance to include anything of tremendous size.

The fact that *story,* "narrative," "tale," and *story,* "level of a building," apparently have the same origin is again due to the influence of the fine arts. The latter word seems to have arisen from the friezes or painted windows representing scenes from history and legend which adorned some levels of buildings and which told a "story."

Flamboyant, "florid," "showy," was originally a term from architecture, where it meant in French "resembling a flame" and referred to the wavy, flamelike patterns of the later Gothic style, an extravagant, overly ornamented type of architecture.

The small room at the top of a house, the *attic,* likewise owes its name to a style of architecture. The word when capitalized means literally "pertaining to Attica," the old name for the section of Greece in which Athens is located, and it referred to a special type of Greek architectural decoration. Several centuries ago it was customary in building to include just under the roof a low story which was decorated with columns and other elements in the "Attic" style and which was consequently known as the Attic story. Later, although all connection with Greece disappeared, the word was kept for any room just under the roof.

Finally the word *character,* which has two apparently widely dissimilar meanings in English, "sign or token" and "distinctive trait or traits," referred in Greek times to an instrument for engraving or to a coin stamp. Thus the first meaning of this word in English comes from the idea of cutting a symbol in stone or metal, while the sense of the second meaning is that our characters are, metaphorically speaking, "stamped" upon us.

ASSIGNMENT

I. Learn the following numeral bases and their meanings:

HEMI-	half	hemisphere
MON-	one, single	monotone, monorail
PROT-	first, original, primitive	protoplasm, protein
DI-, DIPL-	twice, double	dioxide, diploma
DICH-	in two	dichogamy
DEUTER-	second	deuterogamy, deuteragonist
TRI-	three	tripod, tricycle
TETR(A)-	four	tetraethyl
PENT(A)-	five	pentathlon, pentagon, Pentecost
HEX(A)-	six	hexagonal
HEPT(A)-	seven	heptamerous
OCT(A)-	eight	octopus, octane, octagonal
DEC-	ten	decathlon, decaliter
HECT-	one hundred	hectograph
KILO-	one thousand	kilocycle

Two other numeral bases in the series from one to ten which occur rather infrequently are HEN-, "one" (as in *henotheism,* which refers to the worship of one god without excluding belief in the existence of other gods) and ENNEA-, "nine." The suffixed element *-ploid,* "fold" is useful to learn with the numbers: *diploid,* "twofold." *Tetraploid* ("fourfold") has an exclusive biological sense, as has *diploid* and *haploid.* The suffix has, in fact, been almost entirely relegated to the field of genetics.

II. Analyze the following italicized words and define them as they are used in the sentence or phrase.

1. By dint of long thinking about it, it had become a *monomania* with him, and had acquired a fascination which he found it impossible to resist.—Dickens

2. All this was part of the Pharaoh's larger plan to destroy the nation's pantheon of man-beast gods and substitute the world's first *monotheistic* faith, sun worship.—*Time*

3. The room lay in a high turret of the castellated abbey, was *pentagonal* in shape, and of capacious size.—Edgar Allan Poe

4. Playing on the pigeons' *monogamous* habits, they separate competitors from their mates for a week before the race. —*Time*

5. When he pontificated *polysyllabically* over the loudspeaker system, Olivier cracked: "He uses such big words I can't understand him."—*Time*

6. We live in an *homogenized* society that keeps the cream from coming to the top.—Robert Frost

7. Neither Statius nor Ausonius produced more musical *hexameters*.—John Addington Symonds

8. It was appropriate to the situation of the actors, and intended to enhance the pathos of the *protagonist*'s suffering.—John Addington Symonds

9. (a) The place took its name from a stone pillar which stood there, a strange rude *monolith*.—Thomas Hardy

   (b) Whether the Soviet Union can be anything but a *monolithic* state in which all opponents must, of necessity and for public instruction, be physically annihilated.... —*Time*

10. British aircraft companies seldom produce enough *prototypes* of a new plane, thus face delays if a prototype is cracked up. —*Time*

11. ...the unfathomable gloom amid the high trees on each hand, indistinct, shadowless, and spectre-like in their *monochrome* of grey.—Thomas Hardy

12. You could see the strengths and weaknesses of each with *stereoscopic* clarity.—Joseph and Stewart Alsop

13. Household silver became an index of financial status, and decorated with *monograms* and coats of arms, it became a highly personal way for a Dutch burgher to advertise his worth.—*Time*

14. ...subjected to the *dilemma* of suffering their friends to be slain and themselves to be plundered, or openly appealing to arms.—Francis Parkman

15. It is clear that the three plays of this *trilogy* are closely bound together.—John Addington Symonds

16. They recognize no *dichotomy* between mind and body; so all their medicine is, in a sense, psychosomatic.—*Time*

17. The whole establishment had an air of *monastic* quiet and seclusion.—Washington Irving

18. Termites eat wood, but they can't digest it; that is done for them by several species of flagellate *protozoans* in their intestines.—*Harper's Magazine*

19. I have made a special study of cigar ashes—in fact, I have written a *monograph* upon the subject.—A. Conan Doyle

20. In this masterpiece of Shakespeare's art, as in . . . Browning's dramatic *monologues,* a single actor virtually monopolizes the stage.—Arnold Toynbee

III. The following rather technical terms are all connected with religion. Match the words in Column A with the definitions in Column B.

A	B
1. Decalogue	(a) belief in two antagonistic gods, one good and one evil
2. Deuteronomy	(b) the first six books of the Old Testament
3. ditheism	(c) the ruler of a fourth part of a province
4. Heptateuch	(d) the first five books of the Old Testament
5. Hexateuch	(e) the Ten Commandments
6. Monophysite	(f) the first one to suffer death for a cause
7. Pentateuch	(g) the doctrine that the Father, Son, and Holy Spirit are three distinct gods
8. protomartyr	(h) a book of the Bible which contains the second appearance of the Law of Moses
9. tetrarch	(i) one who believes that the nature of Christ is single
10. tritheism	(j) the first seven books of the Old Testament

LESSON XVII

THE LAW

In this lesson we shall consider some of the words in English which were once legal terms but which have since made their way from the law courts to become part of our common language. Ancient Greek legal procedure is reflected by the word *martyr,* which in classical times meant "witness" and was a perfectly ordinary word for a person who testified at a trial. The early Christians, however, used it in reference to those who bore "witness" for Christ and, because so many of them died for their faith, the word has come to mean "one who suffers in behalf of a cause." Also from Greek has come *paraphernalia* (*para,* "beside," and *pherne,* "dowry"), which in a legal sense referred to the property, exclusive of her dowry, belonging to a wife.

One of Rome's greatest contributions to European civilization has been a systematized body of law and, in addition, respect for the body of precedent established by law. *Prejudice* (*pre-,* "before," and *judicum,* "judgment") in Roman legal procedure referred to a previous judgment or decision which affected the case at hand. *Privilege* (*privus,* "private," and *lex, legis,* "law") signified originally a law made in favor of or against an individual. *Peculiar* likewise reflects the pervasive influence of Roman Law; it comes from *peculium,* which was the private property given to a slave, a wife, or a child as his own, and was eventually generalized to mean "pertaining to any individual characteristic." The fact that the word is in turn derived from *pecus,* "cattle," shows its antiquity, for it must go back to the early period when property consisted mainly of sheep and cows (cf. *pecuniary*).

The somewhat primitive legal standards of the Middle Ages are indicated by the word *ordeal,* which in Anglo-Saxon meant "judgment." The term has acquired its modern meaning of "difficult or painful experience" from the fact that in those times it designated a type of trial in which the accused was subjected to physical dangers, such as the plunging of his hand into a cauldron of boiling water or being forced to carry red-hot irons, on the theory that if innocent he would be preserved from harm by the will of Heaven.

Another reminder that at one time the penal code was considerably harsher than it is today is *roué*, "a dissipated person, a grossly immoral individual." The word comes from a verb which in French means "to break on the wheel," a most excruciatingly painful form of execution, and signified that, in the opinion of some, such debauchees should be subjected to this torture. It was first used in regard to the wicked and immoral companions of the Duc d'Orleans in the eighteenth century.

The word *pain* likewise reflects the punitive aspect of the law. It is derived from the Latin *poena* (ultimately from Greek), "penalty," "punishment," (cf. "on *pain* of death"), which became more general in meaning to refer not just to the "pain" inflicted by a court of law, but to pain from any source. *Poena* is familiar in the term *subpoena* (*sub*, "under threat of"), the first words of such a writ when it appeared in Latin, which in effect had the meaning, *"Under threat of punishment* you are hereby ordered to be present in court."

Culprit would seem to indicate that in some ages the prosecution has carried greater weight than the defense. The term is taken from the courtroom procedure of Norman England, where trials were conducted in the French language, and is an abbreviation of the words of the prosecutor at the opening of the case. When the prisoner pleaded "not guilty," the representative of the Crown recited the formula *culpable, prit*, "guilty, ready (to prove our case)," and this became shortened to *cul-* and *prit*.

Size, reflecting jurisdiction over commerce, is a shortened form of *assize* (ultimately from Latin *ad* and *sedere*, "to sit"; cf. *assess*), referring to a "sitting" or session of a legislative body and its ordinances, especially those regulating weights and measures.

Bailiwick (*bailiff* and -*wick*, "village") was once a district under the supervision of a bailiff, formerly a representative of a lord or the king, in charge of collecting taxes and administering justice. Another type of tax collector in England at one time was an *escheator*. In the language of lawyers *escheat* refers to the reversion of property without legal heirs to the government, and these officers, whose duty it was to look after such property, acquired a reputation, deserved or not, of being generally dishonest. From their designation, consequently, has come the word *cheater*.

Matter of fact, despite having undergone a process of weakening in popular usage, as in the merely introductory phrase, "Well, as a matter of fact...," is still in use in strictly legal terminology to mean the part of an inquiry concerned with the truth or falsity of the alleged facts, as distinct from *matter of law*, having to do with the legal interpretation of the case.

Ignoramus, literally "we do not know" in Latin, was formerly an indorsement applied to an indictment when a grand jury found the evidence insufficient to bring the defendent to trial. It acquired its modern meaning of "dunce" from a seventeenth-century play by George Ruggle about an ignorant lawyer who was given the legal-sounding as well as suggestive name of *Ignoramus.*

ASSIGNMENT

I. Learn the following bases and their meanings:

CHORE-	dance	chorus
ER(OT)-	love	erotic
GLYPH-	to carve	hieroglyphic, triglyph
NAUT-	sailor	nautical, Argonaut
NES-	island	Indonesia, Melanesia

II. Analyze the following italicized words and define them as they are used in the sentence or phrase.

    1. ...an appearance of benevolence, kindness, pity, and the championship of the helpless is a gloss that covers a *pathological* misanthropy.—*Harper's Magazine*

    2. At intervals sections of the highway were carefully measured and marked as a means of *odometer* testing.

    3. Before the war Guam was the only United States possession in *Micronesia.*

    4. The Chumash *petroglyph* likely represented a comet.

    5. ...weeds whose red and yellow and purple hues formed a *polychrome* as dazzling as that of cultivated flowers. —Thomas Hardy

    6. ...*Polynesian* navigators in flimsy open canoes, without chart or compass.—Arnold Toynbee

    7. *Demographers* are much concerned about the population explosion.

    8. But the antiquity of the scrolls was soon proved conclusively by *paleographical* and archaeological evidence....—*Time*

    9. An immediate interest kindled within me for the unknown Catherine, and I began forthwith to decipher her faded *hieroglyphics.*—Emily Brontë

10. (a) *Aphasia* usually precedes (b) *ataxia* as the first sign of brain damage due to stroke.

11. *Psychometrists* strongly defend the use of tests to determine college entrance.

12. Agnostics challenged the *theistic* basis of his philosophy.

13. The one had a *kinetic* and the other a static temperament. —Allan Nevins

14. Just to describe the new rash of alphabetese, linguists were forced to invent a new word: *acronym*...which first appeared in dictionaries in 1947.—*Time*

15. *Synesthesia*...is not recognized by most cultures as a normal way of experience.—Selby and Garretson, *Cultural Anthropology*

16. He devised the *choreography,* commissioned the music, directed the dancers and the camera, and he dances a leading part.—*Time*

17. The flowers of the orchids present a multitude of curious structures which a few years ago would have been considered as mere *morphological* differences without any special function.—Darwin

18. His poetry is rather too *erotic* and passionate, you know, for some tastes.—Thomas Hardy

19. The rendezvousing in space of the (a) *cosmonauts* and (b) *astronauts* lifted the space program to a new plateau.

20. A peculiar *pathogenic* bacteria was diagnosed as the culprit that sent 122 people to the hospital from the small town's annual picnic.

LESSON XVIII

LITERARY TERMS

In this lesson we shall consider some of the words which our language has drawn from literature. The literary form which has made the greatest contribution of such terms is drama, and the fact that a number of these words have come down into modern English reflects the great influence of the classical theater on later culture. Thus *hypocrite* was originally a term for an actor. *Episode,* which means literally "a coming in addition" (*epi,* "upon," "in addition to," *eis,* "into," and OD-, "way," "road," Lesson V) in the technical language of Greek tragedy designated a part of the play between two songs of the chorus, roughly the equivalent of an act; in early times dialogue scenes between actors were regarded as interpolations or interruptions in the choral songs, which were originally the sole element of Greek tragedy.

Because of the historical development of Greek drama the meaning of *chorus* has changed considerably. In its earliest form, Greek tragedy was performed by a group of fifty dancers, and the original meaning of *chorus* is "dance in a ring" (cf. English *choreography*). The performers, however, sang songs while they danced, and, as the drama of the Greeks developed a polished literary style, the role of the chorus became primarily that of a singing group. *Orchestra* has undergone a somewhat similar evolution. In the early theater it designated the area where the chorus danced (*orcheisthai,* "to dance"). As it is used today, however, it generally refers to the group of musicians who now sit in this place.

Scene likewise reflects the primitive period of Greek tragedy, when the word referred to the tent or booth located behind the playing area, where the actors changed into their costumes. Eventually, when elaborate theaters of stone were built, the word came to be used for the back of the stage, and later for the stage itself.

From the Roman theater has come the word *person* (also its doublet *parson*), which in Latin meant "actor's mask." In Roman comedy there was an appropriate mask for each of the stock characters (the slave, the old man, and others), and so the word *persona* came to mean "a character in a drama," as in the phrase *dramatis personae.* In the course of its passage into modern English *person* later acquired the meaning of "one who plays a part" and by metaphorical extension "one who plays a part in life." Finally the idea of sustaining a role was lost, so that *person* now means simply "individual." The Roman theater has likewise given us *explode* (*ex-,* "from," and *plaudere, plodere,* "to clap," as in *applaud*), literally "to drive off the stage by loud clapping," referring to a practice of showing displeasure which, although the reverse of our own, was common in the past.

The word *pants* has come from Italian comedy, in which there was a stock character named *Pantalone,* a lean, foolish man who usually appeared costumed in a kind of tight-fitting pair of trousers called after him *pantaloons* and eventually shortened to *pants.*

In the theater of the previous century, before the days of electricity, when an especially brilliant, concentrated light was needed to mark out some star performer, a dazzling white beam was produced by directing a flame of oxygen and hydrogen on a cylinder of lime, and it was consequently known as a *limelight.*

Robot is of relatively recent origin (1923). The term comes from the name given to mechanical men in a play by Karel Capek entitled *R.U.R.* (*Rossum's Universal Robots*) and was originally a Czech word *robota,* "compulsory service."

Words such as these have of course come from forms of literature other than drama. Most college students have wondered at one time or another what the connection is between the *Romance* languages (French, Spanish, etc.) and *romance,* having to do with adventure, excitement, and especially love. In the Middle Ages most literature was in Latin; but some lighter works were written in the native dialects which were beginning to emerge from the language of the Romans, and, since such works were in the Romance dialects, they were called by this name. The best known of them dealt with the exploits of knights who slew dragons and rescued fair damsels in distress, and so *romance* has become a term for the characteristics of such fiction.

Finally, literary criticism figures in the origin of *namby-pamby,* a contemptuous nickname for the eighteenth-century English poet, Ambrose Philips (fancifully based on his name), whose insipid, weakly sentimental style has been immortalized by this epithet.

ASSIGNMENT

I. With the aid of a dictionary determine how at least one of the meanings of the following italicized words has its origin as a literary term.

    1. As H.G. Wells said, human history is "a race between education and *catastrophe.*"—*Newsweek*

    2. This *elegiac* mood and ethical spirit...provide unity between the various sections of the poem.—*A Reader's Companion to World Literature*

    3. He is, you see, too far from the athlete and participation in the effort that is the athlete's release, the athlete's *catharsis.* —*George Sheehan*

    4. All the animals, birds, reptiles, and insects of Africa, and also the plants, understand the *onomatopoeic* Bushman tongue. —Laurens Van Der Post

5. Jefferson's words would be changed into a *panegyric* on absolute government.—George Orwell

6. But my first name is Thomas. Painfully *prosaic*.—Agatha Christie

7. The satirist strikes more directly; he either attacks manners, customs, institutions, and persons without disguise, or he does so under a thin veil of *parable*.—John Addington Symonds

8. They forgot even the rules of *prosody*, and, with the melody of Homer yet sounding in their ears, they confound all measure of feet and syllables.—Edward Gibbon

II. For additional practice, with the help of the list of bases at the end of Part II, analyze the following italicized words and define them as they are used in the sentence or phrase.

1. The features expressed nothing of monastic austerity or of *ascetic* privations; on the contrary, it was a bold bluff countenance.—Sir Walter Scott

2. In the thick of traffic shepherds pass along with *bucolic* slowness and serenity, clad in clothes like those worn by their ancestors.—*Atlantic Monthly*

3. Central belief of the cargo cults is that the world is about to come to a *cataclysmic* end.—*Time*

4. Here was a young man who, from a very humble place, was mounting rapidly; from the *cynosure* of a parish, he had become the talk of a county.—Robert Louis Stevenson

5. My poem was evidently too *didactic*. The public was wise enough. It no longer read for instruction.—Washington Irving

6. It was perhaps true that *hedonism* is an impotent gospel, for now it could be seen that pleasure means nothing to many men.—*Harper's Magazine*

7. . . .part of their centuries-old struggle for *hegemony* in modern Europe.—*Time*

8. The face was well shaped, even excellently. But the mind within was beginning to use it as a mere waste tablet whereon to trace its *idiosyncrasies* as they developed themselves. —Thomas Hardy

9. For a number of years he had been a *peripatetic* scissors grinder.

10. The worst offence of this kind which can be committed by a *polemic* is to stigmatise those who hold the contrary opinion as bad and immoral men.—John Stuart Mill

III. The following italicized words are also derived from Greek; define them as they are used in the sentence or phrase.

1. The frozen snows of January still lay like *adamant* in the cross-town streets.—O. Henry

2. His simple patriotism that puts country above home and family is expressed in one of his *aphorisms.—Time*

3. Is it not almost a self-evident *axiom* that the State should require and compel the education. . .of every human being who is born its citizen?—John Stuart Mill

4. Positively ionized air was discovered to have *deleterious* effects upon human well-being.—*Harper's Magazine*

5. . . .have scarcely been able to refrain from breaking out into fierce *diatribes* against that complicated, enormous, outrageous swindle.—Thackeray

6. This was a disbelief in the evidence of the senses, a despair of *empirical* knowledge.—John Addington Symonds

7. Everywhere, some fragment of ruin suggesting the magnificence of a former *epoch*. . . .—Hawthorne

8. I have experienced this pleasure when I have drunk the liquor of the *esoteric* doctrines.—Thoreau

9. Its steeples and towers, and its one great dome, grow more *ethereal;* its smoky housetops lose their grossness in the pale effulgence.—Dickens

10. When the Vandals disembarked at the mouth of the Tiber, the emperor was suddenly roused from his *lethargy* by the clamours of a trembling and exasperated multitude.—Edward Gibbon

11. Helen, we remember, got her potent *anodyne,* nepenthe, from an Egyptian princess.—Barry B. Powell

12. Marstan had sprung out of his chair in a *paroxysm* of anger. —A. Conan Doyle

13. The progressivists treat the schools as laboratories of experience in which students learn chiefly by *pragmatic* problem solving.—*Time*

14. . . .at his gentlest tells nothing less than the bitter truth and at his worst dismisses humanity with a *sardonic* jeer.—*Time*

15. If the game was chess, the officers had to stand throughout, and Napoleon almost invariably lost unless the other player *sycophantically* threw the game.—*Time*

LESSON XIX

TERMS FROM VARIOUS OCCUPATIONS

In Lesson XI of Part I we saw some of the words which originally belonged to the language of farming and which came to be used figuratively, so that their meanings broadened or changed, words such as *delirium* (literally "out of the furrow") and *rehearse* (literally "to harrow over again"). In this lesson are some terms drawn from various other ways of earning a livelihood.

The work of making cloth is represented by the word *tease,* literally "to separate or pull apart" (the fibers of wool, flax, etc.), and by *heckle,* "to comb out" (flax or hemp in preparation for spinning). *Subtle* (Latin *sub-,* "under," and *tela,* "woven material") originally referred to a fabric which was finely woven, while "to be on tenterhooks" was a figure of speech taken from a finishing process in the manufacture of cloth, where the material is stretched by means of hooks on a wooden frame known as a *tenter,* so that it will dry evenly without shrinking.

Dicker apparently has a very interesting origin; it is thought by some authorities to come from the fur trading carried on between the early Germans and the Romans, which must have involved much the same sort of bargaining that took place in more recent times between frontiersmen and Indians. Furs were customarily handled in groups of ten known as *decuriae* (from Latin DECIM-, "ten" "tenth"; see Part I, Lesson VI), and so *dicker,* a much later form of this word, once meant "to argue over a bundle of ten furs."

Shambles, "a scene of bloodshed or general destruction," is a term formerly used to refer to a butcher shop; it once meant the bench or table (Latin *scamellum,* "little bench") on which the meat was cut and sold.

Ton and *broker* both recall the early wine trade. *Ton* represents the Anglo-Saxon *tunne,* "a large cask" (which is still the meaning of its doublet *tun*). It was first used for "wine cask," then for "weight of a wine cask," and finally acquired its current meaning of unit of weight in general. A *broker* was originally one who "broached" a cask of wine, that is, a retailer who sold wine from the barrel in small amounts. From this beginning the word became generalized in its use to mean any middleman.

Chap has been contributed by merchandising; it is a shortened form of *chapman,* "trader," "merchant" (Anglo-Saxon *ceap,* "trade," "a bargain," which also gives us *cheap*) and came to mean "person" in the same way as the word *customer* in the colloquial expression "a tough customer" (meaning "a tough person to deal with"). *Untrammeled* is a figure of speech drawn from fishing. A *trammel* is a kind of net (Latin *tri-,* "three," and *macula,* "mesh"), so *untrammeled* originally meant "free from the confines of a net." Blacksmithing has contributed *brand-new,* which once meant "fresh from the fire," *brand* here being "flame." Shakespeare in fact speaks of articles "fire-new from the mint."

To turn once again to the language of farming, *pester* (from Latin *pastorium,* "tether," "hobble," related to *pasture*) formerly referred to the practice of shackling the feet of horses so as to prevent them from wandering out of the pasture. *Ruminate,* "to ponder," was once a very picturesque figure of speech. It originally meant "to chew the cud," and so whoever first applied the term to mental activity intended to convey the idea of going over and over a problem in one's mind. As a matter of fact, the zoological term *ruminant* is still used to designate animals that chew the cud.

Season was originally "sowing time" (ultimately from Latin *satio,* "sowing"). *Greenhorn* apparently once referred to a young animal with horns which were new and hence called "green"; so today *greenhorn* is applied to a person who is inexperienced, usually because of youth.

According to one explanation, the expression "gone haywire" has arisen from the nature of the wire used around bales of hay. Such wire is stretched very tight and when cut it coils up into a jumbled mass that is quite suggestive of a machine which has broken down. Another possibility, however, is that the expression originally referred to logging camps with rundown equipment patched together by means of miscellaneous pieces of wire such as those salvaged from bales of hay. In these "haywire camps," as they were called, the machinery was generally out of order.

ASSIGNMENT

I. The following italicized words have entered English from Greek without having become completely anglicized; thus they still retain their Greek, or in some cases their Latin, endings (since, as we have seen, such words have often come into English by way of Latin; see Introduction to Part II). Define them as they are used in the sentence or phrase.

1. The brilliancy of the foliage has passed its *acme.* —Hawthorne

2. We had soup today, in which twenty kinds of vegetables were represented, and manifested each its own *aroma.* —Hawthorne

3. You weaken the *aura* of all good laws every time you break a bad one. —*Harper's Magazine*

4. I like you more than I can say; but I'll not sink into a *bathos* of sentiment. —Charlotte Brontë

5. In this casual and sinisterly impermanent manner the Soviet *colossus* had marked the boundary with its tiny neighbor. —*Harper's Magazine*

6. ...the ultimate and all-embracing movement of a stellar *cosmos* in which our local solar system has now dwindled to the diminutiveness of a speck of dust. —Arnold Toynbee

7. ...there seems to be no intelligible *criterion* by which the merits of the quarrel can be judged. —*Harper's Magazine*

8. ...a Rag and Bottle shop, and general *emporium* of much disregarded merchandise. —Dickens

9. Yet their discipline was such as to draw forth the *encomiums* of the Spanish conquerors. —William Hickling Prescott

10. I cannot forecast to you the action of Russia. It is a riddle wrapped in a mystery inside an *enigma;* but perhaps there is a key. —Sir Winston Churchill

11. ...the standards of conduct which civilization has over *eons* gradually imposed upon human nature. —*Harper's Magazine*

12. What we are headed for is a sort of social structure in which the highbrows are the elite, the middlebrows are the bourgeoisie, and the lowbrows are *hoi polloi.* —*Harper's Magazine*

13. There is not an *iota* of truth in this accusation.

14. ... "image" in Madison Avenue's *lexicon* means what the public thinks about a person or corporation when it is not thinking very hard. —*Time*

15. These appearances, which bewilder you, are merely electrical phenomena not uncommon—or it may be that they have their ghastly origin in the rank *miasma* of the tarn. —Edgar Allan Poe

16. . . . and today he writes of the New Deal with the *nostalgia* usually found in men who have narrowly missed a famous war.—*Time*

17. But conscription—that much favored *panacea* for national security—will not meet the problem.—*Harper's Magazine*

18. Her anxiety . . . had given a strange tremor to her voice and made her eyes more eloquent in their silent *pathos.*—W.H. Hudson

19. Actuated by these sentiments our ancestors arrayed themselves against the government in one huge and compact mass. All ranks, all parties, all Protestant sects, made up that vast *phalanx.*—Macaulay

20. . . . amused them by explaining some of the strange *phenomena* exhibited by the ocean in the tempest, which had filled their superstitious minds with mysterious dread. —William Hickling Prescott

21. The tragedy has been so uncommon, so complete, and of such personal importance to so many people that we are suffering from a *plethora* of surmise, conjecture, and hypothesis. —A. Conan Doyle

22. In a lengthy *prolegomenon* he stated the underlying philosophical ideas on which his work was based.

23. What most men feared was not the moral verdict of society, pronouncing them degraded by vicious or violent acts, but the intellectual estimate of incapacity and the *stigma* of dullness. —John Addington Symonds

24. There were no short cuts to learning, no comprehensive lexicons, no dictionaries of antiquities, no carefully prepared *thesauri* of mythology and history.—John Addington Symonds

25. It took him months to recover from the emotional *trauma* produced by the false accusations brought against him.

II. Give all of the plurals listed in your dictionary for each of the following words:

1. colossus	7. enigma	13. stigma
2. cosmos	8. lexicon	14. synthesis
3. criterion	9. miasma	15. thesaurus
4. diagnosis	10. octopus	16. trauma
5. emporium	11. phalanx	
6. encomium	12. prolegomenon	

LESSON XX

SCIENTIFIC LANGUAGE

In the previous lessons we have encountered a number of scientific terms. The remainder of the book, however, will be devoted exclusively to the study of technical terminology, which to so great an extent has been derived from Greek. Science figures so largely in present-day life that even the general student should have some acquaintance with its language and should acquire the ability to analyze its complex terms.

Many of the words which you will encounter in the following lessons are extremely technical and, you may feel, unnecessarily so. There has always been a tendency to regard the specialized language of scientists as merely the mark of pompousness. In some cases, it is true, technical terms have been manufactured needlessly, but there are several reasons why a specialized vocabulary is desirable.

In the first place, the fact that such words are confined to a specialized sphere is of value in ensuring precision of language. Technical words as a rule have but one application, and this makes them more useful tools for the expression of scientific ideas. Words in general use often have many applications and shades of meaning, and, although their richness of meaning may enhance their value for literary purposes, it is not desirable in scientific writing. *Speechlessness* and *aphasia* (PHA-, "to speak") at first glance seem to refer to the same thing, yet *speechlessness* actually has several meanings; the word may designate stage fright, it may refer to a momentary loss of the power to express oneself because of surprise or anger, it may apply to a condition present from birth where a child has never learned to talk. *Aphasia,* on the other hand, refers to a specific abnormal state involving loss of speech, usually the result of brain damage. Similarly, to say that a man has acromegaly is quite different from saying that he has large hands and feet. *Acromegaly* is a specific diseased condition characterized by the enlargement of the bones of the extremities and caused by excessive activity of the pituitary gland.

The fact that such words are generally unfamiliar and are employed almost exclusively by specialists who know their application tends to keep their meaning precise. Technical terms which come into general use sometimes lose their exactness. The word *allergy* is a good example of this. In medicine it refers to an abnormal sensitivity to certain substances which are harmless to most people; but it is often used by nonphysicians loosely to mean indigestion or simply dislike. Many of the terms from psychology which have passed into popular circulation show this same looseness of application. *Complex,* for instance, has come to mean popularly unusual fear or dislike, and you have no doubt often heard *phobia* and *mania* used in an exaggerated sense.

Finally, technical terms allow for economy of language while still maintaining precision of meaning. It is much shorter to write or say "thrombosis" than "formation of a clot in the heart or a blood vessel which obstructs the circulation," just as "H_2O" is a shorter means of expression than "two atoms of hydrogen and one of oxygen."

ASSIGNMENT

I. The following **suffixes** are used almost exclusively in connection with medicine. Learn them and their meanings.

-itis, "inflammation of," "inflammatory disease of "

APPENDIC- appendix + *-itis* appendicitis
ARTHR- joint + *-itis* arthritis
TONSILL- tonsil + *-itis* tonsillitis

-oma, usually "tumor arising in or composed of "; occasionally, "swelling containing"; rarely, "diseased condition," "result of" (related to *-ma,* "result of"; see Lesson XI)

Usually this suffix is attached to a base which designates a type of body tissue, such as bone, muscle, etc., but the commonest term which ends in *-oma, carcinoma,* a type of cancer, does not follow this pattern. The base CARCIN- means "crab," and the word originated in ancient times when the nature of malignant growths was little understood. One explanation for the term is that the swollen veins surrounding the diseased area resembled the claws of a crab (cf. the term *cancer,* which in Latin means "crab," as in the sign of the zodiac and in the phrase *Tropic of Cancer*).

MELAN- black, dark + *-oma* melanoma

(a highly malignant tumor, i.e., cancer, composed of dark, pigment-bearing cells)

OSTE- bone + -*oma* osteoma
(a benign tumor composed of bone tissue)

HEMAT- blood + -*oma* hematoma
(a swelling containing blood)

TRACH(Y)- rough + -*oma* trachoma
(an infectious disease of the eyes in which granulations form
on the inside of the eyelid)

If -*oma* is followed by an additional suffix, it becomes -*omat-*.

CARCIN-   crab + -*omat-* + -*ous* carcinomatous
TRACH(Y)- rough + -*omat-* + -*ous* trachomatous

-*osis*, "diseased condition of"; sometimes, "act of," "process
of," like -*sis,* of which this is a form (see Lesson XI)

PSYCH-   mind   + -*osis* psychosis
TUBERCUL-   nodule + -*osis* tuberculosis
HYPN-   sleep + -*osis* hypnosis

The adjectival form of this suffix is usually -*otic.*

PSYCH- mind + -*otic* psychotic
HYPN- sleep + -*otic* hypnotic

II. Learn the following bases and their meanings:

ARTHR- "joint," "speech sound or articulation"
   arthritis—inflammation of a joint
   arthropod—a member of a large group of animals with
      jointed legs, including insects and spiders
   anarthria—the lack of ability to articulate words because of
      brain damage

CARDI- "heart"
   electrocardiogram—a record of the heart's action (This is
      often abbreviated EKG.)
   cardiologist—a heart specialist
   pericardium—the membranous sac which encloses the heart

CHONDR- "cartilage"
   hypochondriac—one who has a morbid anxiety about his
      health (The term originally referred to one suffering from

melancholy in general and reflects the discarded notion that melancholy arose in the particular part of the body "under the cartilage" of the breastbone.)

chondrocyte—a cartilage cell

synchondrosis—a joint where connection is made by a plate of cartilage

CYAN- "dark blue"

cyanophil—having an affinity for blue dye

anthocyanin—a pigment found in flowers and plants

cyanide—a derivative of cyanogen, which is involved in the process of making dark-blue dye

CYT- "cell"

cytology—the branch of biology dealing with the nature of cells

hemocytozoan—a parasite living within blood corpuscles

anisocytosis—inequality in the size of red blood cells

ENTER- "intestine"

dysentery—an infectious disease of the intestines

archenteron—the primitive digestive tract of an embryo

exenterate—to surgically remove the bowels from

HEPAT- "liver"

hepatomegaly—enlargement of the liver

hepatization—the change of tissue into a liverlike substance

hepatica—a small plant with leaves which resemble the lobes of the liver

MELAN- "black," "dark"

melanin—the dark pigment found in skin, hair, etc.

melanosis—the abnormal presence of dark pigment in the body tissue

melangeophilous—dwelling in loam

Melanesia (NES-, "island")—a group of islands in the South Pacific, so called from the blackness of the inhabitants' skin

melancholy—literally, "the presence of black bile," a term going back to the humoral theory of physiology (see opening essay of Lesson XVII, Part I), according to which a predominance of black bile was thought to cause sadness

MYC(ET)- "fungus," "mold"

> *mycology*—the branch of botany concerned with the study of fungi

> *mycotrophic*—referring to plants which live in a symbiotic relationship with fungi

> *Aureomycin, Chloromycetin, neomycin*—various antibiotic drugs, the names of which contain this base because they were originally prepared from mold substances (Aureomycin and Chloromycetin are both trade names.)

NEPHR- "kidney"

> *nephritis*—inflammation of the kidneys

> *pronephros*—the foremost of the three pairs of embryonic kidney structures

> *nephrolith*—a kidney stone

OST(E)- "bone"

> *osteopath*—originally, a practitioner whose method of treatment was based on the theory that most diseases are caused by disarrangement of the bone structure and consequent interference with nerves and blood vessels

> *osteotome*—a surgical instrument for cutting bone

> *acrostealgia*—pain in the bones of an extremity

SCLER- "hard"

> multiple *sclerosis*—a disease in which there is a gradual hardening of tissue in brain and spinal chord

> *arteriosclerosis*—hardening of the walls of the arteries

> *sclerometer*—an instrument for determining the hardness of materials

III. Analyze the following words and define them:

1. endocarditis	11. scleroid
2. periostitis	12. macrocyte
3. osteoclast	13. enteritis
4. sclerodermatous	14. cyanosis
5. cytolysis	15. cardiograph
6. parenteral	16. enarthrosis
7. exostosis	17. necrosis
8. melanism	18. diathermy
9. mycosis	19. hemophilia
10. hepatitis	20. embolism

IV. The following words contain elements which have been studied in this or previous lessons. Match Column B with Column A.

A	B
1. hematocytolysis	(a) inability to see the color blue
2. anenterous	(b) inflammation of the kidney associated with a kidney stone
3. acyanopsia	(c) impairment of speech articulation
4. megalocardia	(d) pertaining to a condition of the skin characterized by increase in dark pigment
5. hepatoma	(e) having no intestine
6. lithonephritis	(f) the dissolution of blood cells
7. dysostosis	(g) the enlargement of the heart
8. dysarthria	(h) a tumor of the liver
9. acromycosis	(i) defective formation of bone
10. melanodermic	(j) the growth of fungus on the hands and feet

LESSON XXI

COMBINING FORMS USED IN MEDICAL TERMS

Learn the following **combining forms** and their meanings:

-ectomy, "surgical removal of" (from the base TOM-, "to cut"; see Lesson III)

APPEND-	appendix	+ -*ectomy*	appendectomy
TONSILL-	tonsil	+ -*ectomy*	tonsillectomy

-tomy, "surgical operation on," "surgical cutting of"

GLOSS(o)-	tongue	+ -*tomy*	glossotomy
GASTR(o)-	stomach	+ -*tomy*	gastrotomy
LOB(o)-	lobe (of the brain)	+ -*tomy*	lobotomy

-rrhea (*-rrhoea*), "abnormal discharge"

dia-		+ -*rrhea*	diarrhea
PY(o)-	pus	+ -*rrhea*	pyorrhea
LOG(o)-	word	+ -*rrhea*	logorrhea

(a term from abnormal psychology which refers to excessive and usually incoherent loquacity)

ASSIGNMENT

I. Learn the following bases and their meanings:

ADEN- "gland"

> *adenoid*—(1) like a gland (2) a growth of lymphoid tissue in the throat
>
> *lymphadenitis*—inflammation of a lymph gland
>
> *ectadenia*—ectodermal reproductive glands in insects

ANGI- "vessel"

> *cholangiotomy*—incision into the bile ducts
>
> *sporangium*—a spore case
>
> *angiitis*—inflammation of a blood or lymph vessel

CEPHAL- "head"

> *mesocephalic*—referring to a head with a medium ratio of length to breadth
>
> *cephalopod*—one of a class of molluscs to which belong squid, octopuses, etc., having tentacles (i.e., "limbs") around the front of the head
>
> *en-* + CEPHAL- "brain"; *electroencephalograph*—an instrument for measuring brain waves
>
> *archencephalon*—the primitive forebrain

CHOL(E)- "bile," "gall"

> *cholangitis*—inflammation of the bile ducts
>
> *cholelith*—a gallstone
>
> *cholagogue*—an agent which induces the flow of bile
>
> *choleric*—prone to anger, since, according to the humoral theory of physiology, a predominance of yellow bile, usually simply termed bile, made a person wrathful (cf. *melancholy,* in the preceding lesson)

HYSTER- "uterus," "hysteria" (The two meanings arise from the belief of the ancients that, since hysteria was observed mostly in women, it must somehow be associated with the organ peculiar to women.)

> *hysterotomy*—a surgical incision into the uterus
>
> *hysteroepilepsy*—hysteria associated with symptoms of epilepsy

LIP- "fat"

> *lipase*—an enzyme which breaks down fats during the digestive process
>
> *lipophil*—having an affinity for fatty tissue
>
> *lipuria*—the presence of fat in the urine

MAST-, MAZ- "breast"

mastectomy—the surgical removal of a breast

mastoid—a nipple-shaped projection of the temporal bone behind the ear

mastodon—a prehistoric mammal named from the nipple-like projections on its teeth (ODONT-)

OO- "egg"

ootheca—an egg case

oosphere—an egg before fertilization

OO- + PHOR- ("to bear"), "ovary"; *oophoritis*—inflammation of an ovary

OT- "ear"

otoscope—an instrument for examining the ear

otorrhea—a discharge from the ear

dichotic—affecting the two ears differently, so that, for instance, a single sound will be heard simultaneously in one way by one ear and in another way by the other ear

PHLEB- "vein"

phlebectomy—surgical removal of a vein

phlebosclerosis—hardening of the walls of a vein

PY- "pus"

arthroempyesis—the formation of pus in a joint

pyogenesis—the formation of pus

pyonephritis—inflammation of a kidney accompanied by the presence of pus

UR- "urine"

melanuria—the presence of black pigment in the urine

dysuria—difficulty in urination

II. Analyze the following words and define them:

1. diuretic	11. enuresis
2. angioma	12. adenoma
3. lipolysis	13. phlebitis
4. acephalous	14. pyuria
5. empyema	15. oogenesis
6. oolite	16. hysterectomy
7. hydrocephalous	17. angiologist
8. parotitis	18. encephalitis
9. phlebotomy	19. pyorrhea
10. mastoidectomy	20. polyuria

III. Match Column B with Column A:

1. otomycosis
2. cholangiography
3. barotalgia
4. adenectopia
5. antipyogenic
6. lipohemarthrosis
7. eucephalous
8. hematuria
9. endophlebitis
10. hemangioma

(a) having a well-developed head (applied to certain insect larvae)
(b) a tumor composed of blood vessels
(c) the presence of blood and fatty substance in a joint
(d) inflammation of the inner coat of a vein
(e) the presence of blood in the urine
(f) the growth of a fungus inside the ear
(g) the presence of a gland in an abnormal place
(h) preventing the formation of pus
(i) pain in the ear caused by (air) pressure
(j) X-ray of the bile ducts

LESSON XXII

COMBINING FORMS USED IN MEDICAL TERMS

Learn the following **combining forms** and their meanings:

-*path,* "one who suffers from a disease of," "one who treats a disease" (from the base PATH- "to feel," "to suffer"; see Lesson X)

PSYCH(o)-   mind   + -*path*   psychopath
OSTE(o)-   bone   + -*pathy*   osteopath

-*pathy,* "disease of," "treatment of disease of or by"

NEUR(o)-   nerve   + -*pathy*   neuropathy
(a disease or disorder of the nervous system)

HYDR(o)-   water   + -*pathy*   hydropathy
(the treatment of disease by means of water)

OSTE(o)-   bone   + -*pathy*   osteopathy

-iasis, "diseased condition" (often referring to an infestation by parasites)

PSOR- itch + *-iasis* psoriasis
(a chronic itching disease of the skin)

ELEPHANT- elephant + *-iasis* elephantiasis
(a disease resulting from an infestation of worms which causes the skin of the affected part to resemble an elephant's hide)

AMEB- amoeba + *-iasis* amebiasis
(an infestation by amoebas)

-therapy, "treatment of or by"

CHEM(o)-	chemical	+ *-therapy*	chemotherapy
HELI(o)-	sun	+ *-therapy*	heliotherapy
PSYCH(o)-	mind	+ *-therapy*	psychotherapy

ASSIGNMENT

I. Learn the following bases and their meanings:

BRACHY- "short"
>*brachyglossal*—having a short tongue
>*brachypodous*—having a short foot or stalk
>*brachylogy*—shortness of expression

BRADY- "slow"
>*bradycardia*—abnormal slowness of the heart action
>*bradylogia*—abnormal slowness of speech
>*bradykinesia*—abnormal slowness of movement

CHLOR- "green," "yellowish-green"; also, "chlorine" (a yellowish-green gas)
>*chlorophyll*—the green coloring matter in plants
>*achlorhydria*—the absence of hydrochloric acid in the stomach

DOLICH- "long"
>*dolichofacial*—having an abnormally long face
>*dolichomorphic*—having a long form

ERYTHR- "red"
>*erythrocyte*—a red blood corpuscle
>*erythrophilous*—having an affinity for red dye
>*hemoerythrin*—a red pigment found in the blood of certain animals

EURY(S)- "wide," "broad"

> *eurybaric*—able to withstand wide variations in pressure
> *eurycephalic*—having an unusually broad head

LEUC-, LEUK- "white"

> *leukemia*—a disease characterized by an abnormal increase in the number of white blood cells
> *leukoderma*—absence of skin pigmentation occurring in patches or bands
> *leucoma*—a white opacity in the cornea of the eye as a result of an ulcer or injury

MER- "part"

> *hexamerous*—having six parts
> *dysmerogenesis*—the production of unlike parts
> *merogony*—development of normal young from part of an egg

PLATY- "flat," "broad"

> *platyhelminth*—a flatworm
> *platysma*—a broad sheet of muscle
> *amphiplatyan*—flat at both ends

STEN- "narrow"

> *stenography*—shorthand writing
> *stenothermic*—capable of existing only within a narrow range of temperature
> *stenopetalous*—having narrow petals

TACH(Y)- "speed"; "swift"

> *tachylogia*—extreme rapidity of speech
> *tachistoscope*—an instrument for providing very brief exposure of visual material

XANTH- "yellow"

> *xanthoderma*—yellowness of the skin
> *xanthodont*—referring to certain rodents with yellow-colored teeth
> *xanthin*—a yellow pigment found in flowers

II. Analyze the following words and define them:

1. brachycephalic	5. erythrocytometer
2. leucocytosis	6. stenosis
3. hemostat	7. hydrotherapy
4. tachylyte	8. erythrism

9. doliochocephal
10. pentamerous
11. homeopathy
12. arthromere
13. aneurism
14. tachometer
15. physiotherapist
16. osteophyte
17. chlorosis
18. isomerous
19. idiopathic
20. urolith

III. Match Column B with Column A

1. eurythermic
2. erythrophobia
3. orthodolichocephalus
4. angiostenosis

5. bradyarthria

6. xanthophore

7. merotomy
8. platycephalic
9. chloropsia
10. tachycardia

(a) division into parts
(b) a yellow pigment-bearing cell
(c) slowness of speech articulation
(d) capable of withstanding wide variations of temperature
(e) defect of vision in which all objects appear green
(f) excessively fast beating of the heart
(g) fear of the color red
(h) the narrowing of a blood vessel
(i) having a long straight head
(j) characterized by a flat head

IV. While most people are not likely to be called upon to coin new words, one useful method of becoming familiar with scientific terminology is to try to form words on the basis of a knowledge of bases and affixes. For each of the following definitions, therefore, give a single word with this meaning. Since the words are all in current use, they have been listed as they appear in dictionaries. (Answers are at the end of Lesson XXV. But no peeking.)

Example: inflammation of a gland—<u>adenitis</u>

1. a tumor composed of fatty tissue
2. pain in a joint
3. narrowing of the heart
4. blueness of the extremities
5. a fungus infection of the skin
6. surgical incision into the liver
7. inflammation of the ear
8. smallness of the heart
9. condition of having a black tongue
10. the study of bones

LESSON XXIII

COMBINING FORMS

Learn the following **combining forms** and their meanings:

-emia, "condition of the blood"; occasionally, "congestion of blood in" (from HEM- "blood"; see Lesson V)

LEUK- white + *-emia* leukemia
(a disease marked by the presence of large numbers of white corpuscles in the blood)

an- + OX- oxygen + *-emia* anoxemia
(a condition in which there is deficiency of oxygen in the blood)

hypo- + GLYC- sugar + *-emia* hypoglycemia
(a condition in which there is a deficiency of glucose in the blood)

TULAR- + *-emia* tularemia
(an infectious disease commonly found among animals but transmissible to man, named from Tulare County, California, where it was discovered)

-hedron, "solid figure with a (specified) number of faces"

POLY-   many   + *-hedron*   polyhedron
OCTA-   eight   + *-hedron*   octahedron
ICOSA- twenty + *-hedron*   icosahedron

ASSIGNMENT

I. Learn the following bases and their meanings:

AC(O)U- "to hear"
    acoustics—the study of sound
    paracusia—any defect in the hearing
    acoumetry—the measurement of hearing ability

MENING- "membrane"; specifically, the membranes around the brain and spinal cord, the meninges

> *meningoencephalitis*—inflammation of the brain and its surrounding membranes
>
> *meningomyelitis*—inflammation of the spinal cord and its surrounding membranes

MY(S)-, MYOS- "muscle"

> *myograph*—an instrument for recording muscular action
>
> *myomere*—a muscle segment
>
> *amyotaxia*—lack of muscular coordination
>
> *myositis*—inflammation of a muscle

MYEL- "bone marrow," "the spinal cord" (The two meanings arise from the failure of early anatomists to differentiate between the two substances, since the spinal cord as well as marrow is found within bone.)

> *poliomyelitis* (POLI- "gray")—inflammation of the gray matter of the spinal cord
>
> *myelocyte*—a cell of bone marrow
>
> *myelencephalon*—the posterior portion of the brain

NEUR- "nerve," "the nervous system"

> *neuralgia*—pain along the course of a nerve
>
> *neurosis*—a type of mental disorder
>
> *neuropsychiatry*—a branch of medicine concerned with both the mind and the nervous system
>
> *neurosurgery*—surgery of the nervous system

OPHTHALM- "eye"

> *ophthalmia*—inflammation of the eyeball or surrounding tissue
>
> *ophthalmologist*—a physician who specializes in the treatment of diseases of the eye
>
> *photophthalmia*—inflammation of the eyes caused by excessively bright light

PHREN- "mind," "diaphragm" (The two meanings arise from the fact that the ancients generally regarded the region of the diaphragm as the seat of the emotions and intellect.)

> *phrenogastric*—pertaining to the stomach and diaphragm
>
> *hebephrenia* (HEBE- "youth")—a form of mental illness occurring at puberty
>
> *bradyphrenia*—slowness of mental activity

phrenology—an outmoded system of diagnosing personality by analyzing the surface irregularities of the skull; popular in the 18th and 19th centuries

(*Frenzy* and *frantic* are also derived from the Greek word *phren.*)

PLEG- "paralysis"; PLEX- "(paralytic) stroke"

paraplegia—paralysis of the lower half of the body

diplegia—paralysis of the same part on both sides of the body

apoplexy—a stroke; a sudden paralysis and loss of consciousness caused by the rupture or blocking of a blood vessel in the brain

R(R)HIN- "nose"

rhinitis—inflammation of the nose

otorhinolaryngologist—a specialist in diseases of the ear, nose, and throat

rhinoceros (CER- "horn")—so called from the horn on its nose

rhinencephalon—the portion of the brain concerned with the sense of smell

SOM(AT)- "body"

chromosome—any of several deeply staining bodies in a cell which determine hereditary characteristics

somatology—in anthropology, the study of the physical characteristics of the human body

merosome—a body segment

STHEN- "strength"

asthenopia—weakness of the eyes

anisosthenic—referring to pairs of muscles of unequal power

adenohypersthenia—greater than normal activity of a gland

THYM- "mind," "strong feeling"

dysthymia—melancholy, despondency

hyperepithymia—exaggerated desire

prothymia—alertness

TON(US)- "a stretching," "tension"

tonic—a medicine which invigorates and braces

ophthalmotonometer—an instrument for measuring tension within the eyeball

angiohypertonia—abnormal constriction of blood vessels

peritonitis—inflammation of the peritoneum, the membrane that encloses, i.e., is "stretched around," the internal organs

II. Analyze the following words and define them:

1. meningitis	11. calisthenics
2. exophthalmic	12. myocarditis
3. platyrrhinian	13. schizophrenia
4. uremia	14. psychosomatic
5. neurasthenia	15. decahedron
6. atony	16. neurologist
7. ophthalmoscope	17. osteomyelitis
8. hemiplegia	18. isotonic
9. cyclothymia	19. pyemia
10. rhinoscope	20. catatonic

III. Match Column B with Column A:

1. myasthenia	(a) perception of bodily sensations
2. ophthalmoplegia	(b) an excess of fat in the blood
3. oligophrenia	(c) paralysis of a single limb or part of the body
4. hyperacusia	(d) paralysis of the eye
5. somatotopagnosia	(e) lack of muscle tone
6. rhinophonia	(f) muscular weakness
7. hyperlipemia	(g) feeble-mindedness
8. monoplegia	(h) inability to identify one's body or its parts
9. somesthesia	(i) exceptionally acute hearing
10. amyotonia	(j) a nasal tone in speaking

LESSON XXIV

SUFFIXES USED IN SCIENTIFIC TERMINOLOGY

Learn the following **suffixes** and their meanings:

-in, -ine, "chemical substance" (of Latin derivation)

anti- +	TOX-	poison	+ *-in*	antitoxin
	MELAN-	black, dark	+ *-in*	melanin

(a dark pigment found in skin, hair, etc.)

HEMO(o)- blood + CYAN- blue + -*in* hemocyanin
(a pigment found in the blood of some invertebrates)

epi- + NEPH- kidney + -*ine* epinephrine
(another name for adrenalin; Latin REN- "kidney")

-*ium,* "part," "lining or enveloping tissue," "region"

endo- + CARDI- heart + -*ium* endocardium
(the membrane lining the cavities of the heart)

peri- + NEPHR- kidney + -*ium* perinephrium
(a tissue surrounding a kidney)

epi- + NEUR- nerve + -*ium* epineurium
(a sheath of tissue surrounding a peripheral nerve)

ASSIGNMENT

I.   Learn the following bases and their meanings:

BLAST- "bud," "formative substance," "embryonic cell"

> *blastomere*—any of the cells formed during the first few divisions of a fertilized ovum

> *blastula*—an embryo in an early stage of development, consisting of one or several layers of cells around a central cavity

> *myoblast*—an embryonic cell which develops into muscle tissue

COCC(US)- "berry," "seed," "spherical bacterium"

> *pentacoccous*—having five seeds or carpels

> *streptococcus*—(STREPT- "twisted," here meaning "twisted chain")—any of a particular genus of bacteria some species of which cause serious disease and which are named from their arrangement in chains

> *meningococcemia*—the presence in the blood of the bacteria which cause meningitis

CYST- "bladder," "sac," "sac containing morbid matter"

> *cholecystitis*—inflammation of the gallbladder

> *cystolithiasis*—condition caused by a stone in the urinary bladder

cystectomy—surgical removal of a cyst

statocyst—a fluid-filled sac found in many invertebrates which serves as an organ of balance

DACTYL- "digit," "finger or toe"

dactylosymphysis—adhesion of fingers or toes

hexadactylism—the condition of having six fingers or toes

brachydactyly—the condition of having abnormally short digits

DROM- "a running," "a course"

hippodrome (HIPP- "horse")—originally, a track for horse races

dromomania—a morbid desire to wander

homodromy—a condition of having spirals which turn in the same direction

HIST(I)- "tissue"

histamine—a substance occurring in all animal and vegetable tissue

histometaplastic—changing tissue into that of another type

histozoic—living within tissue, as a parasite

ICHTHY- "fish"

ichthyosaur—a prehistoric marine reptile with a fish-like body

Chondroichthyes—a class of vertebrates, mainly fish, with cartilaginous skeletons

ORNIS-, ORNITH- "bird"

ornithophilous—pollinated through the agency of birds

archaeornis—a type of prehistoric bird of the European Upper Jurassic

ichthyornis—a type of prehistoric bird with vertebrae resembling those of fishes

PHAG- "to eat"

sarcophagus—(SARC- "flesh")—a stone coffin, so called because early sarcophagi were made of limestone, which caused the body to disintegrate rapidly

geophagy—the eating of earth

glossophagine—securing food with the tongue

PLAS(T)-"to form"

> *plasma*—the fluid part of the blood (literally, "something formed")
>
> *encephalodysplasia*—defective development of the brain
>
> *-plasty*—surgical operation to form, plastic surgery, as in *arthroplasty*—formation of an artificial joint
>
> *hyperplasia*—excessive development of tissue

PTER(YX)- "wing," "fin"

> *helicopter*—literally, "spiral (HELIC-) wing"
>
> *arthropterous*—referring to fishes with jointed fin-rays
>
> *Lepidoptera* (LEPID- "scale")—an order of insects to which belong butterflies and moths
>
> *coleopterous* (COLE- "sheath")—belonging to an order of insects having hard anterior wings which cover the membranous posterior ones
>
> *ichthyopterygia*—paired fish fins

STOM(AT)- "mouth," "opening"

> *amphistomous*—applied to certain worms which have suckers at both ends of the body
>
> *stomatoplasty*—plastic surgery on the mouth
>
> *exostome*—an opening in the outer wall of an ovule
>
> *-stomy*—an operation to make an artificial opening in an organ, as *enterostomy* –the making of an opening through the abdominal wall into the intestine for the purpose of drainage

II. Analyze the following words and define them:

1. pericardium	14. osteoplasty
2. syndrome	15. orthopterous
3. anthropophagous	16. polydactylism
4. protoplasm	17. histology
5. anastomosis	18. phagocyte
6. erythroblast	19. chiropter
7. syndactyl	20. epigastrium
8. ichthyosis	21. pterodactyl
9. phytophagous	22. osteoblast
10. neuropterous	23. ichthyology
11. micrococcus	24. neoplasm
12. anadromous	25. hemolysin
13. ornithology	

III. Match Column B with Column A:

1. rhinoplasty	(a) the dissolution of tissue
2. ornithosis	(b) stone-eating (as certain birds)
3. lithophagous	(c) fish-eating
4. endomysium	(d) having two wings
5. cholecystokinin	(e) the condition of having abnormally long fingers or toes
6. pteropod	(f) the making of an opening into the gallbladder
7. ichthyophagous	(g) the connective tissue between fibers and muscle
8. dipterous	(h) a hormone which causes the gallbladder to contract
9. macrodactylism	(i) plastic surgery on the nose
10. histolysis	(j) a disease found in birds
11. cholecystostomy	(k) a fossil fish
12. ichthyolite	(l) small molluscs having feet with winglike lobes

LESSON XXV

DIMINUTIVE SUFFIXES

Learn the following **diminutive suffixes** and their meanings:

-ium, -ion, "little" (often difficult to distinguish from *-ium* in the preceding lesson)

BACTER- staff, rod + *-ium*   bacterium
POD-   foot   + *-ium*   podium
(in zoology, a part which serves as a foot)

THEC-   case   + *-ium*   thecium
(a part of a fungus which contain sporules)

ASTER-   star   + *-ion*   asterion
(the meeting point of various sutures or seams in the skull, forming a star-shaped pattern)

STOM-   mouth   + *-ion*   stomion
(a skin pore of a sponge)

-idium, "little"

    BAS- base + *-idium* basidium
    (a fungus cell which bears spores on a stalk)
    OO- egg + PHOR- to bear + *-idium* oophoridium
    (a spore case in certain plants)
    STOM- mouth + *-idium* stomidium
    (the terminal pore of a tentacle)

-arium, -arion, "little"

    CON- cone + *-arium* conarium
    (an old term for the pineal gland)
    HIPP- horse + *-arion* Hipparion
    (a genus of extinct mammals related to the horse)

-isk, -iscus, "little"

    ASTER- star   + *-isk* asterisk
    MEN- moon, month + *-iscus* meniscus
    (a crescent-shaped object, in particular, a type of lens; also, the curved upper surface of a column of liquid)

ASSIGNMENT

I. Learn the following bases and their meanings:

    ACTIN- "ray," "radiating structure"

        actinobiology—the branch of biology which studies the effects of radiation upon living organisms

        actinodromous—referring to a leaf with veins radiating from a common center

        actinodermatitis—inflammation of the skin caused by the actinic rays in sunlight

    ANTH- "flower"

        chrysanthemum—literally, "golden (CHRYS-) blossom"

        anthology—originally, a collection of choice passages, (that is, the "flowers") of literary works

        anthema—a skin eruption, literally, a "blossoming"

        anthophilous—attracted by flowers, as certain insects

    CARP- "fruit"

        amphicarpous—producing two kinds of fruit

        carpolith—a fossil fruit

        angiocarp—a fruit with external covering

    DENDR- "tree," "tree-like structure"

        dendrolatry—the worship of trees

        dendron—the branching process of a nerve cell

philodendron—an ornamental climbing plant (one which "clings to trees")

GON- "generative," "reproductive," "sexual" (related to GEN-, "to be produced"; see Lesson VII)

archegonium—the female reproductive organ in certain plants

gonorrhea—a venereal disease

gonoblast—a type of reproductive cell in animals

GYMN- "naked"

gymnasium—(in ancient Greece clothes were not worn during athletic exercises)

gymnorhinal—referring to birds with nostril region not covered with feathers

gymnanthous—having uncovered flowers, with no floral envelope

HIPP- "horse"

hippopotamus (POTAM- "river"; cf. *Mesopotamia*)—literally "river horse"

hippodrome—originally, a course for race horses

HYGR- "wet," "moist"

hygroscope—an instrument which indicates humidity, hence *hygroscopic*—absorbing moisture from the air

hygrophyte—a plant which lives in a moist environment

euryhygric—able to withstand wide variations in humidity

PHYLL- "leaf"

chlorophyll—the green coloring matter found in leaves

phyllophagous—eating leaves

oligophyllous—having few leaves

THEC(A)- "case" (related to THE- "to place," "to put"; see Lesson X; originally, "a case in which to put something")

bibliotheca—a library

amphithecium—the external layer of cells in the spore case of certain plants

pterotheca—the wing case of a chrysalis

neurothecitis—inflammation of the sheath of a nerve

THROMB- "a clot"

thrombin—a substance in the blood which causes clotting

thromboangiitis—clot formation accompanied by inflammation of a blood vessel

thrombocyte—a blood platelet, a type of cell important in clotting

TOX- "poison"

intoxicate—originally, to poison

toxin—a poisonous substance produced by microorganisms or by plants and animals

antitoxin—a substance which counteracts a toxin

zootoxin—a toxin derived from an animal

XYL- "wood"

xylophone—a percussion instrument played by striking wooden bars

xylocarp—a hard, woody fruit

xylophyte—a woody plant

II. Analyze the following words and define them:

1. perianth	13. xanthophyll
2. schizocarpous	14. monocarpic
3. phyllopod	15. ootheca
4. gonidium	16. thrombosis
5. xylotomous	17. anthocyanin
6. actinomorphic	18. acrocarpous
7. carpophagous	19. pseudopodium
8. prothrombin	20. exanthema
9. heterophyllous	21. dendrite
10. xylophagous	22. toxicology
11. toxemia	23. phyllotaxy
12. oogonium	24. nephridium

III. Match Column B with Column A:

A	B
1. gonidangium	(a) referring to a moisture-loving plant
2. geocarpy	(b) having bare wings
3. melanophyllous	(c) the reversion of flower petals to ordinary green leaves
4. podotheca	(d) the determination of dates by the study of tree rings
5. actinotherapy	(e) the practice of eating horse meat
6. epixylous	(f) having hard leaves
7. hygrophilous	(g) the ripening of fruits underground
8. hippophagy	(h) a structure containing minute reproductive bodies
9. chloranthy	(i) growing upon wood
10. gymnopterous	(j) treatment by means of rays
11. dendrochronology	(k) a foot covering (of birds or reptiles)
12. sclerophyllous	(l) having dark-colored leaves

IV. For each of the following definitions give a single word with this meaning. Since these words are all in current use, they have been listed as they appear in dictionaries.

1. paralysis of the tongue
2. having hidden flowers
3. eating only one thing
4. pertaining to the formation of bone
5. having small wings
6. fear of flowers
7. with winged fruit
8. bearing leaves
9. deficient hearing
10. inflammation of the nerve of the eye

———————

ANSWERS TO EXERCISE IV OF LESSON XXII

1. lipoma
2. arthralgia
3. cardiostenosis
4. acrocyanosis
5. dermatomycosis

6. hepatomy
7. otitis
8. microcardia
9. melanoglossia
10. osteology

ANSWERS TO EXERCISE IV OF LESSON XXV

1. glossoplegia
2. cryptanthous
3. monophagous
4. osteoplastic, osteogenic
5. micropterous

6. anthophobia
7. pterocarpous
8. phyllophorous
9. hypacusia
10. opthalmoneuritis

INDEX OF WORDS APPEARING IN CONTEXT (GREEK)

Roman numerals after the entries indicate the lesson in which the word is to be found. Words from Lessons XX through XXV are not included here.

A

academy ii
Achilles' heel i
acme xix
acromegaly xiii
acronym xvii
acrophobia xiii
Acropolis xiii
adamant xviii
Adonis i
aegis i
aesthete x
aesthetic vii
agnostic vi
allergy x
amazon i
amnesty iv
amorphous viii
amphibious iv
anachronism iv
analgesic iv
analogy iv
analytical iv
anarchy xiii
anathema xi
anatomy iv
android xii
anecdote x
anemic v
anesthetic vii
anodyne xviii
anomaly vi
antagonistic v
anthropocentric vii

anthropoid vii
anthropologist xii
anthropomorphic vii
antibiotics iv
antinomianism xv
antipathies x
antiphonies xv
antipodal iv
antithesis xi
antonym vi
apathy x
aphasia xvii
aphorisms xviii
apocryphal iv
apogee iv
apostates x
apostolic v
apostrophizes xv
apotheosis xi
apotheosized iv
Arcadian ii
archaeologists xii
archaic vii
archetype xii
archiepiscopal xiv
aroma xix
ascetic xviii
asteroids vii
astral viii
astronauts xvii
ataxia xvii
atheist iv
atlas i

atrophy iv
atypical xv
austere iii
aura xix
autocratic xii
autonomy xii
autopsy xv
axiom xviii

B

ballistic ix
barometer xiv
bathos xix
bedlam ii
bibliographical iii
bibliophile viii
biopsy xii
boycott ii
bucolic xviii

C

cacophony x
calligraphy xiv
canon iii
canonical iii
canonized xv
Cassandra i
cataclysmic xviii
catalytic v
catastrophe xviii
catastrophic xv
catharsis xviii
catholic vii

PREFIXES (GREEK)

The Roman numerals in parentheses indicate the lesson in which each prefix is to be found.

a-, *an-*, not, without (IV)
amphi-, both, on both sides of, around (IV)
ana-, *an-*, up, back, again (IV)
anti-, *ant-*, against, opposite (IV)
apo-, *ap-*, from, off (IV)
cata-, *cat-*, down, against, very (IV)
dia-, *di-*, through, across, between (IV)
dys-, bad, disordered, difficult (V)
ec-, out, out of (V)
ecto-, outside, external (V)
en-, *em-*, *el-*, in, into (V)
endo-, *ento-*, *end-*, *ent-*, within (V)
epi-, *ep-*, upon, to, in addition to (V)

eu-, *ev-*, good, well
ex-, out, out of (V)
exo-, outside, external (V)
hyper-, over, excessive (VI)
hypo-, *hyp-*, below, less than normal (VI)
meta-, *met-*, after, changed (VI)
para-, *par-*, beside, disordered (VI)
peri-, around, near (VI)
pro-, before, in front of (VI)
pros-, toward, in addition to (VI)
syn-, *sym-*, syl-, *sys-*, with, together (VI)

SUFFIXES AND COMBINING FORMS (GREEK)

The Roman numerals in parentheses indicate the lesson in which each suffix is to be found.

-ac, pertaining to, etc. (VII)
-al, pertaining to, like, belonging to, having the character of (VIII)
-an (*-ian*), pertaining to, like, one concerned with (VIII)
-arch, one who rules (XIII)
-archy, rule by (XIII)
-arion, little (XXV)
-arium, little (XXV)
-ast, one who does (X)

-cracy, rule by, etc. (XII)
-crat, one who advocates or practices rule by (XII)
-ectomy, surgical removal of (XXI)
-emia, condition of the blood (XXIII)
-gram, thing written (XIV)
-graph, writing, etc. (XIV)
-graphy, writing, etc. (XIV)
-hedron, solid figure (XXIII)

-ia, quality of, etc. (X)
-iasis, diseased condition (XXII)
-ic, pertaining to, etc. (VII)
-ician, specialist in, etc. (IX)
-ics, art, science, or study of (VII)
-idium, little (XXV)
-in, chemical substance (XXIV)
-ine, chemical substance (XXIV)
-ion, little (XXV)
-iscus, little (XXV)
-isk, little (XXV)
-ism, belief in, etc. (IX)
-ist, one who believes in, etc. (IX)
-ite, one connected with, etc. (IX)
-itis, inflammation of, etc. (XX)
-ium, little (XXV)
-ium, part, etc. (XXIV)
-ize, verbal suffix (XV)
-logy, science of, etc. (XII)
-m, result of (XI)
-ma, result of (XI)
-mania, madness about, passion for (XIII)
-maniac, one having a madness or passion for (XIII)
-mat, result of (XI)
-me, result (XI)
-meter, measure (XIV)
-metry, art or science of measuring (XIV)
-nomy, science of, etc. (XII)
-oid, like (VII)

-oma, tumor, etc. (XX)
-osis, diseased condition of, etc. (XX)
-ous (*-ious*), full of, pertaining to, like (VIII)
-path, one who suffers from a disease of, etc. (XXII)
-pathy, disease of, etc. (XXII)
-phobe, one who fears or hates (XIII)
-phobia, abnormal fear or hatred of (XIII)
-ploid, -fold (XVI, footnote)
-rrhea (*-rrhoea*), abnormal discharge (XXI)
-scope, instrument for viewing, etc. (XIV)
-se, act of, etc. (XI)
-sia, act of, etc. (XI)
-sis, act of, etc. (XI)
-st, one who does (XI)
-sy, act of, etc. (XI)
-t, he who, etc. (X)
-te, he who, etc. (X)
-therapy, treatment of or by (XXII)
-tic, pertaining to, etc. (VII)
-tics, art, science, or study of (VII)
-tomy, surgical operation on, etc. (XXI)
-y, quality of, etc. (X)

BASES (GREEK)

The Roman numerals in parentheses following the meanings indicate the lesson in which each base is to be found.

A

ACO(U)-, to hear (XXIII)
ACR-, highest, the extremities (XIII)

ACTIN-, ray, radiating structure (XXV)
ACU-, to hear (XXIII)
ADEN-, gland (XXI)

AESTHE-, to feel, perceive (VII)
AGOG(UE)-, to lead (IX)
AGON-, struggle, contest (V)
ALG-, pain (IV)
ALL-, other (X)
ANDR-, man, male (XI)
ANGEL-, messenger, message (V)
ANGI-, vessel (XXI)
ANTH-, flower (XXV)
ANTHROP-, human being (VII)
ARCHA(E)-, ARCHE-, ancient, primitive, beginning (VII)
ARTHR-, joint, speech sound or articulation (XX)
ASCE-, to exercise (XVIII)
AST(E)R-, star (VII)
AUT-, self (XII)

B

BALL-, to throw, put (VI)
BAR-, weight, pressure (XIV)
BI-, life (IV)
BIBLI-, book (III)
BLAST-, bud, formative substance, embryonic cell (XXIV)
BLE-, to throw, put (VI)
BOL-, to throw, put (VI)
BRACHY-, short (XXII)
BRADY-, slow (XXII)
BUCOL-, cowherd (XVIII)

C

CAC-, bad (X)
CAL(L)-, beauty (XIV)
CANON-, a rule (III)
CARDI-, heart (XX)
CARP-, fruit (XXV)
CAU(S)-, to burn (X)
CENTR-, center (V)
CEPHAL-, head (XXI)
CH(E)IR-, hand (IX)
CHLOR-, green, yellowish-green; chlorine (XXII)

CHOL(E)-, bile, gall (XXI)
CHONDR-, cartilage (XX)
CHORE-, dance (XVII)
CHROM(AT)-, color (VIII)
CHRON-, time (IV)
CINE-, to move (XI)
CLA-, to break (X)
CLYS-, to wash (XVIII)
COCC(US)-, berry, seed, spherical bacterium (XXIV)
COSM-, universe, order (IX)
CRA-, to mix (XVIII)
CRI-, to judge, decide, separate (VIII)
CRYPH-, CRYPT-, hidden, secret (III)
CYAN-, dark blue (XX)
CYCL-, circle, wheel (III)
CYN(OS)-, dog (XVIII)
CYST-, bladder, sac, sac containing morbid matter (XXIV)
CYT-, cell (XX)

D

DACTYL-, digit, finger or toe (XXIV)
D(A)EMON-, spirit, evil spirit (IV)
DEC(A)-, ten (XVI)
DEM-, people (V)
DENDR-, tree, treelike structure (XXV)
DERM(AT)-, skin (VI)
DEUTER-, second (XVI)
DI-, twice, double (XVI)
DICH-, in two (XVI)
DIDAC-, to teach (XVIII)
DIPL-, twice, double (XVI)
DO-, to give (X)
DOG-, opinion, teaching (VI)
DOLICH-, long (XXII)
DOX-, opinion, teaching (VI)

DROM-, a running, a course (XXIV)
DYN(AM)-, force, power (X)

E

EGO-, I (Latin) (XIII)
EM-, blood (V)
ENTER-, intestine (XX)
ER(OT)-, love (XVII)
ERG-, work (X)
ERYTHR-, red (XXII)
ESTHE-, to feel, perceive (VII)
ETHN-, race, cultural group (VIII)
EURY(S)-, wide, broad (XXII)

G

GAM-, marriage (V)
GASTR-, stomach (XII)
GE-, earth (IV)
GEN(E)-, to originate, produce (XI)
GEN(E)-, kind, race (XI)
GER(ONT)-, old age, old people (VII)
GLOSS-, GLOT(T)-, tongue, language (III)
GLYPH-, to carve (XVII)
GNO(S)-, to know (VI)
GON-, generative, reproductive, sexual (XXV)
GON-, angle, angled figure (XV)
GON-, to produce, originate (VII)
GYMN-, naked (XXV)
GYN(E)-, GYN(A)EC-, woman, female (XI)

H

HAEM(AT)-, blood (V)
HECT-, a hundred (XVI)
HEDON-, pleasure (XVIII)

HEGEMON-, leader (XVIII)
HELI-, sun (XII)
HEM(AT)-, blood (V)
HEMER-, day (V)
HEMI-, half (XVI)
HEPAT-, liver (XX)
HEPT(A)-, seven (XVI)
HETER-, other, different (IX)
HEX(A)-, six (XVI)
HIER-, sacred (XIII)
HIPP-, horse (XXV)
HIST(I)-, tissue (XXIV)
HOD-, way, road (V)
HOL-, whole (VII)
HOM(E)-, same (VI)
HYDR-, water (XIII)
HYGR-, wet, moist (XXV)
HYSTER-, uterus, hysteria (XXI)

I

IATR-, physician, medicine (VII)
ICHTHY-, fish (XXIV)
ICON-, image (III)
IDE-, thought, idea (XII)
IDI-, one's own, peculiar (XI)
IS-, equal (XIV)

K

KAL(L)-, beauty (XIV)
KILO-, one thousand (XVI)
KINE-, to move (XI)

L

LAB-, to take, seize (XV)
LAT(E)R-, to worship excessively, be fanatically devoted to (X)
LECT-, to speak, choose (VIII)
LEM-, LEP-, to take, seize (XV)
LEUC-, LEUK-, white (XXII)

LIP-, fat (XXI)
LITE-, stone (XI)
LITH-, stone (XI)
LOG(UE)-, speech, word, pro-
portion, reasoning (IV)
LY-, to loosen (IV)

M

MACR-, large, long (XIV)
MANC-, MANT-, to divine by
means of (XII)
MAST-, MAZ-, breast (XXI)
MEGA(L)-, large; a million
(XIII)
MELAN-, black, dark (XX)
MENING-, membrane (XXIII)
MER-, part (XXIII)
MES-, middle (XV)
MICR-, small, one millionth
part of (XII)
MIM-, to imitate (III)
MIS-, hatred (XI)
MNE-, to remember (IV)
MON-, one, single (XVI)
MORPH-, form, shape (VI)
MY(S)-, muscle (XXIII)
MYC(ET)-, fungus, mold (XX)
MYEL-, bone marrow, the
spinal cord (XXIII)
MYOS-, muscle (XXIII)

N

NAUT-, sailor (XVII)
NE-, new, new and different
form of (IX)
NECR-, the dead, corpse, dead
tissue (XII)
NEPHR-, kidney (XX)
NES-, island (XVII)
NEUR-, nerve (XXIII)

O

OCT(A)-, eight (XVI)

OD-, song, poem (III)
OD-, way, road (V)
ODONT-, tooth (IX)
OLIG-, few (XIII)
ONYM-, name, word (VI)
OO-, egg (XXI)
OPHTHALM-, eye (XXIII)
OP(T)-, eye; to see (IX)
ORA-, to see (XIV)
ORNIS-, ORNITH-, bird
(XXIV)
ORTH-, straight, correct (IX)
OST(E)-, bone (XX)
OT-, ear (XXI)

P

PAED-, child (IX)
PAL(A)E-, old (XII)
PAN(T)-, all, every (IV)
PATE-, to walk (XVIII)
PATH-, to feel, suffer; disease
(X)
PATR-, father (XIII)
PATRI-, family, clan (XIII)
PED-, child (IX)
PEDIA-, education (IX)
PENT(A)-, five (XVI)
PEP(T)-, to digest (VII)
PETR-, rock (XIV)
PHA-, to speak (XI)
PHAG-, to eat (XXIV)
PHA(N)-, to show, appear
(VIII)
PHE(M)-, to speak (XI)
PHER-, to bear, go (VI)
PHIL-, to love (VIII)
PHLEB-, vein (XXI)
PHON-, sound, voice (VIII)
PHOR-, to bear, go (VI)
PHOT-, light (XIV)
PHRA-, to speak (XV)
PHREN-, mind, diaphragm
(XXIII)

PHY-, to grow (X)
PHYLL-, leaf (XXV)
PHYSI-, nature (X)
PLAS(T)-, to form (XXIV)
PLATY-, flat, broad (XXII)
PLEG-, paralysis (XXIII)
PLEX-, paralytic stroke (XXIII)
POD-, foot (IV)
POLEM-, war (XVIII)
POL(IS)-, city, state (IX)
POLY-, many, much (VIII)
PROT-, first, original, primitive (XVI)
PSEUD-, false (XII)
PSYCH-, mind (XII)
PTER(YX)-, wing, fin (XXIV)
PY-, pus (XXI)
PYR-, fire (III)

R

R(R)HIN-, nose (XXIII)

S

SCHIS-, SCHIZ-, to split (XI)
SCLER-, hard (XX)
SOM(AT)-, body (XXIII)
SOPH-, wise (XIII)
STA-, to stand, stop (X)
STAL-, to send, draw (V)
STEN-, narrow (XXII)
STERE-, solid, three-dimensional (XI)
STHEN-, strength (XXIII)
STLE-, to send, draw (V)
STOL-, to send, draw (V)
STOM(AT)-, mouth (XXIV)
STROPH-, to turn (XV)

T

TACH(Y)-, swift; speed (XXII)

TACT-, to arrange, put in order (VI)
TAPH-, tomb (V)
TAUT-, the same (VIII)
TAX-, to arrange, put in order (VI)
TECHN-, art, skill, craft (VII)
TELE-, afar, operating at a distance (XIII)
TETR(A)-, four (XVI)
THANAS-, THANAT-, death (V)
THE-, to place, put (X)
THE-, god (IV)
THEC(A)-, case (XXV)
THERM-, heat (VIII)
THROMB-, clot (XXV)
THYM-, mind, strong feeling (XXIII)
TOM-, to cut (III)
TON(US)-, a stretching, tension (XXIII)
TOP-, place (XIV)
TOX-, poison (XXV)
TRI-, three (XVI)
TROP-, to turn (XII)
TROPH-, to nourish, grow (IV)
TYP-, stamp, model (XI)

U

UR-, urine (XXI)
UR-, tail (XVIII)
URG-, work (X)

X

XANTH-, yellow (XXII)
XEN-, stranger, foreigner (XIII)
XYL-, wood (XXV)

Z

ZO-, animal (XIII)